CAMBRIDGE TEXTS IN THE
HISTORY OF PHILOSOPHY

HUME
Dialogues concerning Natural Religion

CAMBRIDGE TEXTS IN THE HISTORY OF PHILOSOPHY

Series editors

KARL AMERIKS
Professor of Philosophy, University of Notre Dame

DESMOND M. CLARKE
Professor of Philosophy, University College Cork

The main objective of Cambridge Texts in the History of Philosophy is to expand the range, variety, and quality of texts in the history of philosophy which are available in English. The series includes texts by familiar names (such as Descartes and Kant) and also by less-well-known authors. Wherever possible, texts are published in complete and unabridged form, and translations are specially commissioned for the series. Each volume contains a critical introduction together with a guide to further reading and any necessary glossaries and textual apparatus. The volumes are designed for student use at undergraduate and postgraduate level and will be of interest not only to students of philosophy, but also to a wider audience of readers in the history of science, the history of theology, and the history of ideas.

For a list of titles published in the series, please see end of book.

DAVID HUME

Dialogues concerning Natural Religion and Other Writings

EDITED BY
DOROTHY COLEMAN
Northern Illinois University

CAMBRIDGE
UNIVERSITY PRESS

CAMBRIDGE UNIVERSITY PRESS
Cambridge, New York, Melbourne, Madrid, Cape Town, Singapore, São Paulo

Cambridge University Press
The Edinburgh Building, Cambridge CB2 8RU, UK

Published in the United States of America by Cambridge University Press, New York

www.cambridge.org
Information on this title: www.cambridge.org/9780521603591

© Cambridge University Press 2007

First published 2007

Printed in the United Kingdom at the University Press, Cambridge

A catalogue record for this publication is available from the British Library

ISBN 978-0-521-84260-0 hardback
ISBN 978-0-521-60359-1 paperback

For my daughter, Alexandra

Contents

Contents

Acknowledgments

For both critical and encouraging comments on my Introduction and editorial notes I am indebted to James King, David Raynor, M. A. Stewart, and John Wright. Thanks also to David Raynor for drawing my attention to Edward Gibbon's remark on Hume's *Dialogues*, and to J. V. Price for pointing out to me that Matthew Prior is the source for "Not satisfied with life, afraid of death" in Part 10 of the *Dialogues*. I also thank the Hume Society for accepting my paper, "Hume's Philosophy of Ridicule," for its 29th Hume Conference in Helsinki, August, 2002, where the discussion helped direct my approach to the Introduction. I am grateful to Desmond Clarke and Hilary Gaskin for inviting me to undertake this project and for their helpful editorial advice. I owe special thanks to James Dye for preparing the translations of Bayle that are part of the supplementary readings for this volume. Not least, I am grateful to my late afternoon tea companions, Andrea Bonnickson, Annette Johns, and Sharon Sytsma, for their friendship and support throughout this project.

Introduction

David Hume's *Dialogues concerning Natural Religion* (1779) is one of the most influential works in the philosophy of religion and the most artful instance of philosophical dialogue since the dialogues of Plato. Some consider it a successful criticism of rational theology, some find it a failure, others regard it as a defense of some form of natural religion, and yet others emphasize its influence on the development of fideism, religious belief that disclaims rational justification. The great eighteenth-century historian, Edward Gibbon, said that of all Hume's philosophical works it is "the most profound, the most ingenious, and the best written."[1] All readers, regardless of their final assessments, can appreciate its penetrating analyses as well as its entertaining wit and ironic humor.

The topic of the *Dialogues* is natural religion, that is, religious belief, sentiment, and practice founded on evidence that is independent of supernatural revelation. The work presents a fictional conversation among three friends – Cleanthes, Philo, and Demea – that is overheard and later narrated by Pamphilus, Cleanthes' pupil, to his friend Hermippus. Although the names of the characters come from antiquity,[2] the temporal setting

---

[1] Translated from M. Baridon, "Une lettre inédite d'Edward Gibbon à Jean-Baptiste Antoine Suard," *Etudes anglaises* 24 (1971), 80: "[J]e ne crains pas de prononcer que de tous les ouvrages Philosophiques de M. H. celui-ci [the *Dialogues*] est le plus profond, le plus ingenieux et le mieux écrit."

[2] Hume probably named Philo after Philo of Larissa, Cicero's teacher. He probably named Cleanthes after the second head of the school of Stoicism, Cleanthes of Assos (c. 331–c. 232 BC), a religious enthusiast. The names of the other characters may also have eponymous sources, but their etymological significance is more obvious. "Demea," from the Greek *demos*, meaning "people," is an appropriate name for one who defends popular or traditional religion. "Pamphilus," from the Greek *pan* (all) and *philos* (friend), meaning "friend of all," is appropriate for a Shaftesburean narrator who states that "opposite sentiments, even without any decision, afford an agreeable amusement."

is an eighteenth-century one, and the main characters represent philosophical or religious types. They all profess, for different reasons, that the existence of God is evident; but Philo, a skeptic, and Demea, an orthodox theist, urge that the nature of God is incomprehensible, while Cleanthes, an empirical theist, dismisses their skepticism as excessive. He proposes an argument based on the systematic order in nature – commonly known as the argument from design – to establish both the existence of God and his possession of human-like intelligence. Cleanthes later adds that the beneficial aspects of nature's order provide compelling evidence of God's moral perfection, which, if left doubtful or uncertain, would spell "an end at once of all religion" (10.28).

Hume has Philo present a series of powerful criticisms of Cleanthes' argument up to the final section of the dialogue, where he endorses a qualified inference to an intelligent cause of nature that stops short of attributing moral qualities to it. Although Philo dominates the conversation and is standardly taken to represent Hume's views, Hume makes Cleanthes the putative apparent hero of the piece (LE2, 120), and has Pamphilus pronounce at the end that "upon a serious review of the whole, I cannot but think, that *Philo*'s principles are more probable than *Demea*'s; but that those of *Cleanthes* approach still nearer to the truth" (12.34). This conclusion is dramatically foreshadowed in characterizations attributed to Hermippus in the *Dialogues*' prologue that contrast the "rigid, inflexible orthodoxy of Demea," the "careless scepticism of Philo" and the "accurate philosophical turn of Cleanthes" (Prologue, 6).

The most controversial problem in interpreting Hume's *Dialogues* is what to make of Philo's acceptance of the design argument in Part 12, the concluding section of the work. Many readers find it difficult to reconcile his previous criticisms of the argument with his final confession that "no one has a deeper sense of religion impressed on his mind, or pays more profound adoration to the divine being, as he discovers himself to reason, in the inexplicable contrivance and artifice of nature" (12.2). In one sense the puzzle is about whether Philo is consistent. In another sense the puzzle is about whether Hume is consistent or whether Philo consistently represents Hume's own beliefs. This introduction will suggest a solution to this and other puzzles in the course of elucidating the

---

"Hermippus," from the Greek *herma* (stone boundary markers topped with a bust of Hermes) is an appropriate name for one who contrasts the characters of the three conversationalists.

Dialogues' argumentative structure, its relation to Hume's other writings, and its broader historical context.

Natural religion, philosophical dialogue, and skepticism

A variety of religious and moral interests motivated the preoccupation with natural religion during Hume's time. The perceived enemies of religion were the ancient Greek atomist, Epicurus, and two seventeenth-century philosophers, Baruch Spinoza and Thomas Hobbes.[3] Epicurus maintained that the order of the universe arose from chance and that the gods have no interest in human affairs. Hobbes argued that all occurrences in nature, including human thoughts and volitions, are reducible to the motions of matter governed by general laws. He also denied that the attributes of God could be known. Spinoza argued that God and nature are the same and that God's actions are logically necessary consequences of his nature, not free actions involving deliberation and choice. Although some theists accepted certain aspects of these theories, most considered them practically equivalent to atheism because a God who takes no interest in the world or human affairs, whose nature is unknowable, or whose actions are mediated through or identical with physical processes that occur by chance or necessity but not by choice, does not appear to be a God who can evoke religious sentiments of reverence and worship.

With the exception of extreme fideists, most theists considered natural religion a useful tool for answering doubts regarding theism posed by these philosophical systems. Moderate theists, such as Latitudinarians, also invoked natural religion to defend tolerance of opposing sects whose main doctrines could be justified by natural religion. On the other hand, deists attacked all forms of revealed religion, believing that true religion begins and ends with natural religion. Many theists also appealed to natural religion either to justify moral obligation or strengthen moral

---

[3] For example, the subtitle of Samuel Clarke's *Demonstration of the Being and Attributes of God* is *More particularly in answer to Mr. Hobbes, Spinoza, and their followers*, and Clarke targets the Epicurean doctrine of chance in the same work. See Clarke, *A Demonstration of the Being and Attributes of God and Other Writings*, ed. Ezio Vailati (Cambridge and Yew York: Cambridge University Press, 1998), pp. 3; 11, 19. Berkeley specifies that his philosophy opposes those who take refuge in "the doctrines of an eternal succession of unthinking causes and effects, or in a fortuitous concourse of atoms; those wild imaginations of Vanini, Hobbes, and Spinoza; in a word the whole system of atheism," *Three Dialogues between Hylas and Philonous*, in *Works*, ed. T. E. Jessop and A. A. Luce (London and New York: T. Nelson, 1948–57), II:213. He also targets Epicurus, Hobbes, and Spinoza in his *Alciphron*, Fourth Dialogue, Sec. 16, in *Works*, III:163.

motivation. Even free-thinking philosophers, such as Shaftesbury and Francis Hutcheson, who claimed that atheists are as capable of virtue as theists, contended that belief in divine rewards and punishments in an afterlife is morally preferable to atheism because it reinforces virtuous motives when they are opposed by a sense of the apparent futility of virtue and evident advantages of vice.[4] Most of Hume's contemporaries, then, would have considered his criticism of natural religion offensive to both religion and morality.

This offensiveness explains why the *Dialogues*, although first drafted in 1751, was not published until 1779, three years after Hume's death. Hume wanted to publish the work during his lifetime, but his friends discouraged him from doing so because they feared it would raise new charges of atheism, skepticism, and immoralism against him. Although Hume had never denied the existence of God or an ultimate cause of nature and had never explicitly questioned the validity of the design argument prior to the *Dialogues*, many of his critics believed that the basic principles of his philosophy as laid out in his *Treatise of Human Nature* (1739–40), *Enquiry concerning Human Understanding* (1748), and *Enquiry concerning the Principles of Morals* (1751) undermined morality and religion. As a result, he was twice passed over for academic appointments and an effort was made to excommunicate him from the Church of Scotland. Although mindful of his friends' concerns, Hume believed that "nothing can be more cautiously or artfully written" than his *Dialogues* (*LDH* II:334). Encouraged by those who considered it his best work, Hume made provisions in his will for his nephew to publish it within three years of his death, reasoning that no one could fault a nephew for dutifully carrying out his uncle's last wishes.

Caution probably led Hume to cast his criticism of natural religion in the form of a dialogue so that he could avoid speaking in his own voice, but this was only one of several motives. Among them was his intention to correct, by example, the prejudicial manner in which modern dialogues on religion tended to represent the character of skeptics.

---

[4] Anthony Ashley Cooper, Third Earl of Shaftesbury, "An Inquiry Concerning Virtue or Merit," in *Characteristics of Men, Manners, Opinions, Times*, ed. Lawrence E. Klein (Cambridge: Cambridge University Press, 1999), 190–192; Francis Hutcheson, *An Essay on the Nature and Conduct of the Passions and Affections, with Illustrations on the Moral Sense*, 3rd edn. (facs. rpt., Gainesville: Scholars' Facsimiles & Reprints, 1969), VI.iv.

The opening sentence of the *Dialogues'* prologue alludes to Shaftesbury's call in the early part of the century for a revival of Socratic dialogue-writing that pursues pedagogical ends through unrestrained, reasoned debate.[5] Shaftesbury lamented that modern philosophical dialogue-writing had devolved into the hands of dogmatic clerics who criticized heterodox opinions through misrepresentation, false ridicule, and allegations of immoralism. These writers apparently feared that representing arguments against orthodoxy in a favorable light would give them an undeserved public influence dangerous to the interests of true religion.[6] Shaftesbury defended tolerant inquiry on methodological grounds. He urged that dialogue-writers must address opposing opinions through accurate representations and logical rebuttal to assure that inquiry does not perpetuate errors. Still, Shaftesbury did not rule out the use of raillery and ridicule altogether. Believing that wit and humor are natural and pleasurable components of free-spirited conversation, he defended a polite form of raillery in dialogue-writing such as that used in private conversation among sensible friends whose moral virtues are never in question despite their minor flaws.[7] He also defended what he called "defensive raillery," the use of irony when "the spirit of curiosity would force a discovery of more truth than can conveniently be told."[8]

Similarly, Hume emphasized the importance of avoiding the "vulgar error" in dialogue-writing that puts "nothing but nonsense into the mouth of the adversary" (LE2, 120). He has his conversationalists engage in

---

[5] See Shaftesbury, *"Soliloquy, or Advice to An Author," "The Moralists,"* and *"Miscellany V"* in *Characteristics*, 87–93, 233–235, and 458–463. Hume owned a copy of the 1723 edition of the *Characteristics*, which he signed and dated in 1726 when he was fifteen. Shaftesbury's philosophical views about dialogue and soliloquy may have inspired the young Hume's decision to compose a manuscript, completed before he was twenty, that recorded the progress of his thoughts on religion. Hume recounted that the manuscript began with an "anxious search after arguments to confirm the common opinion" of God's existence. Then "doubts stole in, dissipated, returned, were again dissipated, returned again; and it was a perpetual struggle of a restless imagination against inclination, perhaps against reason." He burned the manuscript not long before sending the sample of his *Dialogues* to Gilbert Elliot in 1751. See LE2, 120.

[6] Critics of orthodoxy were also commonly guilty of abusive ridicule and misrepresentation. In their defense, they maintained that treating orthodoxy with a gravity their opponents were not willing to reciprocate would only reinforce false perceptions of their opponents' religious authority. For more on the topic of religion and ridicule, see John Redwood, *Reason, Ridicule and Religion: The Age of Enlightenment in England*, 1660–1750 (Cambridge, MA: Harvard University Press, 1976).

[7] Shaftesbury, "Sensus Communis, an Essay on the Freedom of Wit and Humour," in *Characteristics*, 36.

[8] Ibid., 30–31.

ridicule and raillery while having their friendship testify to their mutual respect despite their philosophical differences. Cleanthes accuses Philo of unreasonable skepticism, and Philo engages in defensive irony, both in his tenuous alliance with Demea until the end of Part 11 and in his palliative concession to Cleanthes in Part 12. However, despite adopting such Shaftesburean conventions, Hume rejected Shaftesbury's depiction of skepticism in his own dialogue, *The Moralists*, believing that it still portrayed skepticism in a prejudicial light.

To depict skepticism regarding natural religion in a realistic but religiously acceptable manner, Shaftesbury patterned the skeptic of his dialogue, Philocles, after his friend and philosophical nemesis, Pierre Bayle. Bayle, the most influential skeptic of the age, was thought by many to practice Pyrrhonism, an extreme form of skepticism named after the most radical ancient Greek skeptic, Pyrrho of Elis. Finding no opinions to be certain, Pyrrhonians recommended suspension of judgment to achieve peace of mind. Although caricatured as fools who would walk off cliffs because they distrusted the evidence of their senses, they implemented suspense of judgment in their daily life by simply deferring to customary behavior. Bayle repudiated the modern tendency to assimilate skepticism with atheism by proposing Pyrrhonism as a justification for fideistic acceptance of revealed religion as interpreted through traditional religious authorities. Shaftesbury regarded Bayle as "one of the best of Christians" and an exemplar of moral virtue,[9] but he was convinced that Pyrrhonian skepticism is flawed by a misplaced prioritization of values which undermines the skeptic's ability to form a fully consistent and settled character, a conviction he may have considered confirmed by Bayle's conversion to Catholicism, and then conversion back to Protestantism. Accordingly, in *The Moralists*, he has Philocles explain that he loved ease "above all else"[10] and regarded skepticism as more "at ease" and tolerant than dogmatical philosophy because it allowed him to indulge his relish for counterargument without binding him to the rigor of a systematic method that aims for final answers.

In many respects, Hume, like Shaftesbury, models the skeptic of his dialogues on Bayle, largely because Bayle influenced much of his

---

[9] Shaftesbury, Letter to Mr. Darby, February 2, 1708, in Benjamin Rand, ed., *The Life, Unpublished Letters, and Philosophical Regimen of Anthony, Earl of Shaftesbury* (London: Swan Sonnenschein, 1900), 385–386.
[10] Shaftesbury, "The Moralists," Pt. 1, Sec. 2, in *Characteristics*, 241.

own thinking. Several of Philo's remarks – particularly those regarding the incomprehensibility of God, alternative cosmological hypotheses, Epicurus' formulation of the problem of evil, the doctrine of Manicheanism, the suggestion that belief in the existence of God by itself has no influence on our lives, and the idea that philosophical skepticism is the best foundation for belief in revealed religion – can be found in Bayle's writings. Philo also employs the skeptical technique of refutation revived by Bayle. Skeptics tentatively accept premises their dogmatic opponents think are certain and draw conclusions from them which contradict the claims of their opponents. Their aim is not to endorse these conclusions, but to show that the assumed premises fail to support their opponents' contentions.

Whether Bayle is actually a Pyrrhonian skeptic has always been controversial.[11] What is not controversial is that Hume repudiated the Pyrrhonian form of skepticism which many thought Bayle endorsed. Hume advocated Academic skepticism (*EHU* 12.3.24–25), a moderate form of ancient skepticism known mostly through the writings of Cicero, but which began during the third period of Plato's Academy, after which it is named. Academic skeptics held that while nothing is certain, opinions can vary in their degree of probability, and thus a reasonable skeptic accepts whatever beliefs appear most probable. To emphasize his affinity with Academic skepticism, Hume modeled his dialogue on Cicero's *The Nature of the Gods*, voicing his doubts about religion through a character who, like the skeptic in Cicero's dialogue, is an Academic skeptic and who, unlike Shaftesbury's skeptic, is neither flawed by misplaced priorities nor converted by theological arguments Hume considered weak.

Alluding to Hume's skeptical arguments in the *Treatise* and first *Enquiry*, Philo states in Part 1 that difficulties in justifying fundamental principles and contradictions existing in common concepts of causality and matter make judgments about objects of human experience probable rather than certain. Like Hume, he maintains that human beings are psychologically impelled to form beliefs on the basis of probability and that philosophical reasoning is no more than an "exacter and more scrupulous"

---

[11] Although most of Bayle's contemporaries took him to be a Pyrrhonian skeptic, many believe that he is an Academic, not a Pyrrhonian, skeptic. See Maria Neto, "Bayle's Academic Skepticism," in Richard H. Popkin, James E. Force, and David S. Katz, eds., *Everything Connects: In Conference With Richard H. Popkin* (Leiden: Brill Academic Publishers, December, 1998); Thomas M. Lennon, *Reading Bayle* (Toronto: University of Toronto Press, 1999).

method for determining degrees of probability than what we employ in everyday experience (1.9). Like Hume, he repudiates extreme skepticism, recommending only cautious steps in all philosophical reasoning and the limitation of inquiry to topics suited to the reach of our faculties. While finding that there are many subjects for which there is "commonly but one determination, which carries probability or conviction with it" (8.1), Philo proposes that topics concerning objects beyond human experience, such as the nature of God, are so uncertain that it is not reasonable to trust any speculations about them. The *Dialogues* thus portrays skepticism regarding religion, from Philo's point of view, as "entirely owing to the nature of the subject" (8.1), not to excessive doubt or misplaced priorities. However, since the very point of dispute between philosophical theists and skeptics is whether questions about the nature of God are in fact beyond the scope of human reason and experience to determine, Philo's skepticism is, from Cleanthes' point of view, excessive at least with respect to religion, and so he teases Philo for acting like a Pyrrhonian. The task Hume sets for Philo is to explain why the evidence for theism does not warrant belief.

Arguments for the existence and nature of God

Philosophical arguments for the existence and nature of God can be divided into two kinds, *a priori* and *a posteriori*. Following terminology that became common at the beginning of Hume's century, *a priori* arguments for theism purport to prove their conclusions by deducing them as logically necessary consequences of premises taken to be intuitively certain. The ontological argument, for example, infers the existence and attributes of God as logically necessary consequences of the nature of perfect being. The cosmological argument demonstrates the existence and nature of a necessarily existent being from an *a priori* assumption about what kinds of things require a cause.[12] Empirical or *a posteriori* arguments for theism, such as the design argument, only inductively infer that it is

---

[12] In the scholastic terminology in use from Aquinas down through the Renaissance and, less commonly, into the early eighteenth century, the cosmological argument was considered an *a posteriori* argument because it reasons back from effects to causes rather than from causes to effects. Hume was among those who describe the argument as *a priori*. For the variety of uses of the terms *a priori* and *a posteriori* in eighteenth-century writers, see J. P. Ferguson, *The Philosophy of Dr. Samuel Clarke and its Critics* (New York: Vantage Press, 1974), Ch. 2.

probable that an intelligent designer of nature exists, given the evidence of experience.[13]

Many religious apologists in Hume's day considered *a priori* arguments essential to natural religion because only they can conclusively overrule objections against the existence and attributes of God.[14] However, by the time Hume composed the *Dialogues*, interest in *a priori* religious apologetics had started to wane. Even by the end of the seventeenth century, few gave any credit to the ontological argument, as most philosophers became convinced that, even if necessary existence is an essential attribute of a perfect being, it is questionable whether a being possessing that quality actually exists. At the beginning of the eighteenth century, Samuel Clarke breathed new life into the cosmological argument, but acknowledged that it could not settle the "main question between us and the atheists," namely, whether the ultimate, self-existent cause of nature is an intelligent being.[15] There is no obvious necessary connection, he explained, between intelligence and self-existence as there is between self-existence and such attributes as unity, immutability, and infinity. To settle the question between theist and atheist, Clarke thought that the cosmological argument had to be supplemented by a design argument.

Stunning discoveries in physics, astronomy, optics, biology, and other branches of science added new evidence of systematic order in nature that in turn fueled a growing interest in empirical methods of investigation in theology. Newtonianism popularized the view that while all empirical hypotheses fall short of logical certainty, in many instances, most notably Newton's three laws of motion, the evidence supporting them can be so

---

[13] Other *a posteriori* arguments for God's existence include the argument from universal consent and the argument from miracles. The first claims that the existence of God is evident from the pervasiveness of religious belief throughout human culture; the second infers the existence of God from the evidence of apparent violations of laws of nature. In the *Dialogues*, variations on the argument from universal consent appear in Cleanthes' suggestion that belief in an intelligent deity is instinctually triggered by contemplating nature's order (3.7–9), and also Demea's suggestion that belief in a providential deity is triggered by hope and fear (10.1). The argument from miracles is not discussed in *Dialogues* because it does not fall within the province of natural religion, which considers only evidence that is independent of supernatural revelation. However, Hume criticizes this argument in detail in Section 10 of his *Enquiry concerning Human Understanding*.

[14] For example, Clarke, "The Answer to a Seventh Letter Concerning the Argument *a priori*," in *A Demonstration*, 119–121. Clarke considered the *a priori* component of his cosmological argument to be the inference of divine attributes from the nature of a necessarily existent being, once the existence of such a being is demonstrated *a posteriori* (in the scholastic sense – see note 12) from facts about the world.

[15] Clarke, *A Demonstration*, Sec. VIII, p. 38.

strong as to leave no room for any practical doubt. While most apologists for rational theology followed Clarke in combining the design argument and cosmological argument, many began to consider the premises of the cosmological argument either empirical generalizations or psychologically determined beliefs rather than necessary truths. Others believed they could defend theism on the basis of an empirical design argument alone. The two most influential examples of the latter approach are found in Shaftesbury's dialogue, *The Moralists* (1709), and George Berkeley's dialogue, *Alciphron* (1732). To reflect Shaftesbury's and Berkeley's view that an empirical design argument is sufficient to support religion, as well as Clarke's view that *a priori* proofs are necessary for conclusively rebutting objections to theism, Hume's *Dialogues* evaluates the design argument as a stand-alone argument and also considers whether the cosmological argument can compensate for its limitations.

Cleanthes' design argument

The common feature in design arguments is to infer the existence of an intelligent designer from some aspect of the order in nature. More complete versions of the argument begin with arguments *to* design, that is, citations of various instances of order to support the claim that nature is a systematically ordered, harmonious whole.[16] The version in Hume's *Dialogues* assumes that nature's systematic order is a well-established empirical fact. Design arguments use various analogies to elucidate the concept of intelligently designed order. For example, Shaftesbury's version in *The Moralists* compares the order in nature to personal identity or the unity of the self, while Berkeley's version in the *Alciphron* compares the order in nature to human speech.[17] The version presented by

---

[16] For example, William Derham, *Physico-Theology: or, A Demonstration of the Being and Attributes of God, from the Works of Creation* (London, 1713); Bernhard Nieuwent, *The Religious Philosophers: or the Right Use of Contemplating the Works of the Creator*, an influential Dutch work published in English five times between 1718 and 1745.

[17] See Shaftesbury, "The Moralists," Pt. 3, Sec. 1, in *Characteristics*, 300–304; Berkeley, *Alciphron*, Fourth Dialogue, Secs. 6–7, in *Works* III:148–149. Hume alludes to Shaftesbury's analogy in a footnote to his discussion of personal identity in the *Treatise* (1.4.6. n. 50). Hume may be alluding to Berkeley's analogy in *D* 3.7, when he has Cleanthes remark that "no language can convey a more intelligible irresistible meaning, than the curious adjustment of final causes" (3.7). Berkeley argued that nature is a language conveying meaning to us through visual or "optical" signs exactly as one person speaks to another in conversation through linguistic signs. We know God exists, he believed, because "God talks to us" using the visual language of nature.

Cleanthes in Part 2 relies on the machine analogy rooted in the systems of Galileo and Newton and popularized by Hume's fellow countryman, George Cheyne. In *Philosophical Principles of Religion: Natural and Revealed*, Cheyne wrote: "By nature, I understand this vast, if not infinite, *Machine* of the Universe . . . consisting of an infinite Number of lesser *Machines*, every one of which is adjusted by Weight and Measure."[18] Although Cheyne, like Clarke, believed that the connection between intelligence and order is a necessary one, Hume adapted Cheyne's analogy to conform to an empirical cast of the design argument. Blending the thoughts of various writers,[19] Hume has Cleanthes reason that since order in nature resembles order in machines, and since experience teaches that like effects have like causes, "we are led to infer, by all the rules of analogy, that the causes also resemble; and that the author of nature is somewhat similar to the mind of man; though possessed of much larger faculties, proportioned to the grandeur of the work, which he has executed" (2.5).

While Demea protests that Cleanthes' empirical argument gives advantages to atheists by conceding the existence of God is not *a priori* certain, Philo objects that it falls far short of empirical certainty. To show this he introduces three objections to the argument which draw from Hume's account of causal reasoning in the *Treatise* and *Enquiry*. First, in inferences from analogy any deviation from an exact resemblance between objects weakens the probability of inferences based on their resemblance. Since the scale, mass, duration, and situation of the universe are vastly different from those of any artifacts of human making, any inference from their similarity falls significantly short of practical certainty. Second, while not all forms of matter are capable of creating ordered effects – piles of brick and mortar never arrange themselves into a house, for example – nature affords numerous instances of forms of matter that are: plants and animals and their seeds and eggs regularly produce other ordered plants, animals, seeds and eggs. If experience shows that ordered effects

---

[18] George Cheyne, *Philosophical Principles of Religion: Natural and Revealed*, 5th edn. (London, 1736), 2. Cf. *D* 2.5.

[19] Hume's decision to present the argument this way reflects his conviction that "a man cannot escape ridicule, who repeats a discourse as a school-boy does his lesson, and takes no notice of any thing that has been advanced in the course of the debate" (*Essays*, 109). On the other hand, his lack of interest in *a priori* arguments may explain why, aside from Demea's characteristic tendency to appeal to pious authorities, he has Demea provide no more than a "school-boy" summary of Clarke's cosmological argument in Part 9.

are produced by non-intelligent as well as intelligent causes, it is arbitrary to conclude that every ordered effect, including nature as a whole, must ultimately be produced by an intelligent cause (2.18–23).

These first two objections lead to the third: the most conclusive causal inferences are those based on observations of constant conjunctions between exactly similar types of objects. To be empirically certain that differences between nature and machines make no difference to the similarity of their causes, and to be empirically certain that causes of ordered effects other than intelligence cannot be the cause of nature, we would need to observe a constant conjunction between intelligent causes and the generation of universes. However, we do not have this kind of evidence regarding the universe since it is a unique, single entity. Philo concludes that the inference to an intelligent designer is at best weakly probable rather than empirically certain.

The instinctive feeling of intelligent design

Hume was aware that the design argument, despite its shortcomings, garnered a wide appeal which many of his contemporaries considered additional evidence in its favor. Consequently, he addresses this feature of the argument in Part 3, where Cleanthes characterizes the inference to an intelligent designer, not as a conclusion drawn by weighing evidence, but as an instinctive, immediate *feeling* that strikes with "a force like that of sensation" (3.7)[20] when contemplating nature's order. Cleanthes concludes that even if the inference is "irregular" or "contradictory to the principles of logic" by Philo's account, it is sufficiently supported by "common sense and the plain instincts of nature," evidence he claims Philo must accept if he professes to be a "reasonable" skeptic (3.8). Hume has Pamphilus describe Philo as "a little embarrassed and confounded" (3.10) by Cleanthes' ridicule and re-characterization of his argument in psychological terms. His reaction is dramatically appropriate given the shift in Cleanthes' argument and the unpopularity of skepticism regarding religion, but some readers have inferred that Pamphilus' observation,

[20] *A force like that of sensation*: Phrasing used by Colin MacLaurin, *An Account of Sir Isaac Newton's Philosophical Discoveries* (London, 1748; rpt., New York: Johnson, 1968), 381 and Henry Home, *Essays on the Principles of Morality and Natural Religion* (1751; facs. rpt., New York: Garland Publishing, 1976), 328. Since Home and Hume were close friends, they may have discussed this psychological account of the argument from design prior to or during the time Hume composed the *Dialogues*.

together with Philo's conciliatory remarks in the concluding part of the *Dialogues*, signal that Hume himself was persuaded by this version of the argument.

This interpretation may seem to be supported by the fact that Cleanthes' new emphasis on common instinct curiously resembles Hume's defense of belief in causation in the *Treatise* and his first *Enquiry*. Causal beliefs, he argued, ultimately depend on natural instinct, not rational argument. While reasonable and unreasonable causal beliefs are distinguishable by the degree to which they are supported by observations of constant conjunctions between events, the inference to a causal relation based on this standard is not itself reasoned. It cannot result from immediate or demonstratively necessary inferences because, however constant the relation between two objects has been, it is logically possible that their conjunction will not continue. Nor is the inference based on probable reasoning, since probable reasoning already presupposes that regular conjunctions observed in the past will continue in the future. Causal inference, Hume concluded, must be founded on instinct rather than reason (*T* 1.3.2,14; *EHU* 5.22).

However, Hume also saw that not all instincts are alike. He distinguished between "principles which are permanent, irresistible, and universal; such as the customary transition from causes to effects, and from effects to causes: and the principles, which are changeable, weak, and irregular." Universal instincts are essential for survival, but irregular instincts are not:

> The former are the foundation of all our thoughts and actions, so that upon their removal, human nature must immediately perish and go to ruin. The latter are neither unavoidable to mankind, nor necessary, or so much as useful in the conduct of life; but, on the contrary, are observed only to take place in weak minds, and being opposite to the other principles of custom and reasoning, may easily be subverted by a due contrast and opposition. For this reason, the former are received by philosophy, and the latter rejected. (*T* 1.4.4.1)

Hume specifically comments on the relation between universal instincts and Cleanthes' argument in his March, 1751 letter to Gilbert Elliot. He delicately suggests to Elliot that the instinct to infer an intelligent designer from nature's order may be more like the anthropomorphic instinct to see human shapes in clouds than the instinct to believe in causes and external objects:

I could wish that Cleanthes' argument could be so analyzed, as to be rendered quite formal and regular. The propensity of the mind towards it, unless that propensity were as strong and universal as that to believe in our senses and experience, will still, I am afraid, be esteemed a suspicious foundation. It is here I wish for your assistance. We must endeavour to prove that this propensity is somewhat different from our inclination to find our own figures in the clouds, our face in the moon, our passions and sentiments even in inanimate matter. Such an inclination may, and ought to be controlled, and can never be a legitimate ground of assent. (LE2, 121; cf. *NHR*, 127–128)

Furthermore, in *The Natural History of Religion*, Hume unambiguously argued that belief in intelligent, invisible power, while common, is not universal (*NHR*, 124). He also proposed that religious belief originates in and is perpetuated by hopes and fears concerning unknown causes rather than by contemplation of nature's order (*NHR*, 126). Even if Hume allowed that the feeling of intelligent design is in some sense instinctive, he did not accept it as an irresistible psychological principle, much less as one whose absence would lead to the extinction of human life.

Advocates of the design argument themselves acknowledged that the feeling of intelligent design, while common, is not entirely universal, typically conceding that incurious "savages" and excessively curious skeptics fail to experience it. Hume understood that he must still address the suggestion that the argument for intelligent design is accepted at least by all sensible people who seriously consider it (cf. *NHR*, 134). To do this Hume has Philo and Demea draw Cleanthes' attention to alternative explanations of observed order, all of which can be considered "sensible" following Cleanthes' principles.

Alternative hypotheses

Demea's rebuttal of Cleanthes' argument revisits the lively controversy between theists such as Peter Browne and Berkeley concerning what it means to say that God is an intelligent being or mind.[21] Like Berkeley,

---

[21] See Peter Browne, *The Procedure, Extent, and Limits of the Human Understanding* (London, 1728; facs. rpt., New York and London: Garland Publishing, 1976), 81–85. His views were criticized by (among others) Berkeley in *Alciphron* (originally published in 1732), Fourth Dialogue, Secs. 17–22, in *Works*, III:163–170. Browne responded to Berkeley and other critics in *Things Divine and Supernatural Conceived by Analogy with Things Natural and Human* (London, 1733; facs. rpt., New York and London: Garland Publishing, 1976).

Cleanthes maintains that it means that God is intelligent in the same sense as the human – the difference is not a difference in kind, only one of degree. Like Browne, Demea argues that since perceptions, thoughts, sentiments, and volitions and their successive order of existence in human consciousness depend on physical circumstances of the human condition, human intelligence cannot literally resemble a being for whom physical circumstances do not apply. While Browne accepts that God and human thought are analogous powers, he denies their similarity consists in some proportion of knowable qualities. The difference between human intelligence and divine intelligence is not just one of degree, but an incomprehensible difference of kind. Like Browne, Demea nevertheless maintains that since intelligence is something we value in human nature, it is natural and appropriate to attribute intelligence to the ultimate cause of nature as a figurative expression of awe or respect for a power incomprehensibly greater than our own, provided it is acknowledged that when the terms "intelligent" and "mind" are used in this way, they do not denote anything literally resembling human thought (*D* 3.13). Philo also ascribes intelligence to God in a similarly limited, pious manner of speaking (*D* 1.3), but only ironically, presuming that he agreed with Berkeley's assessment that "nothing can be inferred from such an account of God, about conscience, or worship, or religion"[22] a consequence which suits Philo's skepticism regarding religion. However, Cleanthes, like Berkeley, rejects Browne's mysticism precisely because it would be no different from skepticism or atheism in its consequences.

Putting aside this controversy between theists, Philo shows that Cleanthes' facile manner in applying rules of analogy more strongly supports a variety of pagan hypotheses that have important explanatory advantages. In Part 5, he amusingly proposes polytheistic scenarios of universes created by intelligent but juvenile, senile, or underling deities. While fanciful, they have the advantage of explaining apparent imperfections in the universe. In Part 6, he proposes a pantheistic hypothesis according to which God is the soul of the universe and the universe is God's body. The suggestion has the advantage of conforming to the uniform evidence of experience that minds exist only in bodies. In Part 7, he proposes that the same features of the world which lead Cleanthes

---

[22] Berkeley, *Alciphron*, in *Works* III:165. His criticism of the view that God's mind is different in kind from human intelligence continues up through p. 170.

to see nature as a machine can be found in the effects of biological generation. If nature's order resembles an organism more than a machine, then, by Cleanthes' principles, it would follow that the universe more probably originated in a primordial plant, animal, egg, or seed. Fanciful as these suggestions appear, they have the advantage of being consistent with uniform experience that intelligent beings originate through biological generation, not the other way around.

Philo's arguments in Parts 5–7 have a playful mood, humorously reducing Cleanthes' prideful empiricism to what Cleanthes would consider poetical superstitions, but in Part 8 he adopts a more serious tone. He proposes that, given infinite time and a finite quantity of matter, the observed natural order, including intelligent life, would inevitably arise from the motion and collision of unorganized material particles. According to this hypothesis, nature's order is the result of necessity, not of chance or intelligent design. While it does not explain why matter possesses an inherent power of motion, it has an important explanatory advantage that Cleanthes' hypothesis lacks. The idea that intelligent life gradually develops from unconscious matter in accordance with general causal laws is consistent with the evidence that while many forms of matter exist that are not intelligent, intelligent life has never been found to exist without matter. Cleanthes' hypothesis reverses this universally observed order of causal dependence, suggesting that material reality originates from an immaterial mind.[23]

Despite Philo's professed skepticism about understanding ultimate causes, the conspicuous change in tone in Part 8 leads some readers to speculate that Hume may have believed the ultimate cause or causes of nature are material. This interpretation may seem to be supported by the following remark from his *Natural History of Religion*:

> Could men anatomize nature, according to the most probable, at least the most intelligible philosophy, they would find, that these causes are nothing but the particular fabric and structure of the minute parts of their own bodies and of external objects; and that, by a regular and constant machinery, all the events are produced, about which they are so much concerned. (*NHR*, 127)

---

[23] However, Part 8 does not consider Berkeley's claim that matter, being passive, cannot originate motion, while mind, which we experience as an active principle, can. See Berkeley, *A Treatise concerning the Principles of Human Knowledge*, Pt. 1, Secs. 25–28 in *Works*, II:51–53. Hume addresses this type of view in *T* 1.3.14.8–13 and *EHU* 7.9–25.

Nevertheless, the context of this statement is a general one about unknown causes, not specifically about ultimate causes. The remark does not close off the possibility that the "particular fabric and structure" of minute particles of matter and the "regular and constant machinery" of the universe have a more ultimate, perhaps even intelligent cause, since it does not explain why the fabric and structure of material particles and the laws of physics are what they are. His remark further suggests that explanations that pretend to identify ultimate causes would be less intelligible because of the difficulty in explaining what makes such causes ultimate. The following quotation from the *Treatise* is further evidence that Hume, no less than his fictional Philo, is skeptical of any pretense to identify ultimate causes:

> And tho' we must endeavour to render all our principles as universal as possible, by tracing up our experiments to the utmost, and explaining all effects from the simplest and fewest causes, 'tis still certain we cannot go beyond experience; and any hypothesis, that pretends to discover the ultimate or original qualities . . . ought at first to be rejected as presumptuous and chimerical. (*T*, Intro., 8)

The reason why Hume considers the fabric and structure of material particles and general laws of physics the most "intelligible" account of unknown causes is voiced by Philo: they do not reverse the universally observed dependence of thought on matter. Nevertheless, since Hume does not believe such explanations are complete, Philo accurately represents Hume's skepticism when he states that the material hypothesis of Part 8, if taken as a pretended ultimate explanation of nature, is only one of "a hundred contradictory views." It is natural, then, that Hume has Philo conclude Part 8 by saying that all pretended ultimate explanations, including Cleanthes' hypothesis, "prepare a complete triumph for the sceptic," who claims that "a total suspense of judgement is here our only reasonable resource" (8.12).

Demea's cosmological argument

Demea proposes that Philo's alternative hypotheses show that empirical speculation concerning the ultimate cause of nature is too uncertain to provide any guidance for religious worship. If Cleanthes' principles leave in doubt whether the cause of nature is one or many, finite or infinite, transcendent or immanent, material or immaterial, "What devotion or worship address to them?" he asks, or "What veneration or obedience pay them?" With all these attributes in question, natural theology "becomes altogether useless" (6.1).

To remedy this deficiency, Demea offers to defend theism with an *a priori* cosmological argument for a necessarily existent being that resembles Samuel Clarke's argument.[24] Like Clarke, Demea maintains that the argument conclusively proves divine attributes such as unity and infinity that empirical arguments leave uncertain.

Cleanthes poses five objections to show that Demea's argument does not support theism. All are consistent with Hume's principles. His first objection, which he claims is entirely decisive, is a general statement denying that claims about what exists can be proven by *a priori* demonstration (9.5). His next two objections concern the concept of necessary being. He claims, first, that the concept has no consistent meaning, and then suggests that, by one account of its meaning, the material universe may be this necessary being (9.6–7). His final two criticisms challenge Demea's assumption that an eternal series of contingent events must have a cause (9.8–9).

Cleanthes' third criticism specifically addresses an argument Clarke had given to support his claim that the ultimate cause of nature cannot be material. The argument is sometimes referred to as the argument from contingency. Clarke noted that the material universe, with respect both to its parts and to the form in which its parts are arranged, is logically contingent rather than necessary because both the whole and each of its parts can be conceived not to exist or to exist in a different form. He concluded that the reason why a material universe exists rather than nothing, and the reason why the arrangement of matter in this universe exists rather than some other, must be an immaterial cause, not a material one. Cleanthes responds by saying that the existence of an immaterial deity also appears logically contingent:

> [T]he mind can at least imagine him to be non-existent, or his attributes to be altered. It must be some unknown, inconceivable

---

[24] Demea describes the argument as *a priori*, but Clarke describes it as *a posteriori*. The difference is explained by the fact that Clarke used these terms in their older scholastic sense. See note 12. For Clarke's argument, see *A Demonstration*, Secs. I–III, pp. 8–28.

qualities, which can make his non-existence appear impossible, or his attributes unalterable: And no reason can be assigned, why these qualities may not belong to matter. As they are altogether unknown and inconceivable, they can never be proved incompatible with it. (9.7)

Some readers question whether Cleanthes' criticisms of the cosmological argument are convincing, but Hume did not need them to be convincing if he believed that the cosmological argument, even if sound, has no religious significance. Even if it proves divine attributes such as infinity, unity, or necessary existence, it would not prove divine intelligence, and another issue – the focus of Parts 10 and 11 – would still divide theists from skeptics and atheists. Meanwhile, Hume concludes the discussion of the cosmological argument by having Philo say, without either endorsing or rejecting Cleanthes' criticisms, that he will set aside these abstract reflections to observe that

> the argument *a priori* has seldom been found convincing, except to people of a metaphysical head, who have accustomed themselves to abstract reasoning . . . Other people, even of good sense and the best inclined to religion, feel always some deficiency in such arguments, though they are not perhaps able to explain distinctly where it lies. A certain proof, that men ever did, and ever will, derive their religion from other sources than from this species of reasoning. (9.11)

The problem of evil

His cosmological argument dismissed, Demea's zeal to defend religious worship leads him to propose a psychological justification of religion in place of a rational one, a shift that parallels Cleanthes' shift to an instinctive justification in Part 3. He now asserts that consciousness of "imbecility and misery," not reasoning, leads people to believe "in a being, on whom all nature is dependent" who is capable of protecting humanity from misfortune. "Our hopes and fears," Demea asserts, make us "endeavour, by prayers, adoration, and sacrifice, to appease those unknown powers, whom we find, by experience, so able to afflict and oppress us" (10.1). Since Hume himself argues in his *Natural History of Religion* that religious worship originates in and is perpetuated by hope and fear spurred by ignorance, it is not surprising that he has Philo join Demea in cataloguing a long list of natural and moral evils[25] that pollute human life and concur that "the best and indeed the only method of bringing everyone to a due sense of religion is by just representations of the misery and wickedness of men" (10.2).

Demea's and Philo's gloomy assessment of the human condition introduces a new problem for natural religion – how to reconcile the existence of evil with the orthodox conception of God as an all-powerful, all-knowing, and morally perfect being. Several different strategies are available to theists to defuse this problem. One is to deny the reality of evil. Following this account, which Philo attributes to William King and Gottfried Leibniz (10.6), what we consider evil from our limited perspective is actually good in so far as it is part of a system that could not be improved by its elimination. Demea rejects this approach, finding that it contradicts "the united testimony of mankind, founded on sense and consciousness," that affirms the reality of evil. Instead, he proposes a solution he claims has been urged by "all pious divines and preachers," namely, that evil is real, but still compatible with God's perfect goodness because whatever evil exists will be rectified at some future time, if not in this life, then in life after death. Like Shaftesbury,[26] Cleanthes rejects this solution because expectations about what will exist in the future or an afterlife are arbitrary without evidence from present experience. Nevertheless, he also understands that if experience shows that humankind is "unhappy or corrupted" in this life, "there is an end at once of all religion. For to what purpose establish the natural attributes of the deity, when the moral are still doubtful and uncertain?" (10.28). To defuse the problem of evil, Cleanthes claims that Philo and Demea's depiction of the hopelessness of the human condition is exaggerated. The evidence of human experience shows that happiness predominates over misery, and this predominance in turn proves God's perfect benevolence.

Philo cautions Cleanthes that he is putting "this controversy on a most dangerous issue," and is "unawares introducing a total scepticism into the most essential articles of natural and revealed theology" (10.33). His warning initially draws from Hume's treatment of this topic in a manuscript fragment surviving from around the time he was finishing his *Treatise*. Despite his stated inclination to believe that misery predominates over

[25] *Natural evil* is pain and suffering produced by unconscious forces of nature; *moral evil* is evil produced by human choice.
[26] Shaftesbury, "The Moralists," in *Characteristics*, 245.

happiness, Hume argued in the fragment that "the facts are here so complicated and dispersed, that a certain conclusion can never be formed from them" (Fragment, 111). It is understandable, then, that Hume would have Philo say that "a talent of eloquence and strong imagery is more requisite than that of reasoning and argument" (10.2) to represent the miserable state of the human condition. It is also understandable why, even after declaring his inclination to believe that misery predominates over happiness, Philo says he will not "insist upon these topics" (10.33). Both Hume and Hume's Philo deal with the question concerning divine benevolence on other grounds.

Hume approached the question in two ways. One approach draws from his account of moral passions and judgment. In this regard, the question is how best to explain the existence of moral judgments and motives: are they common to all conscious creatures or do they depend on more particular characteristics and circumstances? Hume sided with the second alternative. In his *Treatise* and *Enquiry concerning the Principles of Morals*, he argued that moral judgments depend on feelings and sentiments rooted in human nature. Although he did not spell out the religious consequences of this position in his published writings, he did so in a letter to Francis Hutcheson. "Since morality, according to your opinion as well as mine, is determined merely by sentiment," he wrote,

> it regards only human nature and human life. This has been often urged against you, and the consequences are very momentous . . . If morality were determined by reason, that is the same to all rational beings: But nothing but experience can assure us, that the sentiments are the same. What experience have we with regard to superior beings? How can we ascribe to them any sentiments at all? They have implanted those sentiments in us for the conduct of life like our bodily sensations, which they possess not themselves. (LH, 114)

Hume's second approach considers the issue solely within the context of the problem of evil. From this standpoint, the question is: what hypothesis best explains the distribution of happiness and misery actually found in the world? Is the mixture of good and evil best explained in terms of moral intentions of a deity, or by morally indifferent forces of nature?

In his early fragment, Hume argued that even if it is granted that pleasure predominates over pain, the ambiguity of the evidence suggests this predominance is at best marginal. Since a marginal predominance could result from a mixture of causes that are indifferent to human happiness, parsimony makes it probable that the ultimate cause or causes of nature have no moral intentions. However, by the time he wrote his *Enquiry concerning Human Understanding*, Hume came to believe that the problem of evil is not a problem about the quantity of evil at all. Framing the *Enquiry*'s discussion of this issue as a dialogue between a first-person narrator and his Epicurean friend, Hume has the friend argue that if the question of God's moral perfection is not assumed but subjected to the test of empirical evidence, even the least mixture of evil with good counts as evidence against it.

It may seem that Hume is endorsing a non-skeptical conclusion in the fragment and the *Enquiry* that is inconsistent with his view, voiced through Philo, that no judgments about the nature of ultimate causes warrant belief. However, the difficulty disappears if Hume's remarks are seen in the context of the same argumentative strategy adopted by Philo in the *Dialogues*. The purpose of these arguments is not to endorse non-skeptical conclusions but to show that, accepting the assumption of his non-skeptical, theistic opponents that empirical evidence is strong enough to justify conclusions about the moral qualities of ultimate causes, the evidence supports a conclusion that contradicts their opinion that God is perfectly benevolent.

Whereas Hume's fragment emphasizes the *quantity* of evil, and the *Enquiry* emphasizes the *mere existence* of evil, the *Dialogues* emphasizes the fact that evil *appears avoidable*. The shift is necessary because in Part 11 Cleanthes introduces the heterodox idea that God's powers are finite rather than infinite, explaining that while God is supremely wise, powerful, and benevolent, he is limited by necessity. Intractable qualities of matter and the general physical laws that govern them would require God to permit some evil in order to achieve benevolent ends. He then proposes that God is perfectly benevolent because the predominance of happiness over misery proves that God avoids unnecessary evil.

To undermine Cleanthes' argument, Philo sets out to show that evil *appears* avoidable to us even on Cleanthes' assumption that everything depends on a finite God. For example, one of the causes of evil is the conformity of everything in nature to general laws. This cause does not appear to be necessary because we find no contradiction in supposing that a finite, but still vastly superior and supreme cause could govern nature through particular volitions rather than general laws. Since the conformity of things to general laws does not appear to be necessary to us, and since, by Cleanthes' hypothesis, everything ultimately depends on God, the evil that results from general laws therefore appears avoidable as well. However, by human standards of benevolence, the only standards known to us, a being that does not act so as to avoid unnecessary evil is not benevolent. Philo accepts that if it could be known by *a priori* reasoning that God possesses morally perfect intentions, it could also be known that evil, despite these appearances, is consistent with divine moral perfection. However, supposing (as Cleanthes does) that there is no such *a priori* knowledge, judgments about his moral qualities must be drawn from the evidence of human experience, the way things appear. With regard to the moral qualities of the ultimate cause or causes of the universe, there are only four logical possibilities to consider: (1) they are perfectly good, (2) they are perfectly evil, (3) they are a mixture of good and evil, or (4) they are neither good nor evil. The existence of both good and evil in nature weighs against the first two hypotheses. The evidence that all events obey a uniform system of general laws does not support the hypothesis that contrary moral agencies, one malevolent, the other benevolent, underlie the natural course of events. The fourth hypothesis, Philo concludes, "seems by far the most probable" (11.15).

Hume also has Philo respond, at least implicitly, to Joseph Butler's treatment of the problem of evil in his influential work, *The Analogy of Religion*, first published in 1736.[27] Butler proposes that the mixture of pleasure and pain in nature as such has no bearing on the moral qualities of God. He argues that suffering can be good if it is a punishment for vice or necessary for developing moral character. Moreover, he argues that moral evil, while never good, is an evil a morally perfect being would permit only if it is necessary to bring about a greater good, namely human freedom and rectitude. Philo's response is implicit in his comment that

> what I have said concerning natural evil will apply to moral, with little or no variation; and we have no more reason to infer, that the rectitude of the supreme being resembles human rectitude than that his benevolence resembles the human. (11.16)

Philo's statement suggests that even if we suppose that everything depends on a supreme but limited God, there is no contradiction in

---

[27] Joseph Butler, *The Analogy of Religion*, ed. Ernest C. Mossner (New York: F. Ungar Pub. Co., 1961), Pt. I, Chs. III–IV.

further supposing that virtue could be learned in ways other than through suffering or that even a limited God could have created human beings with a disposition to always choose what is good. Since moral evil exists and appears avoidable, we have no basis for inferring the existence of a supremely intelligent and powerful being, whether finite or infinite, who acts from moral motives such as righteousness.

Philo's final criticism is ostensibly directed against Cleanthes' anthropomorphism, but the form of the argument – a cosmological argument – suggests that Demea is its principal target. Philo explains that since every event must have a cause, the existence of human vice must have a cause, and that cause must have another, and so on, either *ad infinitum* or ending in the ultimate cause of all things. Demea interrupts before Philo can complete his argument, but the intended conclusion is clear. If everything ultimately depends for its existence on God, whether as something he directly causes or only permits through other causes he creates, then God is ultimately the cause of moral evil, and thus responsible for it. Demea complains that he had allied himself with Philo "in order to prove the incomprehensible nature of the divine being, and refute the principles of *Cleanthes*, who would measure everything by human rule and standard." Now, Demea says, "Philo is betraying that holy cause," by defending conclusions about God's moral qualities on the basis of human standards (11.18). Demea would have no reason to be disturbed by this argument unless he had been assuming, like Cleanthes, that God is not responsible for human sin and that if God were responsible for sin, he would not be an appropriate object of worship. He would then have perceived that Philo's argument is as much a refutation of his own way of thinking as it is of Cleanthes'. No longer relishing the conversation, Demea departs from the company, excusing himself on some pretense.

Verbal disputes and true religion

Demea's departure is a reminder that there are social limits to tolerance of raillery and skepticism regarding religion. Consequently, after Demea leaves, Philo adopts a conciliatory tone, at least on the point of intelligent design, when he says:

> notwithstanding the freedom of my conversation, and my love of singular arguments, no one has a deeper sense of religion impressed

on his mind, or pays more profound adoration to the divine being, as he discovers himself to reason, in the inexplicable contrivance and artifice of nature. A purpose, an intention, a design strikes every-where the most careless, the most stupid thinker, and no man can be so hardened in absurd systems, as at all times to reject it. (12.2)

He then lists some instances of apparent design, contrasts the claims of theists and atheists, and concludes that "the whole of natural theology" reduces to "one simple, though somewhat ambiguous, at least undefined proposition" to which both atheists and theists can assent: "*that the cause or causes of order in the universe probably bear some remote analogy to human intelligence*" (12.33).

Philo's remarks seems surprising, and their artful wording makes it deliciously easy to interpret them entirely ironically.[28] However, Philo is not speaking entirely in jest. Professing his "unfeigned" sentiments, he modifies his original skeptical principle. No longer urging suspension of judgment concerning all theological topics because they go beyond the reach of human faculties to determine, he adopts a more moderate form of Academic skepticism which accepts every fact "when it is supported by all the arguments, which its nature admits of; even though these arguments be not, in themselves, very numerous or forcible" (12.4). The change in his position does not concede very much: it allows him to continue to maintain that the nature of God is incomprehensible. He describes the design of nature through which God reveals himself as "inexplicable" and describes the conclusion of the design argument as "ambiguous" or "at least undefined." His earlier criticisms have prepared the way for this ambiguity because they showed that all ordered effects resemble each other to the extent that they exhibit mutual adaptation among their parts. Since like effects have like causes, the resemblance of these effects provides at least *some*, even if not forceful evidence that the ultimate cause of nature resembles all the diverse causes of order within nature, including human intelligence. At the same time, the vast differences among ordered effects

---

[28] For example, the inference to an intelligent designer "strikes everywhere the most careless, the most stupid thinker," but not a cautious reasoner. No one who is "hardened in absurd systems" can "at all times . . . reject" it, though cautious reasoners can. "Astronomers," like Newton, and almost all the scientists of Hume's day, may have "insensibly," that is, "without thinking" and without evidence, taken their principles to be a foundation for religious piety, but the authority of science is "much the greater" when it does "not directly profess that intention." No one pays "more adoration to God as he discovers himself to reason" than Philo, since reason discovers nothing about divine nature. (See 12.2.)

are also evidence that there is a proportionate difference among their causes, and, in particular, a proportionate difference between the cause of nature as a whole and human intelligence. To this extent, atheists as much as theists can accept that the ultimate cause or causes of nature remotely resemble human intelligence because the statement is too ambiguous to have religiously significant content. Its ambiguity also explains why Hume would feel no compunction about resorting to irony in his other works, where he sometimes states the design argument as if he endorsed a theistic interpretation of it.[29]

To further explain the ambiguity of the design argument's conclusion, Philo proposes that the dispute about whether God is a mind or intelligent being can be regarded as merely verbal. A dispute is verbal if it is about words rather than about ideas or things. Since "mind" or "intelligence" can be taken in a broad as well as narrow sense, atheists as well as theists can agree that the cause of nature remotely resembles human intelligence while still disagreeing about the degree of resemblance. Even disagreements about degrees of qualities are verbal because there are no precise standards or definitions to demarcate degrees of qualities. To emphasize the differences in degree between the cause of nature and human intelligence, atheists are inclined to say that their resemblance is *very remote*; to emphasize that nature's cause is more like human thought than it is like instinct, biological reproduction, or natural selection, theists are inclined to say it is *not very remote* – but both sides could just as easily switch expressions. When theists wish to emphasize divine superiority over human intelligence, they will say their resemblance is *very remote*, and if atheists wish to emphasize the unity of all things they will be inclined to say the resemblance is *not very remote*. Since these are ambiguous expressions that can be used by atheists and theists alike, they cannot be taken as endorsements of either view.

It is not obvious whether Hume was willing to accept the less restricted version of Academic skepticism that Philo describes in Part 12. Yet, provided it is understood in a way that makes no difference to the thesis that the nature of God is incomprehensible, he most likely regarded a merely verbal assent to this less restricted Academic skepticism as an acceptable practical compromise for an irreligious skeptic who desires to makes

---

[29] Cf. *T* 1.3.14n; *Letter from a Gentleman*, 25–26; *NHR*, "Introduction" and Sec. xv, pp. 124–125, 134.

himself appear more reasonable to a "dogmatic" (non-skeptical) theist. In either case, it is significant that Hume, who was accused of unreasonable skepticism by theists and atheists alike, inserted a long discursive footnote in Part 12 proposing, in his own voice, that the dispute between skeptics and dogmatists can also be regarded as verbal.

Some find it puzzling that Hume does not have Philo suggest a verbal analysis of the dispute concerning the moral qualities of the cause of nature. Since moral qualities have degrees, it seems that the terms for moral qualities can also be used in a broad sense, so that anyone can agree that the cause of nature remotely resembles human virtue while also disagreeing about their degree of resemblance. Hume has a good reason not to have Philo make this concession, even following his less restricted form of Academic skepticism. The resemblance between nature and human artifacts provides at least some empirical evidence that the cause of nature is proportionately similar to human thought, but there is less evidence that nature resembles the effects of human benevolence and rectitude, for the reasons given by Philo in Part 11. Since a resemblance between the cause of nature and human virtue is less probable than its resemblance to human intelligence, Philo is willing to accept the latter but not the former.

Despite the ambiguity of Philo's single theological tenet, it is not entirely without consequences. First, it has important negative implications. It does not support any attempt to justify scientific, moral, and religious practices on theological principles. Second, it may produce certain sentiments such as "astonishment" because of the "greatness of the object"; "melancholy" because of "its obscurity"; and "contempt of human reason" because it "can give no solution more satisfactory" with regard to the question of what nature God possesses (12.33). None of these, however, constitute scientific, moral, or religious attitudes as these are normally understood.

To oppose Cleanthes' claim that belief in immortality and a system of divine rewards and punishments is necessary for morality, Philo provides a moral defense of his understanding of true religion that expands on that given in the dialogue of Section 11 of Hume's *Enquiry concerning Human Understanding*. Like the *Enquiry*'s unnamed "friend," Philo argues that morality derives from instincts inherent in human nature and that therefore virtue depends neither on the acceptance of religious beliefs nor on philosophical arguments that may or may not support them. Whereas Shaftesbury defended tolerance of free inquiry on methodological grounds, Hume defends it on the moral ground that philosophical arguments alone cannot undermine moral interests. While tolerant of all theological arguments, Hume was less tolerant of religious passions, stating that "generally speaking, the errors in religion are dangerous; those in philosophy only ridiculous" (*T* 1.4.7.13). Philo reflects this Humean view when he observes that religious passions, particularly the sense of obligation owed to God, tend to subvert natural standards of morality, sometimes to the extreme of defending abhorrent crimes in the name of divine justice.

Philo calls his single, ambiguous theological tenet "true religion" (12.9) because it does not include determinate beliefs, sentiments, and practices regarding ultimate causes which are insufficiently supported by reason and evidence or which subvert ordinary moral standards. However, Philo also gives voice to Hume's view that apart from a select few like himself, most people will be motivated by hope and fear to seek consolation in popular forms of religion. This is not an endorsement of fideism, only a statement of fact about what influences most people's religious beliefs. While some may hope to find rational justification for these beliefs, their recourse to popular religion will be sounder if they first understand why a determinate understanding of the nature of ultimate causes is beyond the scope of human reason.

Readers of the *Dialogues* often wonder whether Hume's religious views might be best summed up as a species of theism, deism, atheism or skepticism. Using any one of these labels without significant qualification would be misleading. Hume is a skeptic about religion based on Academical, not Pyrrhonian principles. He suspends belief concerning all theological opinions more precise or determinate than the assertion that the cause or causes of order in nature remotely resemble human intelligence, a trivial statement having no positive consequences for religious practice. He can be called a philosophical theist only in a verbal sense. He did not consider himself a deist,[30] probably because he considered arguments for an intelligent designer to be neither very probable nor religiously significant. For most practical purposes he could be called an atheist, but he denied

---

[30] Lord Charlemont reported that Hume once said, "I am no deist. I do not style myself so, neither do I desire to be known by the appellation" (Royal Irish Academy, MS 12/R/7f523). Spelling modernized.

that his philosophical principles implied atheism, and he never denied the existence of God or an ultimate cause even when in the private company of professed atheists with whom he could express his views freely.[31]

Conclusion

The Dialogues concerning Natural Religion is a serious philosophical work whose aim is to delineate the limits of natural religion, but readers should not forget that it is also a literary work whose aim is to entertain – even to make its readers smile. There is something comical in Hume's portrayal of each of the characters: Demea's penchant for parroting pious authorities, Philo's vehement manner, which Pamphilus describes as "somewhat between jest and earnest," and Cleanthes' exasperation with Philo's persistent objections to beliefs he considers too obvious for any sensible person to question. A humorous inversion of the proverbial rake's progress, the *Dialogues* develops more like a picaresque tale in which Cleanthes' richly exaggerated expectations for the design argument are gradually whittled down, through his misadventures with the roguish Philo, to a single, purely speculative, and ambiguous proposition which has no positive consequences for religion, science, or morality. While Philo began with the remark that anyone who doubts the existence of God deserves the greatest ridicule, the *Dialogues'* end puts one more in mind of Hume's remark that "next to the ridicule of denying an evident truth, is that of taking much pains to defend it" (*T* 1.3.16.3).

Some readers, though not all, will accept Philo's conclusions. Some will side with Demea's mysticism or fideism. Some will prefer polytheism,

---

[31] Hume defends himself against charges of atheism in *A Letter from a Gentleman*, 21–30. Although probably not compiled by Hume, the pamphlet was likely drawn from a private letter Hume wrote to John Coutts. Additional evidence that Hume was not an atheist include the following: (1) A famous anecdote appearing in the letters of Diderot relates that when Hume attended a dinner-party hosted by d'Holbach in France, he teasingly announced that he did not believe in atheists because he had never seen any. (D'Holbach replied that there were fifteen atheists at the table, and three others who had not yet made up their minds.) See Denis Diderot, *Lettres à Sophie Volland*, ed. André Babelon (Paris: Gallimard, Editions de la Nouvelle revue française, 1938), 2: 77. (2) Gibbon's *Memoirs* remark on the French *philosophes* who "laughed at the scepticism of Hume" and "preached atheism with the bigotry of dogmatists." See Edward Gibbon, *Memoirs: Memoirs of the life and writings of Edward Gibbon*, ed. O. F. Emerson (Boston and London: Ginn & Company, 1898), 135. (3) George Horne recounted that while in Paris Sir James Macdonald wrote to an English acquaintance remarking that "poor Hume, who on your side of the water was thought to have too little religion, is here thought to have too much." *Gentleman's Magazine* 60 (1763), 644.

pantheism, atheism, or other alternatives to theism, and others will be convinced that Cleanthes' views are closest to the truth. Some may simply find that "opposite sentiments, even without any decision, afford an agreeable amusement" (Prologue, 4). Hume hoped that, above all else, his readers would become more tolerant regarding heterodox opinions, particularly those of irreligious skepticism and atheism, which in his time were the least tolerated of all.

Chronology

1711	Hume is born in Edinburgh on April 26.
1711–21	Spends his youth at Ninewells, the family home in Scotland.
1721–25	Attends University of Edinburgh, where he remains until 1725 without taking a degree.
1726–28	Returns to Ninewells, though he winters in Edinburgh. Engages in private study of law while also reading extensively in the classics and general philosophy, especially the works of Shaftesbury, Virgil, Cicero, and stoic philosophy.
1729–31	Hume is transported by "a new scene of thought"; but is also stricken with symptoms of depression. He keeps a notebook recording the progress of his thoughts on religion, which concludes in irreligious skepticism.
1731	Begins planning his *Treatise of Human Nature*.
1734	Still suffering from depression, Hume leaves Scotland to pursue a more active life in business working for a merchant in Bristol; four months later he resumes the life of a scholar and heads for France, stopping in Paris and Rheims before settling in La Flèche, where he begins writing the *Treatise*.
1737–38	Returns to London and prepares his manuscript of the *Treatise* for publication, removing its more irreligious components. His early memoranda, containing notes on his readings, and his early writing on evil that is preserved as a manuscript fragment probably began about this time.

1739	Books I and II of *A Treatise of Human Nature* are published. Hume begins a correspondence with Hutcheson, leading to revisions of his draft of Book III.
1740	*An Abstract . . . of a Treatise of Human Nature* and Book III of the *Treatise* are published.
1741	First volume of *Essays, Moral and Political* is published.
1742	Second volume of *Essays, Moral and Political* is published.
1744–5	Considered for the Chair of Moral Philosophy at University of Edinburgh; charges of atheism block his appointment.
1745	Becomes tutor to the Marquess of Annandale for a year. *A Letter from a Gentleman to his Friend in Edinburgh* is published in answer to charges of atheism.
1746	Appointed Secretary to General St. Clair for a military expedition.
1747	Returns to Ninewells.
1748	*Philosophical Essays concerning Human Understanding* (later re-titled *Enquiry concerning Human Understanding*) is published. Appointed *Aide de camp* to General St. Clair on military embassy to Vienna and Turin. *Three Essays, Moral and Political* and the third edition of *Essays, Moral and Political* are published.
1751	*An Enquiry concerning the Principles of Morals* is published. Hume sends a sample of his *Dialogues concerning Natural Religion* to Gilbert Elliot. He is elected co-secretary to the Edinburgh Philosophical Society (later called the Royal Society of Edinburgh).
1752	Hume is considered for the Chair of Logic at University of Glasgow. Once again, charges of atheism block his appointment. He becomes Keeper of the Advocates' Library. *Political Discourses* and *The Bellman's Petition*, a satire on the clergy, are published. Begins work on *History of England*.
1754	*Essays and Treatises on Several Subjects* and the first volume of *History of England*, covering James I and Charles I, are published.

1755–57	Efforts are made to excommunicate Hume and his friend Henry Home, Lord Kames; both are ultimately exonerated.
1756	Second volume of *History of England*, covering the commonwealth, Charles II, and James II, is published.
1757	"The Natural History of Religion," "Of the Passions," "Of Tragedy," and "Of the Standard of Taste" are published in *Four Dissertations*. Hume makes revisions to his *Dialogues concerning Natural Religion*.
1759	*History of England*, volumes III and IV, covering the reign of the Tudors, are published.
1761	The final volumes of the *History of England*, VI and VII, covering Julius Caesar to 1485, are published. Comtesse de Boufflers writes to Hume, beginning a long and intimate friendship. Hume revises *Dialogues concerning Natural Religion* again, making mainly stylistic changes.
1763–64	Goes to France as Secretary to the British ambassador. He is hailed by Parisian society.
1765	Remains in France as *chargé d'affaires*.
1766	Returns to England with Jean-Jacques Rousseau, who had been banished from Switzerland and France.
1767	Appointed Under-Secretary of State for the Northern Department for one year.
1769	Returns to Edinburgh.
1774	Composes his essay "The Origin of Government."
1775	Composes an "Advertisement" to be affixed to all copies of the second volume of *Essays and Treatises* that repudiates his *Treatise* as a "juvenile" work.
1776	Makes final revisions to his *Dialogues*. Dies on August 25.
1777	Last complete edition of *Essays and Treatises on Several Subjects*.
1779	Posthumous publication of *Dialogues concerning Natural Religion*.

Further reading

I. Life and correspondence

For biographies of Hume, see E. C. Mossner's *The Life of David Hume*, 2nd edn. (Oxford: Oxford University Press, 1980) and Roderick Graham's *The Great Infidel: A Life of David Hume* (East Linton, Scotland: Tuckwell Press, Ltd., 2005).

For letters by Hume, see *The Letters of David Hume*, ed. J. Y. T. Greig, 2 vols. (Oxford: Clarendon Press, 1932); and *New Letters of David Hume*, ed. Raymond Klibansky and Ernest C. Mossner (Oxford: Clarendon Press, 1954). For letters to Hume, see *Letters of Eminent Persons Addressed to David Hume*, ed. John Hill Burton (Edinburgh, 1849; facs., Bristol: Thoemmes, 1989).

II. General introductions to Hume

See Norman Kemp Smith's *The Philosophy of David Hume* (London: Palgrave Macmillan, 2005). For a briefer introduction, but one that also covers the full range of Hume's philosophical thought, see Terence Penelhum, *David Hume: An Introduction to His Philosophical System* (West Lafayette, IN: Purdue University Press, 1992).

Introductory anthologies include Peter Millican, ed., *Reading Hume on Human Understanding* (Oxford: Clarendon Press, 2002); David Norton, ed., *The Cambridge Companion to David Hume* (New York: Cambridge University Press, 1993); and Saul Traiger, ed., *The Blackwell Guide to Hume's "Treatise"* (Oxford: Blackwell Publishing, 2005).

III. Hume's philosophy of religion

For an overview, see John Gaskin's *Hume's Philosophy of Religion*, 2nd edn. (Atlantic Highlands, NJ: Humanities Press International, Inc., 1988), and his more recent essays: "Hume on Religion," in Norton's *Cambridge Companion*, 313–344 and "Religion: The Useless Hypothesis," in Millican's *Reading Hume on Human Understanding*, 349–370.

Advanced readings

Keith Yandell, *Hume's "Inexplicable Mystery": His Views on Religion* (Philadelphia: Temple University Press, 1990) and Miguel Badia Cabrera, *Hume's Reflection on Religion* (Dordrecht and Boston: Kluwer, 2001); D. Z. Phillips and Timothy Tessin, eds. *Religion and Hume's Legacy* (London and New York: Macmillan Press, Ltd., and St. Martin's Press, Inc., 1999); James Fieser, ed., *Early Responses to Hume's Writings on Religion* (Bristol: Thoemmes, 2001).

There is wide disagreement about how best to classify Hume's position on religion. The most controversial view is that Hume is a theist who takes belief in God to be a fundamental belief analogous to belief in causation or external existence. See R. J. Butler, "Natural Belief and the Enigma of Hume," *Archiv für Geschichte der Philosophie* 42 (1960), 73–100; Beryl Logan, *A Religion without Talking* (New York: Peter Lang, 1996); and Stanley Tweyman, *Scepticism and Belief in Hume's Dialogues concerning Natural Religion* (Dordrecht, Boston and Lancaster: Martinus Nijhoff Publishers, 1986), 10–19; 121–146. Gaskin argues against this view in *Hume's Philosophy of Religion*, 116–131.

On Hume's use of irony in his religious writings, see James Fieser, "Hume's Concealed Attack on Religion and his Early Critics," *Journal of Philosophical Research* 20 (1995), 83–101; and J. V. Price, *The Ironic Hume* (Austin: University of Texas Press, 1965), Ch. 4.

For discussions of the historical background to Hume's criticism of religion, see Robert H. Hurlbutt, *Hume, Newton, and the Design Argument*, rev. edn. (Lincoln: University of Nebraska Press, 1985); Anders Jeffner, *Hume and Butler on Religion* (Stockholm: Aktiebolaget, 1966); Richard H. Popkin, "The Breakdown of the Newtonian Synthesis of Science and Religion: Hume, Newton, and the Royal Society," in James E. Force, ed.,

Essays on the Context, Nature, and Influence of Isaac Newton's Theology (Norwell: Kluwer, 1990); Isabel Rivers, *Reason, Grace, and Sentiment, II: Shaftesbury to Hume* (Cambridge: Cambridge University Press, 2000); Elmer Spraque, "Hume, Henry More, and the Design Argument," *Hume Studies* 14 (1988), 305–327; and M. A. Stewart, "Religion and Rational Theology," in A. Broadie, ed., *The Cambridge Companion to the Scottish Enlightenment* (Cambridge: Cambridge University Press, 2003).

IV. Hume's *Dialogues*

Book-length commentaries

David O'Connor, *Hume on Religion* (London and New York: Routledge, 2001); William Lad Sessions, *Reading Hume's Dialogues: A Veneration for Religion* (Bloomington: Indiana University Press, 2002); and Stanley Tweyman, *Scepticism and Belief in Hume's Dialogues concerning Natural Religion* (Dordrecht, Boston, and Lancaster: Martinus Nijhoff Publishers, 1986).

Some advanced readings

The design argument: See John Beaudoin in "On Some Criticisms of Hume's Principle of Proportioning Cause to Effect," *Philo* 2 (1999), 26–40; Simon Blackburn, "Playing Hume's Hand," in *Religion and Hume's Legacy*, 3–16; Paul Draper, "Hume's Reproduction Parody of the Design Argument," *History of Philosophy Quarterly* 8 (1991), 135–148; Manfred Kuehn, "Kant's Critique of Hume's Theory of Faith," in M. A. Stewart and John P. Wright, eds., *Hume and Hume's Connexions* (University Park, PA: Pennsylvania State University Press, 1995), Ch. 12; Beryl Logan, "The Irregular Argument in Hume's *Dialogues*," *Hume Studies* 18 (1992): 483–500; Isabel Rivers, "Galen's Muscles, Wilkins, Hume, and the Educational Use of the Argument from Design," *Historical Journal* 36 (1993), 577–597; Cameron Shelley, "The First Inconvenience of Anthropomorphism: The Disanalogy in Part IV of Hume's Dialogues," *History of Philosophy Quarterly* 19 (2002), 171–189; Yandell, *Hume's "Inexplicable Mystery,"* Chs. 8–10.

The cosmological argument: See Joseph K. Campbell, "Hume's Refutation of the Cosmological Argument," *International Journal for Philosophy of Religion* 40 (1996), 159–173; James Dye, "A Word on Behalf of Demea," *Hume Studies* 15 (1989), 120–140; Edward. J. Khamara, "Hume 'versus' Clarke on the Cosmological Argument," *Philosophical Quarterly* 42 (1992), 34–55; Thomas M. Olshewsky, "Demea's Dilemmas," *British Journal for the History of Philosophy* 11 (2003), 473–483; M. A. Stewart, "Hume and the 'Metaphysical Argument *A Priori*'," in A. J. Holland, ed., *Philosophy, its History and Historiography* (Dordrecht and Boston: Reidel, 1985); and Kenneth Williford, "Demea's Theistic Proof," *Hume Studies* 29 (2003), 99–123; Yandell, *Hume's "Inexplicable Mystery,"* Ch. 11.

   The problem of evil: Advanced studies include Paul Draper, "Pain and Pleasure: An Evidential Problem for Theists," in William Rowe, ed., *God and the Problem of Evil* (Oxford: Blackwell, 2001), 180–202 and "The Skeptical Theist," in D. Howard-Snyder, ed., *The Evidential Argument from Evil* (Bloomington: Indiana University Press, 1996), 12–29; James Dye, "Demea's Departure," *Hume Studies* 18 (1992), 467–481; Klaas Kraay, "Philo's Argument for Divine Amorality," *Hume Studies* 29 (2003), 283–304; David O'Connor, "Skepticism and Philo's Atheistic Preference," *Hume Studies* 29 (2003), 267–282; Nelson Pike, "Hume on Evil," in M. Adams and R. Adams, eds., *The Problem of Evil* (New York and Oxford: Oxford University Press, 1990), 38–52; M. A. Stewart, "An Early Fragment on Evil," in Stewart and Wright, eds., *Hume and Hume's Connexions*, Ch. 8; Stanley Tweyman, "Hume's Dialogues on Evil," *Hume Studies* 13 (1987), 74–85; Stephen J. Wykstra, "The Humean Obstacle to Evidential Arguments from Suffering," in Adams and Adams, eds., *The Problem of Evil*, 138–160; Yandell, *Hume's "Inexplicable Mystery"*, Chs. 12–13.

   Morality and religion: See Miguel A. Badia-Cabrera, "Hume's Scepticism and His Ethical Depreciation of Religion," in Richard H. Popkin, ed., *Skepticism in the History of Philosophy: A Pan-American Dialogue* (Dordrecht: Kluwer, 1996), 99–114; Christopher Bernard, "Hume and the Madness of Religion," in Stewart and Wright, eds., *Hume and Hume's Connexions*; J. B. Schneewind, "Hume and the Religious Significance of Moral Rationalism," *Hume Studies* 26 (2000), 211–223; Yandell, *Hume's "Inexplicable Mystery,"* Ch. 3.

   Hume's use of the dialogue genre: See Michel Malherbe, "Hume and the Art of Dialogue," in Stewart and Wright, eds., *Hume and Hume's Connexions*, 201–223; Jonathan Dancy, "'For Here the Author is Annihilated': Reflections on Philosophical Aspects of the Use of Dialogue Form in Hume's *Dialogues concerning Natural Religion*," in Timothy

J. Smiley, ed., *Philosophical Dialogues: Plato, Hume, Wittgenstein* (Oxford: Oxford University Press, 1995); Michael Prince, *Philosophical Dialogue in the British Enlightenment* (Cambridge: Cambridge University Press, 1996), Ch. 5; Martin Bell, "The Relation between Literary Form and Philosophical Argument in Hume's *Dialogues concerning Natural Religion*," *Hume Studies* 27 (2001), 227–246; and Richard Dees, "Morality above Metaphysics: Philo and the Duties of Friendship in *Dialogues* 12," *Hume Studies* 28 (2002), 131–148. A less recent but still important essay on the Ciceronian structure of Hume's *Dialogues* is Christine Battersby, "The *Dialogues* as Original Imitation: Cicero and the Nature of Hume's Skepticism," in David Fate Norton et al., eds., *McGill Hume Studies* (San Diego: Austin Hill Press, Inc., 1979), 239–252.

Note on the text

The *Dialogues*

The text used for this edition of Hume's *Dialogues concerning Natural Religion* is Hume's original manuscript, transcribed with the permission of the Royal Society of Edinburgh. The manuscript is housed in the National Library of Scotland. Paragraph numbering appears in the margins and all references to the text in the introduction and notes are to part-number and paragraph-number of this edition. For example, 12.7 refers to *Dialogues*, Part 12, paragraph 7, this edition. When clarification is needed, the abbreviation "*D*" precedes the reference. Page numbers from Norman Kemp Smith's second edition of the *Dialogues* (Indianapolis: Bobbs-Merrill, 1947) also appear in the margin of the text. In the absence of a critical edition of the *Dialogues*, Kemp Smith's edition has long served as the scholarly standard. Although it is now out of print, the enormous body of secondary literature referencing this edition alone justifies the cross-referencing.

In keeping with the editorial policy of *Cambridge Texts in the History of Philosophy*, I have modernized the text in several ways: Eighteenth-century spellings are replaced with modern spellings (for example, "betwixt" is replaced with "between"); initial capital letters for most nouns or substantives are changed to lower case; "&" is changed to "and"; contractions (for example, 'tis, explor'd, wou'd) are replaced with expanded spellings. Minor inconsistencies in Hume's spelling and punctuation have also been corrected, but for the most part his original punctuation and use of British variants are preserved.

Hume's footnotes (thirteen in all) are referenced with superscript lower-case letters and appear above the footnotes provided by the editor, which are all referenced with superscript numbers. Editorial additions to Hume's footnotes are in brackets. Editorial footnotes explain Hume's historical allusions and terminology, identify notable precedents for certain phrasings or arguments, and relate the text to Hume's other writings.

Whether a passage in the original manuscript marked as a note in Part 12 should be inserted into the main text has been controversial. In his 1976 edition of the *Dialogues*, J. V. Price incorporated the note into the main text on the grounds that the words "A Note," placed above Hume's recopied version, are "not . . . in Hume's hand," and that Hume, in preparing a final draft of the work, would have been "conscious of incongruity of a discursive note within a dialogue" (250–251). Martin Bell, persuaded by Price's reasoning, also incorporated the note into the main text in his 1990 edition of the *Dialogues* published by Penguin Classics. However, in a more recent assessment of the manuscript evidence, M. A. Stewart concludes that the words "A Note" are indeed written in Hume's hand ("The Dating of Hume's Manuscripts," in Paul Wood, ed., *The Scottish Enlightenment: Essays in Reinterpretation* [Rochester: University of Rochester Press, 2000], 301). On the basis of this reassessment, I have included the passage as a note to the text.

Supplementary texts

Supplementary texts have been included to assist the reader in interpreting Hume's *Dialogues* and his general views about religion. Items 1 through 4 have been edited to include some modernizations and corrections. As with the main text, Hume's footnotes are referenced with superscript lower-case letters. Editorial additions to Hume's footnotes are enclosed in brackets.

1. Transcriptions printed with permission of the Royal Society of Edinburgh:
(A) Selection from Hume's early memoranda, MS 23159. The selection is transcribed from the group of notes appearing under the heading "Philosophy." The selection is referenced with the title "Memoranda," followed by an entry number and its page number in this volume.

(B) Extract from Hume's letter to Francis Hutcheson, March 16, 1740, MS 23151, no. 57. It is referenced with the abbreviation LH, followed by the page number in this volume.

(C) Extract from Hume's letter to William Mure, June 30, 1743, MS 23152, no. 3. It is referenced with the abbreviation LM, followed by the page number in this volume.

2. Transcription printed with the permission of the National Library of Scotland:
Acc. 10805, Hume's manuscript fragment on evil. The fragment is probably from a manuscript Hume was composing around the time he was completing his *Treatise of Human Nature*. The fragment was first published by M. A. Stewart in "Hume's Early Fragment on Evil," in John Wright and M. A. Stewart, eds., *Hume and Hume's Connexions* (University Park, PA: Pennsylvania State University Press, 1995), 160–170. The modernized transcription included in the present volume is referenced with the title "Fragment," followed by its page number in this volume.

3. Transcriptions printed with the permission of the Library of King's College at the University of Cambridge:
(A) Letter to Gilbert Elliot: February 18, 1751 (JMK/PP/87/28, folios 5–6).
(B) Letter to Gilbert Elliot March 10, 1751 (JMK/PP/87/28, folios 7–8).
   The first letter to Elliot is referenced with the abbreviation LE1 and the second with the abbreviation LE2, both followed by their page numbers in this volume.

4. Selections from Hume's *Natural History of Religion* follow the posthumous 1777 edition, which includes Hume's final alterations. These selections are referenced by the abbreviation *NHR*, followed by section number to facilitate cross-referencing to complete editions of the text.

5. Selections from Pierre Bayle, translated by James Dye for this volume. These selections are examples of Bayle's writings on religion which influenced Hume's discussions of the problem of evil and materialist explanations of nature, as well as his adoption of the skeptical strategy of refutation for the *Dialogues*.

(A) *Continuation des pensées diverses*, Ch. CVI, in *Œuvres diverses de Mr. Pierre* Bayle, 4 vols. (The Hague, 1737), III:333–336. Referenced as "Bayle on Materialism vs. Intelligent Design," followed by its page number in this volume. This selection was previously translated under the title "Bayle on Strato's 'Atheism'" by Norman Kemp Smith in his 1947 edition of the *Dialogues* (Appendix B, pp. 80–86), now out of print.

(B) "Manichéens," Note D, *Dictionnaire historique et critique*, 5th edn., 4 vols. (Amsterdam, Leiden, The Hague, Utrecht, 1740), III:305–306. Referenced as "Bayle on Manicheanism," followed by its page number in this volume.

Footnotes in both selections, referenced with superscript numbers, are the translator's.

References to Hume's other writings

References to Hume's *Treatise of Human Understanding* are to the text in the Norton edition (Oxford: Oxford University Press, 2000). References to this text cite book, part, section, and paragraph numbers, preceded by the abbreviation *T*. For example, *T* 1.4.4.1 refers to Hume's *Treatise*, Bk. 1, Part 4, Section 4, paragraph 1.

References to Hume's *Enquiry concerning Human Understanding* are to the student edition by Tom L. Beauchamp (Oxford: Oxford University Press, 2000), which has the same text as Beauchamp's critical edition. References to this text cite section and paragraph numbers, preceded by the abbreviation *EHU*. For example, *EHU* 12.25 refers to Hume's *Enquiry concerning Human Understanding*, Section 12, paragraph 25.

References to *A Letter from a Gentleman to His Friend in Edinburgh* (1745) are to the edition by Ernest C. Mossner and John C. Price (Edinburgh: Edinburgh University Press, 1967).

References to Hume's popular essays are to *Essays, Moral, Political and Literary*, rev. 2nd edn. ed. Eugene Miller (Indianapolis: Library Classics, 1987), abbreviated as *Essays*, with page number following.

References to Hume's personal correspondence not included in the supplementary texts for this volume are to *The Letters of David Hume*, ed. J. Y. T. Greig, 2 vols. (Oxford: Clarendon Press, 1932), abbreviated as *LDH*, with volume and page number following.

Abbreviations

D	*Dialogues concerning Natural Religion*, this edition.
EHU	*Enquiry concerning Human Understanding*, ed. Tom L. Beauchamp (Oxford: Oxford University Press, 2000).
Essays	*Essays, Moral Political and Literary*, rev. 2nd edn. ed. Eugene Miller (Indianapolis: Library Classics, 1987).
Fragment	Hume's manuscript fragment on evil, this edition.
LDH	*The Letters of David Hume*, ed. J. Y. T. Greig 2 vols. (Oxford: Clarendon Press, 1932).
LE1	Letter to Gilbert Elliot, February 18, 1751, this edition.
LE2	Letter to Gilbert Elliot, March 10, 1751, this edition.
Letter from a Gentleman	*A Letter from a Gentleman to His Friend in Edinburgh*, ed. Ernest C. Mossner and John V. Price (Edinburgh: Edinburgh University Press, 1967).
LH	Letter to Francis Hutcheson, March 16, 1740, this edition.
LM	Letter to William Mure, June 30, 1743, this edition.

Memoranda	Selection from Hume's memoranda, this edition.
NHR	Selections from *Natural History of Religion,* this edition.
T	*A Treatise of Human Nature*, ed. David Fate Norton and Mary Norton (Oxford: Oxford University Press, 2000).

Dialogues concerning Natural Religion

Pamphilus to Hermippus

1 It has been remarked, my *Hermippus*, that, though the ancient philosophers conveyed most of their instruction in the form of dialogue, this method of composition has been little practiced in later ages, and has seldom succeeded in the hands of those, who have attempted it.[1] Accurate and regular argument, indeed, such as is now expected of philosophical enquirers, naturally throws a man into the methodical and didactic manner; where he can immediately, without preparation, explain the point, at which he aims; and thence proceed, without interruption, to deduce the proofs, on which it is established. To deliver a SYSTEM in conversation scarcely appears natural; and while the dialogue-writer desires, by departing from the direct style of composition, to give a freer air to his performance, and avoid the appearance of *author* and *reader*, he is apt to run into a worse inconvenience, and convey the image of *pedagogue* and *pupil*.[2] Or if he carries on the dispute in the natural spirit of good company, by throwing in a variety of topics, and preserving a proper balance among the speakers; he often loses so much time in preparations and transitions, that the reader will scarcely think himself compensated, by all the graces of dialogue, for the order, brevity, and precision, which are sacrificed to them.

---

[1] Anthony Ashley Cooper, Third Earl of Shaftesbury (1671–1713), "Soliloquy, or Advice to An Author," "The Moralists," and "Miscellany V" in *Characteristics of Men, Manners, Opinions, Times*, ed. Lawrence E. Klein (Cambridge: Cambridge University Press, 1999), 87–93; 233–235; 458–463.

[2] Cf. Cicero (106–43 BC), *The Nature of the Gods (De Natura Deorum)*, trans. P. G. Walsh (Oxford and New York: Oxford University Press, 1997), 1.5–10.

2 There are some subjects, however, to which dialogue-writing is peculiarly adapted, and where it is still preferable to the direct and simple method of composition.

3 Any point of doctrine, which is so *obvious*, that it scarcely admits of dispute, but at the same time so *important*, that it cannot be too often inculcated, seems to require some such method of handling it; where the novelty of the manner may compensate the triteness of the subject; where the vivacity of conversation may enforce the precept; and where the variety of lights, presented by various personages and characters, may appear neither tedious nor redundant.

[128] 4 Any question of philosophy, on the other hand, which is so *obscure* and *uncertain*, that human reason can reach no fixed determination with regard to it; if it should be treated at all; seems to lead us naturally into the style of dialogue and conversation. Reasonable men may be allowed to differ, where no one can reasonably be positive: Opposite sentiments, even without any decision, afford an agreeable amusement: And if the subject be curious and interesting, the book carries us, in a manner, into company, and unites the two greatest and purest pleasures of human life, study and society.

5 Happily, these circumstances are all to be found in the subject of NATURAL RELIGION. What truth so obvious, so certain, as the *being* of a God, which the most ignorant ages have acknowledged, for which the most refined geniuses have ambitiously striven to produce new proofs and arguments? What truth so important as this, which is the ground of all our hopes, the surest foundation of morality, the firmest support of society, and the only principle which ought never to be a moment absent from our thoughts and meditations? But in treating of this obvious and important truth; what obscure questions occur, concerning the *nature* of that divine being; his attributes, his decrees, his plan of providence? These have been always subjected to the disputations of men: Concerning these, human reason has not reached any certain determination: But these are topics so interesting, that we cannot restrain our restless enquiry with regard to them; though nothing but doubt, uncertainty and contradiction have, as yet, been the result of our most accurate researches.[3]

6 This I had lately occasion to observe, while I passed, as usual, part of the summer season with CLEANTHES, and was present at those

3 Ibid., 1.1–6.

4

conversations of his with PHILO and DEMEA, of which I gave you lately some imperfect account. Your curiosity, you then told me, was so excited, that I must of necessity enter into a more exact detail of their reasonings, and display those various systems, which they advanced with regard to so delicate a subject as that of natural religion. The remarkable contrast in their characters still farther raised your expectations; while you opposed the accurate philosophical turn of *Cleanthes* to the careless scepticism of *Philo*, or compared either of their dispositions with the rigid inflexible orthodoxy of *Demea*. My youth rendered me a mere auditor of their [129] disputes; and that curiosity, natural to the early season of life, has so deeply imprinted in my memory the whole chain and connection of their arguments, that, I hope, I shall not omit or confound any considerable part of them in the recital.

5

Part 1

1 After I joined the company, whom I found sitting in *Cleanthes'* library, *Demea* paid *Cleanthes* some compliments, on the great care, which he took of my education, and on his unwearied perseverance and constancy in all his friendships. The father of *Pamphilus*, said he, was your intimate friend: The son is your pupil, and may indeed be regarded as your adopted son, were we to judge by the pains which you bestow in conveying to him every useful branch of literature and science. You are no more wanting, I am persuaded, in prudence than in industry. I shall, therefore, communicate to you a maxim which I have observed with regard to my own children, that I may learn how far it agrees with your practice. The method I follow in their education is founded on the saying of an ancient, *that students of philosophy ought first to learn logics, then ethics, next physics, last of all, the nature of the gods.*[a] This science of natural theology,[1] according to him, being the most profound and abstruse of any, required the maturest judgement in its students; and none but a mind, enriched with all the other sciences, can safely be entrusted with it.

2 Are you so late, says *Philo*, in teaching your children the principles of religion? Is there no danger of their neglecting or rejecting altogether those opinions, of which they have heard so little, during the whole course of their education? It is only as a science, replied *Demea*, subjected to human reasoning and disputation, that I postpone the study of natural

---

[a] Chrysippus apud Plut. *de repug. Stoicorum* [Plutarch, "On Stoic Self-contradictions," in *Moralia* (Cambridge, MA and London: Harvard University Press, 1976), Ch. 9, 1035a–b.]

[1] "Natural theology" is sometimes contrasted with "natural religion" to designate, not the beliefs, sentiments, and practices that can be explained or supported independently of supernatural revelation, but the study of these justifications or explanations.

theology. To season their minds with early piety is my chief care; and by continual precept and instruction, and I hope too, by example, I imprint deeply on their tender minds an habitual reverence for all the principles of religion.[2] While they pass through every other science, I still remark the uncertainty of each part, the eternal disputations of men, the obscurity of all philosophy, and the strange, ridiculous conclusions, which some of the greatest geniuses have derived from the principles of mere human reason. Having thus tamed their mind to a proper submission and self-diffidence, [131] I have no longer any scruple of opening to them the greatest mysteries of religion, nor apprehend any danger from that assuming arrogance of philosophy, which may lead them to reject the most established doctrines and opinions.

3 Your precaution, says *Philo*, of seasoning your children's minds with early piety, is certainly very reasonable; and no more than is requisite, in this profane and irreligious age. But what I chiefly admire in your plan of education is your method of drawing advantage from the very principles of philosophy and learning, which, by inspiring pride and self-sufficiency, have commonly, in all ages, been found so destructive to the principles of religion. The vulgar,[3] indeed, we may remark, who are unacquainted with science and profound enquiry, observing the endless disputes of the learned, have commonly a thorough contempt for philosophy; and rivet themselves the faster, by that means, in the great points of theology, which have been taught them. Those, who enter a little into study and enquiry, finding many appearances of evidence in doctrines the newest and most extraordinary, think nothing too difficult for human reason; and presumptuously breaking through all fences, profane the inmost sanctuaries of the temple. But *Cleanthes* will, I hope, agree with me, that, after we have abandoned ignorance, the surest remedy, there is still one expedient left to prevent this profane liberty. Let *Demea's* principles be improved and cultivated: Let us become thoroughly sensible of the weakness, blindness, and narrow limits of human reason: Let us duly consider its uncertainty and endless contrarieties, even in subjects of common life and practice: Let the errors and deceits of our very senses be set before us; the insuperable difficulties, which attend first principles in all systems; the contradictions, which adhere to the very ideas of matter, cause and

---

[2] Cf. George Berkeley, *Alciphron*, First Dialogue, Sec. 6, in *The Works of George Berkeley*, ed. A. A. Luce and T. E. Jessop, 9 vols. (London: Thomas Nelson and Sons, Ltd., 1949), III:41.

[3] *The vulgar*: Ordinary or common people.

effect, extension, space, time, motion; and in a word, quantity of all kinds, the object of the only science, that can fairly pretend to any certainty or evidence. When these topics are displayed in their full light, as they are by some philosophers[4] and almost all divines; who can retain such confidence in this frail faculty of reason as to pay any regard to its determinations in points so sublime, so abstruse, so remote from common [132] life and experience? When the coherence of the parts of a stone, or even that composition of parts, which renders it extended; when these familiar objects, I say, are so inexplicable, and contain circumstances so repugnant and contradictory; with what assurance can we decide concerning the origin of worlds, or trace their history from eternity to eternity?

4 While *Philo* pronounced these words, I could observe a smile in the countenances both of *Demea* and *Cleanthes*. That of *Demea* seemed to imply an unreserved satisfaction in the doctrines delivered: But in *Cleanthes'* features, I could distinguish an air of finesse; as if he perceived some raillery or artificial malice in the reasonings of *Philo*.

5 You propose then, *Philo*, said *Cleanthes*, to erect religious faith on philosophical scepticism; and you think, that if certainty or evidence be expelled from every other subject of enquiry, it will all retire to these theological doctrines, and there acquire a superior force and authority. Whether your scepticism be as absolute and sincere as you pretend, we shall learn by and by, when the company breaks up: We shall then see, whether you go out at the door or the window; and whether you really doubt, if your body has gravity, or can be injured by its fall; according to popular opinion, derived from our fallacious senses and more fallacious experience. And this consideration, *Demea*, may, I think, fairly serve to abate our ill-will to this humorous sect of the sceptics. If they be thoroughly in earnest, they will not long trouble the world with their doubts, cavils, and disputes: If they be only in jest, they are, perhaps, bad railers, but can never be very dangerous, either to the state, to philosophy, or to religion.

6 In reality, *Philo*, continued he, it seems certain, that though a man, in a flush of humour, after intense reflection on the many contradictions and imperfections of human reason, may entirely renounce all belief and opinion; it is impossible for him to persevere in this total scepticism, or make it appear in his conduct for a few hours. External objects press in

---

4 Such as by Hume himself: Cf. *T* 1.4.7.1–8 and *EHU* 12.5–22.

upon him: Passions solicit him: His philosophical melancholy dissipates; and even the utmost violence upon his own temper will not be able, during any time, to preserve the poor appearance of scepticism.[5] And for what reason impose on himself such a violence? This is a point in which it will [133] be impossible for him ever to satisfy himself, consistent with his sceptical principles: So that upon the whole nothing could be more ridiculous than the principles of the ancient *Pyrrhonians*;[6] if in reality they endeavoured, as is pretended, to extend throughout the same scepticism, which they had learned from the declamations of their school, and which they ought to have confined to them.

7 In this view, there appears a great resemblance between the sects of the *Stoics*[7] and *Pyrrhonians*, though perpetual antagonists: And both of them seem founded on this erroneous maxim, that what a man can perform sometimes, and in some dispositions, he can perform always, and in every disposition. When the mind, by stoical reflections, is elevated into a sublime enthusiasm of virtue, and strongly smit with any *species* of honour or public good, the utmost bodily pain and sufferance will not prevail over such a high sense of duty; and it is possible, perhaps, by its means, even to smile and exult in the midst of tortures. If this sometimes may be the case in fact and reality, much more may a philosopher, in his school, or even in his closet,[8] work himself up to such an enthusiasm, and support in imagination the acutest pain or most calamitous event, which he can possibly conceive. But how shall he support this enthusiasm itself? The bent of his mind relaxes, and cannot be recalled at pleasure: Avocations lead him astray: Misfortunes attack him unawares: And the *philosopher* sinks by degrees into the *plebeian*.

8 I allow of your comparison between the *Stoics* and *Sceptics*, replied *Philo*. But you may observe, at the same time, that though the mind cannot, in Stoicism, support the highest flights of philosophy, yet even when it sinks lower, it still retains somewhat of its former disposition; and

---

[5] Cf. *T* 1.4.7.9–10; *EHU* 12.23.

[6] *Pyrrhonians*: Followers of the most radical ancient Greek skeptic, Pyrrho of Elis (*c.* 360–270 BC), who recommended suspense of judgment because nothing is certain, including the belief that nothing is certain. Most of what is known about Pyrrhonism is from Sextus Empiricus' (fl. *c.* AD 200) *Outlines of Pyrrhonism*, which, appearing in translation at the end of the sixteenth century, had a profound influence on the development of modern philosophy.

[7] *Stoics*: Followers of Zeno of Citium (335–263 BC), who became known as Stoics because Zeno taught at the *Stoa Poikile*, or Painted Colonnade, in Athens. Equating virtue with happiness, Stoics aspired to indifference to pleasures and pains. Cf. Hume, "The Stoic," in *Essays*, pp. 153–154.

[8] *Closet*: A study or private room.

9

the effects of the Stoic's reasoning will appear in his conduct in common life, and through the whole tenor of his actions. The ancient schools, particularly that of *Zeno*,[9] produced examples of virtue and constancy, which seem astonishing to present times.

[134]
> Vain wisdom all and false Philosophy.
> Yet with a pleasing sorcery could charm
> Pain, for a while, or anguish; and excite
> Fallacious hope, or arm the obdurate breast
> With stubborn patience, as with triple steel.[10]

In like manner, if a man has accustomed himself to sceptical considerations on the uncertainty and narrow limits of reason, he will not entirely forget them when he turns his reflection on other subjects; but in all his philosophical principles and reasoning, I dare not say, in his common conduct, he will be found different from those, who either never formed any opinions in the case, or have entertained sentiments more favourable to human reason.[11]

9 To whatever length anyone may push his speculative principles of scepticism, he must act, I own, and live, and converse like other men; and for this conduct he is not obliged to give any other reason, than the absolute necessity he lies under of so doing.[12] If he ever carries his speculations farther than this necessity constrains him, and philosophizes, either on natural or moral subjects, he is allured by a certain pleasure and satisfaction, which he finds in employing himself after that manner. He considers besides, that everyone, even in common life, is constrained to have more or less of this philosophy; that from our earliest infancy we make continual advances in forming more general principles of conduct and reasoning; that the larger experience we acquire, and the stronger reason we are endowed with, we always render our principles the more general and comprehensive; and that what we call *philosophy* is nothing but a more regular and methodical operation of the same kind. To philosophize on such subjects is nothing essentially different from reasoning on common life; and we may only expect greater stability, if not greater truth, from

[9] *Zeno*: Founder of Stoicism. See note 7.
[10] John Milton (1608–1674), *Paradise Lost* (1667), Bk. 2, 565–569.
[11] Compare with the first species of what Hume calls "*mitigated* scepticism, or ACADEMICAL philosophy," the result of correcting excessive skepticism "by common sense and reflection," a result that expresses itself as "caution, and modesty . . . in all kinds of scrutiny and decision" (*EHU* 12.24).
[12] Cf. *T* 1.4.7.10; *EHU* 12.23.

our philosophy, on account of its exacter and more scrupulous method of proceeding.[13]

10 But when we look beyond human affairs and the properties of the surrounding bodies: When we carry our speculations into the two eternities, before and after the present state of things; into the creation and [135] formation of the universe; the existence and properties of spirits; the powers and operations of one universal spirit, existing without beginning and without end; omnipotent, omniscient, immutable, infinite, and incomprehensible: We must be far removed from the smallest tendency to scepticism not to be apprehensive, that we have here got quite beyond the reach of our faculties. So long as we confine our speculations to trade or morals or politics or criticism, we make appeals, every moment, to common sense and experience, which strengthen our philosophical conclusions, and remove (at least, in part) the suspicion, which we so justly entertain with regard to every reasoning, that is very subtle and refined. But in theological reasonings, we have not this advantage; while at the same time we are employed upon objects, which, we must be sensible, are too large for our grasp, and of all others, require most to be familiarized to our apprehension. We are like foreigners in a strange country, to whom everything must seem suspicious, and who are in danger every moment of transgressing against the laws and customs of the people, with whom they live and converse. We know not how far we ought to trust our vulgar methods of reasoning in such a subject; since, even in common life and in that province, which is peculiarly appropriated to them, we cannot account for them, and are entirely guided by a kind of instinct or necessity in employing them.[14]

11 All sceptics pretend, that, if reason be considered in an abstract view, it furnishes invincible arguments against itself, and that we could never retain any conviction or assurance, on any subject, were not the sceptical reasonings so refined and subtle, that they are not able to counterpoise the more solid and more natural arguments, derived from the senses and experience. But it is evident, whenever our arguments lose this advantage, and run wide of common life, that the most refined scepticism comes to be on a footing with them, and is able to oppose and counterbalance them.

---

[13] Cf. *EHU* 12.25.

[14] Compare this and the next paragraph with the second species of Hume's "*mitigated* scepticism," which corrects excessive skepticism by limiting "enquiries to such subjects as are best adapted to the narrow capacity of human understanding" (*EHU* 12.25).

The one has no more weight than the other. The mind must remain in
[136] suspense between them; and it is that very suspense or balance, which is
the triumph of scepticism.

12 But I observe, says *Cleanthes*, with regard to you, *Philo*, and all
speculative sceptics, that your doctrine and practice are as much at vari-
ance in the most abstruse points of theory as in the conduct of common
life. Wherever evidence discovers itself, you adhere to it, notwithstanding
your pretended scepticism; and I can observe too some of your sect to be
as decisive as those, who make greater professions of certainty and assurance. In reality, would not a man be ridiculous, who pretended to reject
Newton's explication of the wonderful phenomenon of the rainbow,[15]
because that explication gives a minute anatomy of the rays of light; a subject, forsooth, too refined for human comprehension? And what would
you say to one, who having nothing particular to object to the arguments
of *Copernicus* and *Galileo* for the motion of the earth,[16] should withhold
his assent, on that general principle, that these subjects were too magnificent and remote to be explained by the narrow and fallacious reason of
mankind?

13 There is indeed a kind of brutish and ignorant scepticism, as you
well observed, which gives the vulgar a general prejudice against what
they do not easily understand, and makes them reject every principle,
which requires elaborate reasoning to prove and establish it. This species
of scepticism is fatal to knowledge, not to religion; since we find, that
those who make greatest profession of it, give often their assent, not
only to the great truths of theism, and natural theology, but even to the
most absurd tenets, which a traditional superstition has recommended
to them. They firmly believe in witches; though they will not believe nor
attend to the most simple proposition of *Euclid*.[17] But the refined and
philosophical sceptics fall into an inconsistence of an opposite nature.
They push their researches into the most abstruse corners of science;
and their assent attends them in every step, proportioned to the evidence,
which they meet with. They are even obliged to acknowledge, that the
most abstruse and remote objects are those, which are best explained

---

[15] Isaac Newton (1642–1727), *Opticks or a Treatise of the Reflections, Refractions, Inflections & Colours
of Light* (London, 1704), Bk. 1, Pt. 2, Prop. ix, Prob. iv.

[16] *Copernicus* (1473–1543) and *Galileo* (1564–1642) both argued for the heliocentric model of planetary
motion.

[17] *Euclid* (c. 325–265 BC): The most prominent mathematician of antiquity and founder of geometry,
best known for his treatise on mathematics, *The Elements*.

by philosophy. Light is in reality anatomized: The true system of the heavenly bodies is discovered and ascertained. But the nourishment of bodies by food is still an inexplicable mystery: The cohesion of the parts of [137] matter is still incomprehensible. These sceptics, therefore, are obliged, in every question, to consider each particular evidence apart, and proportion their assent to the precise degree of evidence, which occurs. This is their practice in all natural, mathematical, moral, and political science. And why not the same, I ask, in the theological and religious? Why must conclusions of this nature be alone rejected on the general presumption of the insufficiency of human reason, without any particular discussion of the evidence? Is not such an unequal conduct a plain proof of prejudice and passion?

14 Our senses, you say, are fallacious, our understanding erroneous, our ideas even of the most familiar objects, extension, duration, motion, full of absurdities and contradictions. You defy me to solve the difficulties, or reconcile the repugnancies, which you discover in them. I have not capacity for so great an undertaking: I have not leisure for it: I perceive it to be superfluous. Your own conduct, in every circumstance, refutes your principles; and shows the firmest reliance on all the received maxims of science, morals, prudence, and behaviour.

15 I shall never assent to so harsh an opinion as that of a celebrated writer,[b] who says that the sceptics are not a sect of philosophers: They are only a sect of liars. I may, however, affirm (I hope without offence), that they are a sect of jesters or railers. But for my part, whenever I find myself disposed to mirth and amusement, I shall certainly choose my entertainment of a less perplexing and abstruse nature. A comedy, a novel, or at most a history, seems a more natural recreation than such metaphysical subtleties and abstractions.

16 In vain would the sceptic make a distinction between science and common life, or between one science and another. The arguments, employed in all, if just, are of a similar nature, and contain the same force and evidence. Or if there be any difference among them, the advantage lies entirely on the side of theology and natural religion. Many principles of mechanics are founded on very abstruse reasoning; yet no man, who [138] has any pretensions to science, even no speculative sceptic, pretends to

[b] *L'art de penser.* [Antoine Arnauld (1612–94), "First Discourse" in *Logic: or the Art of Thinking* (also known as the *Port Royal Logic*), trans. and ed. by Jill Vance Buroker (Cambridge and New York: Cambridge University Press, 1996), 7.]

entertain the least doubt with regard to them. The *Copernican* system contains the most surprising paradox, and the most contrary to our natural conceptions, to appearances, and to our very senses: Yet even monks and inquisitors are now constrained to withdraw their opposition to it. And shall *Philo*, a man of so liberal a genius, and extensive knowledge, entertain any general undistinguished scruples with regard to the religious hypothesis, which is founded on the simplest and most obvious arguments, and, unless it meet with artificial obstacles, has such easy access and admission into the mind of man?

17 And here we may observe, continued he, turning himself towards *Demea*, a pretty curious circumstance in the history of the sciences. After the union of philosophy with the popular religion, upon the first establishment of Christianity, nothing was more usual, among all religious teachers, than declamations against reason, against the senses, against every principle, derived merely from human research and enquiry. All the topics of the ancient Academics were adopted by the Fathers;[18] and thence propagated for several ages in every school and pulpit throughout Christendom. The Reformers[19] embraced the same principles of reasoning, or rather declamation; and all panegyrics on the excellency of faith were sure to be interlarded with some severe strokes of satire against natural reason. A celebrated prelate[c] too, of the Romish communion, a man of the most extensive learning, who wrote a demonstration of Christianity, has also composed a treatise, which contains all the cavils of the boldest and most determined *Pyrrhonism*. *Locke* seems to have been the first Christian, who ventured openly to assert, that *faith* was nothing but a species of *reason*, that religion was only a branch of philosophy, and that a chain of arguments, similar to that which established any truth in morals, politics, or physics, was always employed in discovering all the principles

[c] Monsr. Huet. [Pierre-Daniel Huet (1630–1721), Bishop of Avranches. In addition to *Demonstratio Evangelica* (1679), Huet wrote *A Philosophical Treatise on the Weakness of Human Understanding* (*Traité philosophique de la foiblesse de l'esprit humain*), published posthumously in 1723 and translated into English in 1725, a work extremely skeptical of the ability of human beings to discover truth. Cf. Hume, *Letter from a Gentleman*, 21.]

[18] *Ancient Academics*: Ancient followers of a moderate form of skepticism that developed during the third period of Plato's Academy from the third to the early first century BC. Academic skeptics denied the possibility of certain knowledge, but they believed that opinions which are formed by weighing the evidence for all sides of a dispute are more probable than opinions formed in other ways. *The Fathers*: Prominent theologians of the first centuries of Christianity.

[19] *Reformers*: Protestant Reformationists.

of theology, natural and revealed.[20] The ill use, which *Bayle*[21] and other libertines made of the philosophical scepticism of the Fathers and first Reformers, still farther propagated the judicious sentiment of Mr. *Locke*: [139] And it is now, in a manner, avowed, by all pretenders to reasoning and philosophy, that atheist and sceptic are almost synonymous. And as it is certain, that no man is in earnest, when he professes the latter principle; I would fain hope, that there are as few, who seriously maintain the former.

18 Don't you remember, said *Philo*, the excellent saying of *Lord Bacon*[22] on this head? – That a little philosophy, replied *Cleanthes*, makes a man an atheist: A great deal converts him to religion. – That is a very judicious remark too, said *Philo*. But what I have in my eye is another passage, where, having mentioned *David*'s fool, who said in his heart there is no God,[23] this great philosopher observes, that the atheists nowadays have a double share of folly: For they are not contented to say in their hearts there is no God, but they also utter that impiety with their lips, and are thereby guilty of multiplied indiscretion and imprudence. Such people, though they were ever so much in earnest, cannot, methinks, be very formidable.

19 But though you should rank me in this class of fools, I cannot forbear communicating a remark, that occurs to me from the history of the religious and irreligious scepticism, with which you have entertained us. It appears to me, that there are strong symptoms of priestcraft in the whole progress of this affair.[24] During ignorant ages, such as those which followed the dissolution of the ancient schools,[25] the priests perceived, that atheism, deism,[26] or heresy of any kind could only proceed from the presumptuous questioning of received opinions, and from a belief,

---

[20] *John Locke* (1632–1704), *An Essay concerning Human Understanding* [1690], ed. P. H. Nidditch (Oxford and New York: Clarendon Press and Oxford University Press, 1979), Bk. 4, Chs. 10 and 18; and *The Reasonableness of Christianity* [1695], ed. John C. Higgins-Biddle (Oxford and New York: Clarendon Press and Oxford University Press, 1999).

[21] *Pierre Bayle* (1647–1706), leading skeptic and author of the influential *Historical and Critical Dictionary* (*Dictionnaire historique et critique*). The dictionary was first published in 1697 and was first translated into English in 1710. It became the most popular work of the eighteenth century.

[22] *Francis Bacon* (1561–1626), "Of Atheism," in *Essays* [1597], in *Collected works of Francis Bacon*, ed. Graham Rees, 12 vols. (London: Routledge and Thoemmes, 1996), VI:413.

[23] "The fool hath said in his heart, there is no God," Psalms of David 14:1.

[24] Cf. Hume, "Of Parties in General," in *Essays*, 62–63.

[25] The Christian emperor Justinian closed the last of the ancient schools of philosophy in Athens in AD 529.

[26] *Deism*: The view that the universe was created by an intelligent God who does not subsequently intervene in nature or human history.

that human reason was equal to everything. Education had then a mighty influence over the minds of men, and was almost equal in force to those suggestions of the senses and common understanding, by which the most determined sceptic must allow himself to be governed. But at present, when the influence of education is much diminished, and men, from a more open commerce of the world, have learned to compare the popular principles of different nations and ages, our sagacious divines have changed their whole system of philosophy, and talk the language of *Stoics*, *Platonists*, and *Peripatetics*,[27] not that of *Pyrrhonians* and *Academics*. If we distrust human reason, we have now no other principle to lead us into [140] religion. Thus, sceptics in one age, dogmatists in another; whichever system best suits the purpose of these reverend gentlemen, in giving them an ascendant over mankind, they are sure to make it their favourite principle, and established tenet.

20 It is very natural, said *Cleanthes*, for men to embrace those principles, by which they find they can best defend their doctrines; nor need we have any recourse to priestcraft to account for so reasonable an expedient. And surely, nothing can afford a stronger presumption, that any set of principles are true, and ought to be embraced, than to observe, that they tend to the confirmation of true religion, and serve to confound the cavils of atheists, libertines, and freethinkers of all denominations.

[27] *Platonists*: Followers of Plato (427–347 BC); *Peripatetics*: Followers of Aristotle (384–322 BC), who taught his students in a *peripatos*, a covered walk in the gymnasium in Athens called the Lyceum, whence his followers were called *Peripatetics*.

Part 2

1 I must own, *Cleanthes*, said *Demea*, that nothing can more surprise me, than the light, in which you have, all along, put this argument. By the whole tenor of your discourse, one would imagine that you were maintaining the being of a God, against the cavils of atheists and infidels; and were necessitated to become a champion for that fundamental principle of all religion. But this, I hope, is not, by any means, a question among us. No man; no man, at least, of common sense, I am persuaded, ever entertained a serious doubt with regard to a truth so certain and self-evident. The question is not concerning the BEING but the NATURE of GOD. This I affirm, from the infirmities of human understanding, to be altogether incomprehensible and unknown to us. The essence of that supreme mind, his attributes, the manner of his existence, the very nature of his duration; these and every particular, which regards so divine a being, are mysterious to men. Finite, weak, and blind creatures, we ought to humble ourselves in his august presence, and, conscious of our frailties, adore in silence his infinite perfections, which eye hath not seen, ear hath not heard, neither hath it entered into the heart of man to conceive them.[1] They are covered in a deep cloud from human curiosity: It is profaneness to attempt penetrating through these sacred obscurities: And next to the impiety of denying his existence, is the temerity of prying into his nature and essence, decrees and attributes.

2 But lest you should think, that my *piety* has here got the better of my *philosophy*, I shall support my opinion, if it needs any support, by a very

---

[1] St. Paul, 1 Corinthians 2:9, referring to Isaiah 64.4: "But as it is written, Eye hath not seen, nor ear heard: neither hath it entered into the heart of man, what things God hath prepared for them that love him."

great authority. I might cite all the divines almost, from the foundation of Christianity, who have ever treated of this or any other theological subject: But I shall confine myself, at present, to one equally celebrated for piety and philosophy. It is Father *Malebranche*, who, I remember, thus expresses himself.[a] "One ought not so much (says he) to call God a spirit, in order to express positively what he is, as in order to signify that he is not matter. He is a being infinitely perfect: Of this we cannot doubt.

[142] But in the same manner as we ought not to imagine, even supposing him corporeal, that he is clothed with a human body, as the *Anthropomorphites*[2] asserted, under colour that that figure was the most perfect of any; so neither ought we to imagine, that the spirit of God has human ideas, or bears *any* resemblance to our spirit, under colour that we know nothing more perfect than a human mind. We ought rather to believe, that as he comprehends the perfections of matter without being material . . . he comprehends also the perfections of created spirits, without being spirit, in the manner we conceive spirit: That his true name is, *He that is*,[3] or in other words, Being without restriction, All Being, the Being infinite and universal."

3 After so great an authority, *Demea*, replied *Philo*, as that which you have produced, and a thousand more, which you might produce, it would appear ridiculous in me to add my sentiment, or express my approbation of your doctrine. But surely, where reasonable men treat these subjects, the question can never be concerning the *being* but only the *nature* of the deity. The former truth, as you well observe, is unquestionable and self-evident. Nothing exists without a cause;[4] and the original cause of this universe (whatever it be) we call GOD; and piously ascribe to him every species of perfection. Whoever scruples this fundamental truth deserves every punishment, which can be inflicted among philosophers, to wit, the greatest ridicule, contempt, and disapprobation. But as all perfection is entirely relative, we ought never to imagine, that we comprehend the attributes of this divine being, or to suppose, that his perfections have any analogy or likeness to the perfections of a human creature. Wisdom,

---

[a] *Recherche de la Vérité*. Liv. 3. Chap. 9. [For a contemporary translation, see Nicolas Malebranche, *The Search After Truth*, trans. Thomas M. Lennon and Paul J. Olscamp (Cambridge: Cambridge University Press, 1997), Bk. 3, Pt. 2, Ch. 9, p. 251.]

[2] "Anthropomorphites," in this context, refers to those who conceive of God in terms of physical human characteristics. Hume later broadens the term to describe those who conceive of God in terms of mental and moral human characteristics.

[3] Exodus 3:14.   [4] Cf. Hume, *Letter from a Gentleman*, 22–26.

thought, design, knowledge; these we justly ascribe to him; because these words are honourable among men, and we have no other language or other conceptions, by which we can express our adoration of him.[5] But let us beware, lest we think, that our ideas anywise correspond to his perfections, or that his attributes have any resemblance to these qualities among men. He is infinitely superior to our limited view and comprehension; and is more the object of worship in the temple than of disputation in the schools.

4 In reality, *Cleanthes*, continued he, there is no need of having recourse to that affected scepticism, so displeasing to you, in order to come at this determination. Our ideas reach no farther than our experience: We **[143]** have no experience of divine attributes and operations: I need not conclude my syllogism: You can draw the inference yourself. And it is a pleasure to me (and I hope to you too) that just reasoning and sound piety here concur in the same conclusion, and both of them establish the adorably mysterious and incomprehensible nature of the supreme being.

5 Not to lose any time in circumlocutions, said *Cleanthes*, addressing himself to *Demea*, much less in replying to the pious declamations of *Philo*; I shall briefly explain how I conceive this matter. Look round the world: Contemplate the whole and every part of it: You will find it to be nothing but one great machine, subdivided into an infinite number of lesser machines, which again admit of subdivisions, to a degree beyond what human senses and faculties can trace and explain.[6] All these various machines, and even their most minute parts, are adjusted to each other with an accuracy, which ravishes into admiration all men, who have ever contemplated them. The curious adapting of means to ends, throughout all nature, resembles exactly, though it much exceeds, the productions of human contrivance; of human design, thought, wisdom, and intelligence. Since therefore the effects resemble each other, we are led to infer, by all the rules of analogy, that the causes also resemble; and that the author of nature is somewhat similar to the mind of man; though possessed of much larger faculties, proportioned to the grandeur of the work, which he

---

[5] Cf. Thomas Hobbes, *The Elements of Law, Natural and Politic* (originally published in 1640), ed. J. C. A. Gaskin (Oxford and New York: Oxford University Press, 1994), Pt. 1, Ch. 11, art. 2–4; Peter Browne, *The Procedure, Extent, and Limits of the Human Understanding* (London, 1728; facs. rpt., New York and London: Garland Publishing, 1976), 81–85.
[6] Cf. George Cheyne, *Philosophical Principles of Natural Religion* (London, 1715), 2–5.

has executed. By this argument *a posteriori*,[7] and by this argument alone, do we prove at once the existence of a deity, and his similarity to human mind and intelligence.

6 I shall be so free, *Cleanthes*, said *Demea*, as to tell you, that from the beginning I could not approve of your conclusion concerning the similarity of the deity to men; still less can I approve of the mediums, by which you endeavour to establish it. What! No demonstration of the being of God! No abstract arguments! No proofs *a priori*! Are these, which have hitherto been so much insisted on by philosophers,[8] all fallacy, all sophism? Can we reach no farther in this subject than experience and probability? I will not say, that this is betraying the cause of a deity: But [144] surely, by this affected candour, you give advantages to atheists,[9] which they never could obtain, by the mere dint of argument and reasoning.

7 What I chiefly scruple in this subject, said *Philo*, is not so much, that all religious arguments are by *Cleanthes* reduced to experience, as that they appear not to be even the most certain and irrefragable of that inferior kind.[10] That a stone will fall, that fire will burn, that the earth has solidity, we have observed a thousand and a thousand times; and when any new instance of this nature is presented, we draw without hesitation the accustomed inference. The exact similarity of the cases gives us a perfect assurance of a similar event; and a stronger evidence is never desired nor sought after. But wherever you depart, in the least, from the similarity of the cases, you diminish proportionably the evidence; and may at last bring it to a very weak *analogy*, which is confessedly liable

---

[7] The terms *a posteriori* and *a priori* did not have fixed meanings in the eighteenth century, but as Hume used them, an *a posteriori* proof or argument is a probable inference about logically contingent facts based on the evidence of experience or observation, whereas *a priori* proofs are demonstrative or certain inferences based on self-evident or logically necessary premises.

[8] Samuel Clarke (1675–1729), "The Answer to a Seventh Letter concerning the Argument *a priori*," in *A Demonstration of the Being and Attributes of God and Other Writings*, ed. Ezio Vailati (Cambridge and New York: Cambridge University Press, 1998), 119.

[9] For Hume's wording, cf. Henry More, *Antidote Against Atheism*, in *A Collection of Several Philosophical Writings*, 2nd edn. (London, 1662; facs. rpt., New York and London: Garland Publishing, Inc., 1978), Ch. 2.4–5, p. 12.

[10] Hume distinguishes between two types of reasoning from experience, namely *proofs* and *probabilities*. Both are, strictly speaking, forms of probable reasoning, since both fall short of the logical certainty of demonstrative reasoning. Proofs, however, because they are drawn from evidence of perfectly resembling and exceptionless regularities, leave no room for doubt based on contrary evidence, and in this sense they can be called "certain," even though they fall short of certainty in the stricter sense, that is, logical or demonstrative certainty. Probabilities, because they are based on imperfect regularities or resemblances, fall short of the certainty conveyed by both empirical proof and logical demonstration. See *T* 1.3.11.2–25; 12.1–25 and *EHU* 6.2–4; 9.1.

to error and uncertainty.[11] After having experienced the circulation of the blood in human creatures, we make no doubt, that it takes place in *Titius* and *Maevius*: But from its circulation in frogs and fishes, it is only a presumption, though a strong one, from analogy, that it takes place in men and other animals. The analogical reasoning is much weaker, when we infer the circulation of the sap in vegetables from our experience, that the blood circulates in animals; and those, who hastily followed that imperfect analogy, are found, by more accurate experiments, to have been mistaken.[12]

8 If we see a house, *Cleanthes*, we conclude, with the greatest certainty, that it had an architect or builder; because this is precisely that species of effect, which we have experienced to proceed from that species of cause. But surely you will not affirm, that the universe bears such a resemblance to a house, that we can with the same certainty infer a similar cause, or that the analogy is here entire and perfect. The dissimilitude is so striking, that the utmost you can here pretend to is a guess, a conjecture, a presumption concerning a similar cause; and how that pretension will be received in the world, I leave you to consider.

9 It would surely be very ill received, replied *Cleanthes*; and I should be deservedly blamed and detested, did I allow, that the proofs of a deity amounted to no more than a guess or conjecture. But is the whole adjustment of means to ends in a house and in the universe so slight a resemblance? The economy of final causes?[13] The order, proportion, and [145] arrangement of every part? Steps of a stair are plainly contrived, that human legs may use them in mounting; and this inference is certain and infallible. Human legs are also contrived for walking and mounting; and this inference, I allow, is not altogether so certain, because of the dissimilarity which you remark; but does it, therefore, deserve the name only of presumption or conjecture?

10 Good God! cried *Demea*, interrupting him, where are we? Zealous defenders of religion allow, that the proofs of a deity fall short of perfect

---

[11] Cf. Hume's remarks on analogical probability in *T* 1.13.15.11 and *EHU* 9.1.

[12] Nehemiah Grew (1641–1712), co-founder of plant anatomy, argued that analogies in the anatomy of plants and animals supported the hypothesis that sap circulates through plants much as blood circulates through the bodies of animals. Stephen Hales disproved the circulation of sap in 1716. Berkeley refers to the debate in his final work, *Siris: A Chain of Philosophical Reflexions and Inquiries* (originally published in 1744), in *Works*, V:41.

[13] *Final causes*: The ultimate purposes, ends, or goals of things. Explanations of things in terms of their final causes fell into disfavor during the rise of modern science beginning in the Renaissance. For Hume's rejection of final causes, see *T* 1.3.14.32.

evidence! And you, *Philo*, on whose assistance I depended, in proving the adorable mysteriousness of the divine nature, do you assent to all these extravagant opinions of *Cleanthes*? For what other name can I give them? Or why spare my censure, when such principles are advanced, supported by such an authority, before so young a man as *Pamphilus*?

11 You seem not to apprehend, replied *Philo*, that I argue with *Cleanthes* in his own way; and by showing him the dangerous consequences of his tenets, hope at last to reduce him to our opinion. But what sticks most with you, I observe, is the representation which *Cleanthes* has made of the argument *a posteriori*; and finding that that argument is likely to escape your hold and vanish into air, you think it so disguised that you can scarcely believe it to be set in its true light. Now, however much I may dissent, in other respects, from the dangerous principles of *Cleanthes*, I must allow, that he has fairly represented that argument; and I shall endeavour so to state the matter to you that you will entertain no farther scruples with regard to it.

12 Were a man to abstract from everything which he knows or has seen, he would be altogether incapable, merely from his own ideas, to determine what kind of scene the universe must be, or to give the preference to one state or situation of things above another. For as nothing, which he clearly conceives, could be esteemed impossible or implying a contradiction, every chimera of his fancy would be upon an equal footing; nor could he assign any just reason, why he adheres to one idea or system, and rejects the others, which are equally possible.

13 Again; after he opens his eyes, and contemplates the world, as it
[146] really is, it would be impossible for him, at first, to assign the cause of any one event; much less, of the whole of things or of the universe. He might set his fancy a-rambling; and she might bring him in an infinite variety of reports and representations. These would all be possible; but being all equally possible, he would never, of himself, give a satisfactory account for his preferring one of them to the rest. Experience alone can point out to him the true cause of any phenomenon.[14]

14 Now according to this method of reasoning, *Demea*, it follows (and is, indeed, tacitly allowed by *Cleanthes* himself) that order, arrangement, or the adjustment of final causes is not, of itself, any proof of design; but only

---

[14] Paragraphs 12 and 13 summarize ideas Hume presents in *EHU* 4.2–11 concerning inferences about logically contingent facts.

so far as it has been experienced to proceed from that principle. For aught we can know *a priori*, matter may contain the source or spring of order originally, within itself, as well as mind does; and there is no more difficulty in conceiving, that the several elements, from an internal unknown cause, may fall into the most exquisite arrangement, than to conceive that their ideas, in the great, universal mind, from a like internal, unknown cause, fall into that arrangement. The equal possibility of both these suppositions is allowed. But by experience we find (according to *Cleanthes*), that there is a difference between them. Throw several pieces of steel together, without shape or form; they will never arrange themselves so as to compose a watch: Stone, and mortar, and wood, without an architect, never erect a house. But the ideas in a human mind, we see, by an unknown, inexplicable economy, arrange themselves so as to form the plan of a watch or house. Experience, therefore, proves, that there is an original principle of order in mind, not in matter. From similar effects we infer similar causes. The adjustment of means to ends is alike in the universe, as in a machine of human contrivance. The causes, therefore, must be resembling.

15 I was from the beginning scandalized, I must own, with this resemblance, which is asserted, between the deity and human creatures; and must conceive it to imply such a degradation of the supreme being as no sound theist could endure. With your assistance, therefore, *Demea*, I shall endeavour to defend what you justly call the adorable mysteriousness of the divine nature, and shall refute this reasoning of *Cleanthes*; provided he allows, that I have made a fair representation of it.

16 When *Cleanthes* had assented, *Philo*, after a short pause, proceeded [147] in the following manner.

17 That all inferences, *Cleanthes*, concerning fact are founded on experience, and that all experimental reasonings are founded on the supposition, that similar causes prove similar effects, and similar effects similar causes;[15] I shall not, at present, much dispute with you. But observe, I entreat you, with what extreme caution all just reasoners proceed in the transferring of experiments to similar cases. Unless the cases be exactly similar, they repose no perfect confidence in applying their past observation to any particular phenomenon. Every alteration of circumstances occasions a doubt concerning the event; and it requires new experiments

---

[15] Cf. Hume, *T* 1.3.15.6; Newton, *The Principia: Mathematical Principles of Natural Philosophy*, trans. I. Bernard Cohen and Anne Whitman (Berkeley: University of California Press, 1999), Bk. 3, Rule 2, p. 795.

to prove certainly, that the new circumstances are of no moment or importance. A change in bulk, situation, arrangement, age, disposition of the air, or surrounding bodies; any of these particulars may be attended with the most unexpected consequences: And unless the objects be quite familiar to us, it is the highest temerity to expect with assurance, after any of these changes, an event similar to that which before fell under our observation. The slow and deliberate steps of philosophers here, if anywhere, are distinguished from the precipitate march of the vulgar, who, hurried on by the smallest similitude, are incapable of all discernment or consideration.

18 But can you think, *Cleanthes*, that your usual phlegm and philosophy have been preserved in so wide a step as you have taken, when you compared to the universe houses, ships, furniture, machines; and from their similarity in some circumstances inferred a similarity in their causes? Thought, design, intelligence, such as we discover in men and other animals, is no more than one of the springs and principles of the universe, as well as heat or cold, attraction or repulsion, and a hundred others, which fall under daily observation. It is an active cause, by which some particular parts of nature, we find, produce alterations on other parts. But can a conclusion, with any propriety, be transferred from parts to the whole? Does not the great disproportion bar all comparison and inference? From observing the growth of a hair, can we learn anything concerning the generation of a man? Would the manner of a leaf's blowing, even though perfectly known, afford us any instruction concerning the vegetation of a tree?

[148]   19 But allowing that we were to take the *operations* of one part of nature upon another for the foundation of our judgement concerning the *origin* of the whole (which never can be admitted), yet why select so minute, so weak, so bounded a principle as the reason and design of animals is found to be upon this planet? What peculiar privilege has this little agitation of the brain which we call thought, that we must thus make it the model of the whole universe? Our partiality in our own favour does indeed present it on all occasions: But sound philosophy ought carefully to guard against so natural an illusion.

20 So far from admitting, continued *Philo*, that the operations of a part can afford us any just conclusion concerning the origin of the whole, I will not allow any one part to form a rule for another part, if the latter be very remote from the former. Is there any reasonable ground to conclude, that the inhabitants of other planets possess thought, intelligence, reason, or

24

anything similar to these faculties in men? When nature has so extremely diversified her manner of operation in this small globe; can we imagine that she incessantly copies herself throughout so immense a universe? And if thought, as we may well suppose, be confined merely to this narrow corner, and has even there so limited a sphere of action; with what propriety can we assign it for the original cause of all things? The narrow views of a peasant, who makes his domestic economy the rule for the government of kingdoms, is in comparison a pardonable sophism.

21 But were we ever so much assured, that a thought and reason, resembling the human, were to be found throughout the whole universe, and were its activity elsewhere vastly greater and more commanding than it appears in this globe: Yet I cannot see, why the operations of a world, constituted, arranged, adjusted, can with any propriety be extended to a world, which is in its embryo-state, and is advancing towards that constitution and arrangement. By observation, we know somewhat of the economy, action, and nourishment of a finished animal; but we must transfer with great caution that observation to the growth of a foetus in the womb, and still more, to the formation of an animalcule[16] in the loins of its male parent. Nature, we find, even from our limited experience, possesses an infinite number of springs and principles, which incessantly discover themselves on every change of her position and situation. And what new [149] and unknown principles would actuate her in so new and unknown a situation, as that of the formation of a universe, we cannot, without the utmost temerity, pretend to determine.

22 A very small part of this great system, during a very short time, is very imperfectly discovered to us: And do we thence pronounce decisively concerning the origin of the whole?

23 Admirable conclusion! Stone, wood, brick, iron, brass, have not, at this time, in this minute globe of earth, an order or arrangement without human art and contrivance: Therefore the universe could not originally attain its order and arrangement without something similar to human art. But is a part of nature a rule for another part very wide of the former? Is it a rule for the whole? Is a very small part a rule for the universe? Is nature in one situation, a certain rule for nature in another situation, vastly different from the former?

---

[16] *Animalcule*: According to early biological theory, a miniature, fully formed individual present in the sperm cell.

24 And can you blame me, *Cleanthes*, if I here imitate the prudent reserve of *Simonides*, who, according to the noted story, being asked by *Hiero, What God was?* desired a day to think of it, and then two days more; and after that manner continually prolonged the term, without ever bringing in his definition or description?[17] Could you even blame me, if I had answered at first, *that I did not know*, and was sensible that this subject lay vastly beyond the reach of my faculties? You might cry out sceptic and railer, as much as you pleased: But having found, in so many other subjects, much more familiar, the imperfections and even contradictions of human reason, I never should expect any success from its feeble conjectures, in a subject, so sublime, and so remote from the sphere of our observation. When two *species* of objects have always been observed to be conjoined together, I can *infer*, by custom, the existence of one wherever I *see* the existence of the other: And this I call an argument from experience. But how this argument can have place, where the objects, as in the present case, are single, individual, without parallel, or specific [150] resemblance, may be difficult to explain. And will any man tell me with a serious countenance, that an orderly universe must arise from some thought and art, like the human; because we have experience of it? To ascertain this reasoning, it were requisite, that we had experience of the origin of worlds; and it is not sufficient surely, that we have seen ships and cities arise from human art and contrivance . . .[18]

25 *Philo* was proceeding in this vehement manner, somewhat between jest and earnest, as it appeared to me; when he observed some signs of impatience in *Cleanthes*, and then immediately stopped short. What I had to suggest, said *Cleanthes*, is only that you would not abuse terms, or make use of popular expressions to subvert philosophical reasonings. You know, that the vulgar often distinguish reason from experience, even where the question relates only to matter of fact and existence; though it is found, where that *reason* is properly analysed, that it is nothing but a species of experience. To prove by experience the origin of the universe from mind is not more contrary to common speech than to prove the motion of the earth from the same principle. And a caviller might raise all the same

---

[17] Simonides (550–470 BC) was a lyric poet of ancient Greece. Hiero was the tyrant of Syracuse. The story is related by Cicero in *The Nature of the Gods*, 1.22 and retold by Pierre Bayle, *The Dictionary Historical and Critical*, trans. Pierre Desmaizeaux, 2nd edn. (1734; facs. rpt., New York: Garland, 1984), s.v. "Simonides," note F, V:141 and by William Wollaston, *The Religion of Nature Delineated* (London, 1724; facs. rpt., Demar, NY: Scholars' Facsimiles and Reprints, 1974), 70.
[18] Cf. *EHU* 11.30.

objections to the Copernican system, which you have urged against my reasonings. Have you other earths, might he say, which you have seen to move? Have . . .

26 Yes! cried *Philo*, interrupting him, we have other earths. Is not the moon another earth, which we see to turn round its center? Is not Venus another earth, where we observe the same phenomenon? Are not the revolutions of the sun also a confirmation, from analogy, of the same theory? All the planets, are they not earths, which revolve about the sun? Are not the satellites moons, which move round Jupiter and Saturn, and along with these primary planets, round the sun? These analogies and resemblances, with others, which I have not mentioned, are the sole proofs of the *Copernican* system: And to you it belongs to consider, whether you have any analogies of the same kind to support your theory.

27 In reality, *Cleanthes*, continued he, the modern system of astronomy is now so much received by all enquirers, and has become so essential a part even of our earliest education, that we are not commonly very scrupulous in examining the reasons, upon which it is founded. It is now become a matter of mere curiosity to study the first writers on that subject, who had the full force of prejudice to encounter, and were obliged to turn their [151] arguments on every side, in order to render them popular and convincing. But if we peruse *Galileo*'s famous dialogues concerning the system of the world,[19] we shall find, that that great genius, one of the sublimest that ever existed, first bent all his endeavours to prove, that there was no foundation for the distinction commonly made between elementary and celestial substances. The schools,[20] proceeding from the illusions of sense, had carried this distinction very far; and had established the latter substances to be ingenerable, incorruptible, unalterable, impassable; and had assigned all the opposite qualities to the former. But *Galileo*, beginning with the moon, proved its similarity in every particular to the earth; its convex figure, its natural darkness when not illuminated, its density, its distinction into solid and liquid, the variations of its phases, the mutual illuminations of the earth and moon, their mutual eclipses, the inequalities of the lunar surface, etc. After many instances of this kind, with regard to all the planets, men plainly saw, that these bodies became proper objects

---

[19] Galileo Galilei, *Dialogue concerning the Two Chief World Systems, Ptolemaic and Copernican* (1632).
[20] *The schools*: Academic units within medieval and early modern universities in which Aristotelian philosophy and science were taught.

of experience; and that the similarity of their nature enabled us to extend the same arguments and phenomena from one to the other.

28 In this cautious proceeding of the astronomers, you may read your own condemnation, *Cleanthes*; or rather may see, that the subject in which you are engaged exceeds all human reason and enquiry. Can you pretend to show any such similarity between the fabric of a house, and the generation of a universe? Have you ever seen nature in any such situation as resembles the first arrangement of the elements? Have worlds ever been formed under your eye? And have you had leisure to observe the whole progress of the phenomenon, from the first appearance of order to its final consummation? If you have, then cite your experience, and deliver your theory.

Part 3

1 How the most absurd argument, replied *Cleanthes*, in the hands of a man of ingenuity and invention, may acquire an air of probability! Are you not aware, *Philo*, that it became necessary for *Copernicus* and his first disciples to prove the similarity of the terrestrial and celestial matter; because several philosophers, blinded by old systems, and supported by some sensible appearances, had denied this similarity? But that it is by no means necessary, that theists should prove the similarity of the works of nature to those of art; because this similarity is self-evident and undeniable? The same matter, a like form: What more is requisite to show an analogy between their causes, and to ascertain the origin of all things from a divine purpose and intention? Your objections, I must freely tell you, are no better than the abstruse cavils of those philosophers who denied motion; and ought to be refuted in the same manner, by illustrations, examples, and instances, rather than by serious argument and philosophy.

2 Suppose, therefore, that an articulate voice were heard in the clouds, much louder and more melodious than any which human art could ever reach: Suppose, that this voice were extended in the same instant over all nations, and spoke to each nation in its own language and dialect: Suppose, that the words delivered not only contain a just sense and meaning, but convey some instruction altogether worthy of a benevolent being superior to mankind: Could you possibly hesitate a moment concerning the cause of this voice? And must you not instantly ascribe it to some design or purpose? Yet I cannot see but all the same objections (if they merit that appellation) which lie against the system of theism, may also be produced against this inference.

3 Might you not say, that all conclusions concerning fact were founded on experience: That when we hear an articulate voice in the dark, and [153] thence infer a man, it is only the resemblance of the effects, which leads us to conclude that there is a like resemblance in the cause: But that this extraordinary voice, by its loudness, extent, and flexibility to all languages, bears so little analogy to any human voice, that we have no reason to suppose any analogy in their causes: And consequently, that a rational, wise, coherent speech proceeded, you know not whence, from some accidental whistling of the winds,[1] not from any divine reason or intelligence? You see clearly your own objections in these cavils; and I hope too, you see clearly, that they cannot possibly have more force in the one case than in the other.

4 But to bring the case still nearer the present one of the universe, I shall make two suppositions, which imply not any absurdity or impossibility. Suppose, that there is a natural, universal, invariable language, common to every individual of human race; and that books are natural productions, which perpetuate themselves in the same manner with animals and vegetables, by descent and propagation. Several expressions of our passions contain a universal language: All brute animals have a natural speech, which, however limited, is very intelligible to their own species. And as there are infinitely fewer parts and less contrivance in the finest composition of eloquence than in the coarsest organised body, the propagation of an *Iliad* or *Aeneid* is an easier supposition than that of any plant or animal.[2]

5 Suppose, therefore, that you enter into your library, thus peopled by natural volumes, containing the most refined reason and most exquisite beauty: Could you possibly open one of them, and doubt, that its original cause bore the strongest analogy to mind and intelligence? When it reasons and discourses; when it expostulates, argues, and enforces its views and topics; when it applies sometimes to the pure intellect, sometimes to the affections; when it collects, disposes, and adorns every consideration

---

[1] *Accidental whistling of the winds*: Hume's wording is drawn from Shaftesbury, "The Moralists," Part II, Sec. 3, in *Characteristics*, 276.

[2] *Iliad*: Homer's epic story of the Trojan war. *Aeneid*: Virgil's epic of the founding of Rome. The idea that evidence of intelligent design is greater in natural organisms than in books was common. Cf. Richard Bentley, *A Defence of Natural and Revealed Religion: Being a Collection of the Sermons Preached at the Lecture founded by . . . Robert Boyle*, 4 vols. (London, 1737), I:49, 87.

suited to the subject:[3] Could you persist in asserting, that all this, at the bottom, had really no meaning, and that the first formation of this volume in the loins of its original parent proceeded not from thought and design? Your obstinacy, I know, reaches not that degree of firmness: Even your sceptical play and wantonness would be abashed at so glaring an absurdity.

6 But if there be any difference, *Philo*, between this supposed case [154] and the real one of the universe, it is all to the advantage of the latter. The anatomy of an animal affords many stronger instances of design than the perusal of *Livy* or *Tacitus*:[4] And any objection which you start in the former case, by carrying me back to so unusual and extraordinary a scene as the first formation of worlds, the same objection has place on the supposition of our vegetating library. Choose, then, your party, *Philo*, without ambiguity or evasion: Assert either that a rational volume is no proof of a rational cause, or admit of a similar cause to all the works of nature.

7 Let me here observe too, continued *Cleanthes*, that this religious argument, instead of being weakened by that scepticism, so much affected by you, rather acquires force from it, and becomes more firm and undisputed. To exclude all argument or reasoning of every kind is either affectation or madness. The declared profession of every reasonable sceptic is only to reject abstruse, remote, and refined arguments; to adhere to common sense and the plain instincts of nature; and to assent, wherever any reasons strike him with so full a force, that he cannot, without the greatest violence, prevent it. Now the arguments for natural religion are plainly of this kind; and nothing but the most perverse, obstinate metaphysics can reject them. Consider, anatomize the eye: Survey its structure and contrivance; and tell me, from your own feeling, if the idea of a contriver does not immediately flow in upon you with a force like that of sensation.[5]

[3] Cf. Henry More, *Divine Dialogues*, 2nd edn. (London, 1713), 11–12. Another edition appeared in 1743.

[4] *Livy* (59 BC–AD 17): Titus Livius, famous historian during the age of Augustus. *Cornelius Tacitus* (AD *c.* 55–117): Roman historian famous for two partially preserved works of history on the Roman Republic and empire, the *Annals* (covering AD 14–68) and the *Histories* (covering AD 69–96).

[5] *A force like that of sensation*: Phrasing used by Colin MacLaurin, *An Account of Sir Isaac Newton's Philosophical Discoveries* (London, 1748; facs. rpt., New York: Johnson, 1968), 381, and by Henry Home, *Essays on the Principles of Morality and Natural Religion* [1751] (New York: Garland Publishing, 1976), 328.

The most obvious conclusion surely is in favour of design; and it requires time, reflection and study to summon up those frivolous, though abstruse, objections, which can support infidelity. Who can behold the male and female of each species, the correspondence of their parts and instincts, their passions and whole course of life before and after generation, but must be sensible, that the propagation of the species is intended by nature? Millions and millions of such instances present themselves through every part of the universe; and no language can convey a more intelligible irresistible meaning, than the curious adjustment of final causes.[6] To what degree, therefore, of blind dogmatism must one have attained, to reject such natural and such convincing arguments?

[155]   8 Some beauties in writing we may meet with, which seem contrary to rules, and which gain the affections, and animate the imagination, in opposition to all the precepts of criticism, and to the authority of the established masters of art. And if the argument for theism be, as you pretend, contradictory to the principles of logic; its universal, its irresistible influence proves clearly, that there may be arguments of a like irregular nature. Whatever cavils may be urged, an orderly world, as well as a coherent, articulate speech, will still be received as an incontestable proof of design and intention.

9 It sometimes happens, I own, that the religious arguments have not their due influence on an ignorant savage and barbarian; not because they are obscure and difficult, but because he never asks himself any question with regard to them. Whence arises the curious structure of an animal? From the copulation of its parents. And these whence? From *their* parents? A few removes set the objects at such a distance, that to him they are lost in darkness and confusion; nor is he actuated by any curiosity to trace them farther. But this is neither dogmatism nor scepticism, but stupidity; a state of mind very different from your sifting,[7] inquisitive disposition, my ingenious friend. You can trace causes from effects: You can compare the most distant and remote objects: And your greatest errors proceed not from barrenness of thought and invention, but from too luxuriant a fertility, which suppresses your natural good sense, by a profusion of unnecessary scruples and objections.

---

[6] Possibly a reference to Berkeley's "Optical Language" version of the argument from design. See Introduction, note 17, p. xx above.

[7] *Sifting*: A metaphor Hume uses to describe his methodology in *EHU* 4.14.

10 Here I could observe, *Hermippus*, that *Philo* was a little embarrassed and confounded:[8] But while he hesitated in delivering an answer, luckily for him, *Demea* broke in upon the discourse, and saved his countenance.

11 Your instance, *Cleanthes*, said he, drawn from books and language, being familiar, has, I confess, so much more force on that account; but is there not some danger too in this very circumstance, and may it not render us presumptuous, by making us imagine we comprehend the deity, and have some adequate idea of his nature and attributes? When I read a volume, I enter into the mind and intention of the author: I become him, in a manner, for the instant; and have an immediate feeling and conception of those ideas, which revolved in his imagination, while employed in that [156] composition. But so near an approach we never surely can make to the deity. His ways are not our ways. His attributes are perfect, but incomprehensible. And this volume of nature contains a great and inexplicable riddle, more than any intelligible discourse or reasoning.

12 The ancient *Platonists*, you know, were the most religious and devout of all the pagan philosophers: Yet many of them, particularly *Plotinus*,[9] expressly declare, that intellect or understanding is not to be ascribed to the deity, and that our most perfect worship of him consists, not in acts of veneration, reverence, gratitude or love; but in a certain mysterious self-annihilation or total extinction of all our faculties. These ideas are, perhaps, too far stretched; but still it must be acknowledged, that, by representing the deity as so intelligible, and comprehensible, and so similar to a human mind, we are guilty of the grossest and most narrow partiality, and make ourselves the model of the whole universe.

13 All the *sentiments* of the human mind, gratitude, resentment, love, friendship, approbation, blame, pity, emulation, envy, have a plain reference to the state and situation of man, and are calculated for preserving the existence, and promoting the activity of such a being in such circumstances. It seems, therefore, unreasonable to transfer such sentiments to a supreme existence, or to suppose him actuated by them; and the phenomena, besides, of the universe will not support us in such a theory. All our *ideas*, derived from the senses, are confessedly false and illusive; and cannot, therefore, be supposed to have place in a supreme intelligence: And as the ideas of internal sentiment, added to those of the external

---

[8] Cf. LE2, 121.
[9] Plotinus (AD 205–270) was an influential Roman neo-Platonist. Demea's remarks on Plotinus follow, nearly verbatim, those of Colin MacLaurin in *An Account of Sir Isaac Newton's Philosophy*, 378.

senses, compose the whole furniture of human understanding, we may conclude, that none of the *materials* of thought are in any respect similar in the human and in the divine intelligence. Now as to the *manner* of thinking; how can we make any comparison between them, or suppose them anywise resembling? Our thought is fluctuating, uncertain, fleeting, successive, and compounded; and were we to remove these circumstances, [157] we absolutely annihilate its essence, and it would, in such a case, be an abuse of terms to apply to it the name of thought or reason. At least, if it appear more pious and respectful (as it really is) still to retain these terms, when we mention the supreme being, we ought to acknowledge, that their meaning, in that case, is totally incomprehensible; and that the infirmities of our nature do not permit us to reach any ideas, which in the least correspond to the ineffable sublimity of the divine attributes.[10]

[10] Cf. Peter Browne, *The Procedure, Extent, and Limits of the Human Understanding* (London, 1728; facs. rpt., New York and London: Garland Publishing, 1976), 83–85.

Part 4

1 It seems strange to me, said *Cleanthes*, that you, *Demea*, who are so sincere in the cause of religion, should still maintain the mysterious, incomprehensible nature of the deity, and should insist so strenuously, that he has no manner of likeness or resemblance to human creatures. The deity, I can readily allow, possesses many powers and attributes, of which we can have no comprehension: But if our ideas, so far as they go, be not just, and adequate, and correspondent to his real nature, I know not what there is in this subject worth insisting on. Is the name, without any meaning, of such mighty importance? Or how do you *mystics*, who maintain the absolute incomprehensibility of the deity, differ from sceptics or atheists, who assert, that the first cause of all is unknown and unintelligible? Their temerity must be very great, if, after rejecting the production by a mind; I mean, a mind resembling the human (for I know of no other); they pretend to assign, with certainty, any other specific intelligible cause: And their conscience must be very scrupulous indeed, if they refuse to call the universal, unknown cause a god or deity; and to bestow on him as many sublime eulogies and unmeaning epithets, as you shall please to require of them.[1]

2 Who could imagine, replied *Demea*, that *Cleanthes*, the calm, philo-sophical *Cleanthes*, would attempt to refute his antagonists, by affixing a nickname to them; and like the common bigots and inquisitors of the age, have recourse to invective and declamation, instead of reasoning?

---

[1] The discussion in paragraphs 1–4 tracks the debate between George Berkeley and Peter Browne about whether divine intelligence can be understood in a human sense. See Browne, *Procedure, Extents and Limits of the Human Understanding*, 83–85; Berkeley, *Alciphron*, Fourth Dialogue, Secs. 17–22, in *Works*, III:163–170.

Or does he not perceive, that these topics are easily retorted, and that *anthropomorphite* is an appellation as invidious, and implies as dangerous consequences, as the epithet of *mystic*, with which he has honoured us? In reality, *Cleanthes*, consider what it is you assert, when you represent [159] the deity as similar to a human mind and understanding. What is the soul of man? A composition of various faculties, passions, sentiments, ideas; united, indeed, into one self or person, but still distinct from each other. When it reasons, the ideas, which are the parts of its discourse, arrange themselves in a certain form or order; which is not preserved entire for a moment, but immediately gives place to another arrangement. New opinions, new passions, new affections, new feelings arise, which continually diversify the mental scene, and produce in it the greatest variety, and most rapid succession imaginable.[2] How is this compatible, with that perfect immutability and simplicity, which all true theists ascribe to the deity? By the same act, say they, he sees past, present, and future: His love and his hatred, his mercy and his justice are one individual operation: He is entire in every point of space; and complete in every instant of duration. No succession, no change, no acquisition, no diminution. What he is implies not in it any shadow of distinction or diversity. And what he is, this moment, he ever has been, and ever will be, without any new judgement, sentiment, or operation. He stands fixed in one simple, perfect state; nor can you ever say, with any propriety, that this act of his is different from that other, or that this judgement or idea has been lately formed, and will give place, by succession, to any different judgement or idea.

3 I can readily allow, said *Cleanthes*, that those who maintain the perfect simplicity of the supreme being, to the extent in which you have explained it, are complete *mystics*, and chargeable with all the consequences which I have drawn from their opinion. They are, in a word, atheists, without knowing it.[3] For though it be allowed, that the deity possesses attributes, of which we have no comprehension; yet ought we never to ascribe to him any attributes, which are absolutely incompatible with that intelligent nature, essential to him. A mind, whose acts and sentiments and ideas are not distinct and successive; one, that is wholly simple, and totally immutable; is a mind, which has no thought, no reason, no will, no sentiment, no love, no hatred; or in a word, is no mind at all. It is an abuse of terms to give it

[2] Cf. *T* 1.4.6.4.   [3] Cf. Berkeley, *Alciphron*, Fourth Dialogue, Sec. 17, in *Works*, III:163.

that appellation; and we may as well speak of limited extension without figure, or of number without composition.

4 Pray consider, said *Philo*, whom you are at present inveighing against. [160] You are honouring with the appellation of atheist all the sound, orthodox divines almost, who have treated of this subject; and you will, at last be, yourself, found, according to your reckoning, the only sound theist in the world. But if idolators be atheists, as, I think, may justly be asserted, and Christian theologians the same; what becomes of the argument, so much celebrated, derived from the universal consent of mankind?[4]

5 But because I know you are not much swayed by names and authorities, I shall endeavour to show you, a little more distinctly, the inconveniences of that anthropomorphism, which you have embraced; and shall prove, that there is no ground to suppose a plan of the world to be formed in the divine mind, consisting of distinct ideas, differently arranged; in the same manner as an architect forms in his head the plan of a house which he intends to execute.

6 It is not easy, I own, to see, what is gained by this supposition, whether we judge of the matter by *reason* or by *experience*. We are still obliged to mount higher, in order to find the cause of this cause, which you had assigned as satisfactory and conclusive.

7 If *reason* (I mean abstract reason, derived from enquiries *a priori*) be not alike mute with regard to all questions concerning cause and effect; this sentence at least it will venture to pronounce, that a mental world or universe of ideas requires a cause as much as does a material world or universe of objects; and if similar in its arrangement must require a similar cause.[5] For what is there in this subject, which should occasion a different conclusion or inference? In an abstract view, they are entirely alike; and no difficulty attends the one supposition, which is not common to both of them.

8 Again, when we will needs force *experience* to pronounce some sen- [161] tence, even on these subjects, which lie beyond her sphere; neither can she perceive any material difference in this particular, between these two kinds of worlds, but finds them to be governed by similar principles, and to depend upon an equal variety of causes in their operations. We have

[4] The argument from universal consent appears in Cicero's *The Nature of the Gods*, 1.44; 2.5, and was popularized in the seventeenth century by Herbert of Cherbury.
[5] Cf. Memoranda, 15, p. 106; "Bayle on Materialism and Intelligent Design," pp. 139–140.

specimens in miniature of both of them. Our own mind resembles the one: A vegetable or animal body the other. Let experience, therefore, judge from these samples. Nothing seems more delicate with regard to its causes than thought; and as these causes never operate in two persons after the same manner, so we never find two persons, who think exactly alike. Nor indeed does the same person think exactly alike at any two different periods of time. A difference of age, of the disposition of his body, of weather, of food, of company, of books, of passions; any of these particulars or others more minute, are sufficient to alter the curious machinery of thought, and communicate to it very different movements and operations. As far as we can judge, vegetables and animal bodies are not more delicate in their motions, nor depend upon a greater variety or more curious adjustment of springs and principles.

9 How therefore shall we satisfy ourselves concerning the cause of that being, whom you suppose the author of nature, or, according to your system of anthropomorphism, the ideal world, into which you trace the material? Have we not the same reason to trace that ideal world into another ideal world, or new intelligent principle? But if we stop, and go no farther; why go so far? Why not stop at the material world? How can we satisfy ourselves without going on *in infinitum*? And after all, what satisfaction is there in that infinite progression? Let us remember the story of the *Indian* philosopher and his elephant.[6] It was never more applicable than to the present subject. If the material world rests upon a [162] similar ideal world, this ideal world must rest upon some other; and so on, without end. It were better, therefore, never to look beyond the present material world. By supposing it to contain the principle of its order within itself, we really assert it to be God; and the sooner we arrive at that divine being so much the better. When you go one step beyond the mundane system, you only excite an inquisitive humour, which it is impossible ever to satisfy.

10 To say, that the different ideas, which compose the reason of the supreme being, fall into order, of themselves, and by their own nature, is really to talk without any precise meaning. If it has a meaning, I would fain know, why it is not as good sense to say, that the parts of the material

---

[6] Cf. Locke, *An Essay concerning Human Understanding*, 2.13.19: "Had the poor Indian Philosopher (who imagined that the earth also wanted something to bear it up) but thought of this word substance, he needed not to have been at the trouble to find an elephant to support it, and a tortoise to support his elephant: the word substance would have done it effectively."

world fall into order, of themselves, and by their own nature? Can the one opinion be intelligible, while the other is not so?

11 We have, indeed, experience of ideas, which fall into order, of themselves, and without any *known* cause: But, I am sure, we have a much larger experience of matter, which does the same; as in all instances of generation and vegetation, where the accurate analysis of the cause exceeds all human comprehension. We have also experience of particular systems of thought and of matter, which have no order; of the first, in madness, of the second, in corruption. Why then should we think, that order is more essential to one than the other? And if it requires a cause in both, what do we gain by your system, in tracing the universe of objects into a similar universe of ideas? The first step, which we make, leads us on for ever. It were, therefore, wise in us to limit all our enquiries to the present world, without looking farther. No satisfaction can ever be attained by these speculations, which so far exceed the narrow bounds of human understanding.

12 It was usual with the *Peripatetics*, you know, *Cleanthes*, when the cause of any phenomenon was demanded, to have recourse to their *faculties* or *occult qualities*,[7] and to say, for instance; that bread nourished by its nutritive faculty, and senna purged by its purgative: But it has been discovered, that this subterfuge was nothing but the disguise of ignorance; and that these philosophers, though less ingenuous, really said the same thing with the sceptics or the vulgar, who fairly confessed, that they knew [163] not the cause of these phenomena. In like manner, when it is asked, what cause produces order in the ideas of the supreme being, can any other reason be assigned by you, anthropomorphites, than that it is a *rational* faculty, and that such is the nature of the deity? But why a similar answer will not be equally satisfactory in accounting for the order of the world, without having recourse to any such intelligent creator, as you insist on, may be difficult to determine. It is only to say, that *such* is the nature of material objects, and that they are all originally possessed of a *faculty* of order and proportion. These are only more learned and elaborate ways of confessing our ignorance; nor has the one hypothesis any real advantage above the other, except in its greater conformity to vulgar prejudices.

13 You have displayed this argument with great emphasis, replied *Cleanthes*: You seem not sensible, how easy it is to answer it. Even in

---

7 *Faculties*: powers; *Occult qualities*: hidden qualities of things known only through their effects.

common life, if I assign a cause for any event; is it any objection, *Philo*, that I cannot assign the cause of that cause, and answer every new question, which may incessantly be started? And what philosophers could possibly submit to so rigid a rule? Philosophers, who confess ultimate causes to be totally unknown, and are sensible, that the most refined principles, into which they trace the phenomena, are still to them as inexplicable as these phenomena themselves are to the vulgar. The order and arrangement of nature, the curious adjustment of final causes, the plain use and intention of every part and organ; all these bespeak in the clearest language an intelligent cause or author. The heavens and the earth join in the same testimony: The whole chorus of nature raises one hymn to the praises of its creator: You alone, or almost alone, disturb this general harmony. You start abstruse doubts, cavils, and objections: You ask me, what is the cause of this cause? I know not; I care not; that concerns not me. I have found a deity; and here I stop my enquiry. Let those go farther, who are wiser or more enterprising.

14 I pretend to be neither, replied *Philo*: And for that very reason, I should never perhaps have attempted to go so far; especially when I am sensible, that I must at last be contented to sit down with the same answer, which, without farther trouble, might have satisfied me from [164] the beginning. If I am still to remain in utter ignorance of causes, and can absolutely give an explication of nothing, I shall never esteem it any advantage to shove off for a moment a difficulty, which, you acknowledge, must immediately, in its full force, recur upon me. Naturalists indeed very justly explain particular effects by more general causes; though these general causes themselves should remain in the end totally inexplicable:[8] But they never surely thought it satisfactory to explain a particular effect by a particular cause, which was no more to be accounted for than the effect itself. An ideal system, arranged of itself, without a precedent design, is not a whit more explicable than a material one, which attains its order in a like manner; nor is there any more difficulty in the latter supposition than in the former.

[8] Cf. *T*, Introduction, para. 4; *EHU* 4.12.

1 But to show you still more inconveniences, continued *Philo*, in your anthropomorphism; please to take a new survey of your principles. *Like effects prove like causes.* This is the experimental argument; and this, you say too, is the sole theological argument. Now it is certain, that the liker the effects are, which are seen, and the liker the causes, which are inferred, the stronger is the argument. Every departure on either side diminishes the probability, and renders the experiment less conclusive. You cannot doubt of the principle: Neither ought you to reject its consequences.

2 All the new discoveries in astronomy, which prove the immense grandeur and magnificence of the works of nature, are so many additional arguments for a deity, according to the true system of theism: But according to your hypothesis of experimental theism they become so many objections, by removing the effect still farther from all resemblance to the effects of human art and contrivance. For if *Lucretius*,[a] even following the old system of the world, could exclaim,

> Quis regere immensi summam, quis habere profundi
> Indu manu validas potis est moderanter habenas?
> Quis pariter coelos omnes convertere? et omnes
> Ignibus aetheriis terras suffire feraces?
> Omnibus inque locis esse omni tempore praesto?

[a] Lib. II, 1095. [Lucretius (Roman poet, 99–55 BC), *On the Nature of Things* (*De rerum natura*), trans. Cyril Bailey (Oxford: Clarendon Press, 1950), Bk. 2, 1095–99: "[W]ho can avail to rule the whole sum of the boundless, who to hold in his guiding hand the mighty reins of the deep, who to turn round all firmaments at once, and warm all fruitful lands with heavenly fires, or to be at all times present in all places."]

If Tully[b] esteemed this reasoning so natural as to put it into the mouth of his Epicurean: *Quibus enim oculis animi intueri potuit vester* PLATO [166] *fabricam illam tanti operis, qua construi a deo atque aedificari mundum facit? quae molitio? quae ferramenta? qui vectes? quae machinae? qui ministri tanti muneris fuerunt? quemadmodum autem obedire et parere voluntati architecti aer, ignis, aqua, terra potuerunt?* If this argument, I say, had any force in former ages; how much greater must it have at present; when the bounds of nature are so infinitely enlarged, and such a magnificent scene is opened to us? It is still more unreasonable to form our idea of so unlimited a cause from our experience of the narrow productions of human design and invention.

3 The discoveries by microscopes, as they open a new universe in miniature, are still objections, according to you; arguments, according to me. The farther we push our researches of this kind, we are still led to infer the universal cause of all to be vastly different from mankind, or from any object of human experience and observation.

4 And what say you to the discoveries in anatomy, chemistry, botany? . . . These surely are no objections, replied *Cleanthes*: They only discover new instances of art and contrivance.[1] It is still the image of mind reflected on us from innumerable objects. – Add, a mind *like the human*, said *Philo*. – I know of no other, replied *Cleanthes*. – And the liker the better, insisted *Philo*. – To be sure, said *Cleanthes*.

5 Now, *Cleanthes*, said *Philo*, with an air of alacrity and triumph, mark the consequences. *First.* By this method of reasoning, you renounce all claim to infinity in any of the attributes of the deity. For as the cause ought only to be proportioned to the effect, and the effect, so far as it falls under our cognizance, is not infinite; what pretensions have we, upon your suppositions, to ascribe that attribute to the divine being? You will still insist, that, by removing him so much from all similarity to human creatures, we give in to the most arbitrary hypothesis, and at the same time, weaken all proofs of his existence.

[b] De nat. Deor. Lib. 1. ["Tully" was the common name for Marcus Tullius Cicero. The quotation is from *The Nature of the Gods*, 1.19: "[W]hat sort of mental vision enabled your teacher Plato to envisage the construction of so massive a work, the assembling and building of the universe by the god in the way which he describes? What was his technique of building? What were his tools and levers and scaffolding? Who were his helpers in so vast an enterprise? How could the elements of air and fire, water and earth knuckle under and obey the will of the architect?" Translation by P. G. Walsh (Oxford and New York: Oxford University Press, 1997).]
[1] Cf. Clarke, *A Demonstration*, 51, 81.

6 *Secondly*. You have no reason, on your theory, for ascribing perfection to the deity, even in his finite capacity; or for supposing him free from every error, mistake, or incoherence, in his undertakings. There are many inexplicable difficulties in the works of nature, which, if we allow a perfect author to be proved *a priori*, are easily solved, and become only seeming difficulties, from the narrow capacity of man, who cannot trace infinite [167] relations. But according to your method of reasoning, these difficulties become all real; and perhaps will be insisted on, as new instances of likeness to human art and contrivance. At least, you must acknowledge, that it is impossible for us to tell, from our limited views, whether this system contains any great faults, or deserves any considerable praise, if compared to other possible, and even real systems. Could a peasant, if the *Aeneid* were read to him, pronounce that poem to be absolutely faultless, or even assign to it its proper rank among the productions of human wit; he, who had never seen any other production?

7 But were this world ever so perfect a production, it must still remain uncertain, whether all the excellencies of the work can justly be ascribed to the workman. If we survey a ship, what an exalted idea must we form of the ingenuity of the carpenter, who framed so complicated, useful, and beautiful a machine? And what surprise must we feel, when we find him a stupid mechanic, who imitated others, and copied an art, which, through a long succession of ages, after multiplied trials, mistakes, corrections, deliberations, and controversies, had been gradually improving? Many worlds might have been botched and bungled, throughout an eternity, ere this system was struck out: Much labour lost: Many fruitless trials made: And a slow, but continued improvement carried on during infinite ages in the art of world-making. In such subjects, who can determine, where the truth; nay, who can conjecture where the probability, lies; amidst a great number of hypotheses, which may be proposed, and a still greater number, which may be imagined?

8 And what shadow of an argument, continued *Philo*, can you produce, from your hypothesis, to prove the unity of the deity? A great number of men join in building a house or ship, in rearing a city, in framing a commonwealth: Why may not several deities combine in contriving and framing a world? This is only so much greater similarity to human affairs. By sharing the work among several, we may so much farther limit the attributes of each, and get rid of that extensive power and knowledge, which must be supposed in one deity, and which, according to you, can

[168] only serve to weaken the proof of his existence. And if such foolish, such vicious creatures as man can yet often unite in framing and executing one plan; how much more those deities or demons,[2] whom we may suppose several degrees more perfect?

9 To multiply causes without necessity is indeed contrary to true philosophy:[3] But this principle applies not to the present case. Were one deity antecedently proved by your theory, who were possessed of every attribute, requisite to the production of the universe; it would be needless, I own (though not absurd) to suppose any other deity existent. But while it is still a question, whether all these attributes are united in one subject, or dispersed among several independent beings: By what phenomena in nature can we pretend to decide the controversy? Where we see a body raised in a scale, we are sure that there is in the opposite scale, however, concealed from sight, some counterpoising weight equal to it: But it is still allowed to doubt, whether that weight be an aggregate of several distinct bodies, or one uniform united mass. And if the weight requisite very much exceeds anything which we have ever seen conjoined in any single body; the former supposition becomes still more probable and natural. An intelligent being of such vast power and capacity, as is necessary to produce the universe, or to speak in the language of ancient philosophy, so prodigious an animal, exceeds all analogy and even comprehension.

10 But farther, *Cleanthes*; men are mortal, and renew their species by generation; and this is common to all living creatures. The two great sexes of male and female, says *Milton*, animate the world.[4] Why must this circumstance, so universal, so essential, be excluded from those numerous and limited deities? Behold, then, the theogony of ancient times brought back upon us.[5]

11 And why not become a perfect anthropomorphite? Why not assert the deity or deities to be corporeal, and to have eyes, a nose, mouth, ears, etc.? *Epicurus* maintained, that no man had ever seen reason but in a human figure; therefore the gods must have a human figure. And this argument, which is deservedly so much ridiculed by *Cicero*,[6] becomes, according to you, solid and philosophical.

---

[2] *Demons*: minor gods or half-gods. From the Greek, *daimon*, meaning "god."
[3] Cf. Newton, *Principia*, Bk. 3, Rule 1, p. 794.
[4] Milton, *Paradise Lost*, Bk. 8, 151.
[5] Cf. Bayle, *Continuation des Pensées Diverses*, art. 8, in *Œuvres Diverses*, III:199.
[6] Cicero, *The Nature of the Gods*, 1.74–89.

12 In a word, *Cleanthes*, a man, who follows your hypothesis, is able, perhaps, to assert, or conjecture, that the universe, sometime, arose from [169] something like design: But beyond that position he cannot ascertain one single circumstance, and is left afterwards to fix every point of his theology, by the utmost license of fancy and hypothesis. This world, for aught he knows, is very faulty and imperfect, compared to a superior standard; and was only the first rude essay of some infant deity, who afterwards abandoned it, ashamed of his lame performance: It is the work only of some dependent, inferior deity; and is the object of derision to his superiors: It is the production of old age and dotage in some superannuated deity; and ever since his death, has run on at adventures, from the first impulse and active force, which it received from him . . . You justly give signs of horror, *Demea*, at these strange suppositions: But these, and a thousand more of the same kind, are *Cleanthes'* suppositions, not mine. From the moment the attributes of the deity are supposed finite, all these have place. And I cannot, for my part, think, that so wild and unsettled a system of theology is, in any respect, preferable to none at all.

13 These suppositions I absolutely disown, cried *Cleanthes*: They strike me, however, with no horror; especially when proposed in that rambling way, in which they drop from you. On the contrary, they give me pleasure, when I see, that, by the utmost indulgence of your imagination, you never get rid of the hypothesis of design in the universe; but are obliged, at every turn, to have recourse to it. To this concession I adhere steadily; and this I regard as a sufficient foundation for religion.

Part 6

1 It must be a slight fabric, indeed, said *Demea*, which can be erected on so tottering a foundation. While we are uncertain, whether there is one deity or many; whether the deity or deities, to whom we owe our existence, be perfect or imperfect, subordinate or supreme, dead or alive; what trust or confidence can we repose in them? What devotion or worship address to them? What veneration or obedience pay them? To all the purposes of life, the theory of religion becomes altogether useless: And even with regard to speculative consequences, its uncertainty, according to you, must render it totally precarious and unsatisfactory.[1]

2 To render it still more unsatisfactory, said *Philo*, there occurs to me another hypothesis, which must acquire an air of probability from the method of reasoning so much insisted on by *Cleanthes*. That like effects arise from like causes: This principle he supposes the foundation of all religion. But there is another principle of the same kind, no less certain, and derived from the same source of experience; that where several known circumstances are *observed* to be similar, the unknown will also be *found* similar. Thus, if we see the limbs of a human body, we conclude, that it is also attended with a human head, though hid from us. Thus, if we see, through a chink in a wall a small part of the sun, we conclude, that, were the wall removed, we should see the whole body. In short, this method of reasoning is so obvious and familiar, that no scruple can ever be made with regard to its solidity.

3 Now if we survey the universe, so far as it falls under our knowledge, it bears a great resemblance to an animal or organized body, and seems

---

[1] Cf. *D* 2.9.

actuated with a like principle of life and motion. A continual circulation of matter in it produces no disorder: A continual waste in every part is incessantly repaired: The closest sympathy is perceived throughout the [171] entire system: And each part or member, in performing its proper offices, operates both to its own preservation and to that of the whole. The world, therefore, I infer, is an animal, and the deity is the SOUL of the world, actuating it, and actuated by it.

4 You have too much learning, *Cleanthes*, to be at all surprised at this opinion, which, you know, was maintained by almost all the theists of antiquity, and chiefly prevails in their discourses and reasonings. For though sometimes the ancient philosophers reason from final causes, as if they thought the world the workmanship of God; yet it appears rather their favourite notion to consider it as his body, whose organization renders it subservient to him. And it must be confessed, that as the universe resembles more a human body than it does the works of human art and contrivance; if our limited analogy could ever, with any propriety, be extended to the whole of nature, the inference seems juster in favour of the ancient than the modern theory.

5 There are many other advantages, too, in the former theory, which recommended it to the ancient theologians. Nothing more repugnant to all their notions, because nothing more repugnant to common experience, than mind without body; a mere spiritual substance, which fell not under their senses nor comprehension, and of which they had not observed one single instance throughout all nature. Mind and body they knew, because they felt both: And order, arrangement, organization, or internal machinery in both they likewise knew, after the same manner: And it could not but seem reasonable to transfer this experience to the universe, and to suppose the divine mind and body to be also coeval, and to have, both of them, order and arrangement naturally inherent in them, and inseparable from them.

6 Here therefore is a new species of anthropomorphism, *Cleanthes*, on which you may deliberate; and a theory, which seems not liable to any considerable difficulties. You are too much superior surely to *systemati-cal prejudices*, to find any more difficulty in supposing an animal body to be, originally, of itself, or from unknown causes, possessed of order and organization, than in supposing a similar order to belong to mind. But [172] the *vulgar prejudice*, that body and mind ought always to accompany each other, ought not, one should think, to be entirely neglected; since it is

founded on *vulgar experience*, the only guide which you profess to follow in all these theological enquiries. And if you assert, that our limited experience is an unequal standard, by which to judge of the unlimited extent of nature; you entirely abandon your own hypothesis, and must thenceforward adopt our mysticism, as you call it, and admit of the absolute incomprehensibility of the divine nature.

7 This theory, I own, replied *Cleanthes*, has never before occurred to me, though a pretty natural one; and I cannot readily, upon so short an examination and reflection, deliver any opinion with regard to it. You are very scrupulous, indeed, said *Philo*: Were I to examine any system of yours, I should not have acted with half that caution and reserve, in starting objections and difficulties to it. However, if anything occur to you, you will oblige us by proposing it.

8 Why then, replied *Cleanthes*, it seems to me, that, though the world does, in many circumstances, resemble an animal body, yet is the analogy also defective in many circumstances, the most material: No organs of sense; no seat of thought or reason; no one precise origin of motion and action. In short, it seems to bear a stronger resemblance to a vegetable than to an animal; and your inference would be so far inconclusive in favour of the soul of the world.

9 But in the next place, your theory seems to imply the eternity of the world; and that is a principle, which, I think, can be refuted by the strongest reasons and probabilities. I shall suggest an argument to this purpose, which, I believe, has not been insisted on by any writer. Those who reason from the late origin of arts and sciences,[2] though their inference wants not force, may perhaps be refuted by considerations, derived from the nature of human society, which is in continual revolution, between ignorance and knowledge, liberty and slavery, riches and poverty; so that it is impossible for us, from our limited experience, to foretell with assurance what events may or may not be expected. Ancient learning and history [173] seem to have been in great danger of entirely perishing after the inundation of the barbarous nations; and had these convulsions continued a little longer or been a little more violent, we should not probably have now known what passed in the world a few centuries before us. Nay, were it not for the superstition of the popes, who preserved a little jargon of *Latin*,

---

[2] Cf. John Wilkins (1614–1720), *Of the Principles and Duties of Natural Religion*, 4th edn. (London, 1699), 71; Cheyne, *Philosophical Principles of Natural Religion*, 63; Berkeley, *Alciphron*, Sixth Dialogue, Sec. 23, in *Works* III:264.

in order to support the appearance of an ancient and universal church, that tongue must have been utterly lost: In which case, the western world, being totally barbarous, would not have been in a fit disposition for receiving the *Greek* language and learning, which was conveyed to them after the sacking of *Constantinople*.[3] When learning and books had been extinguished, even the mechanical arts would have fallen considerably to decay, and it is easily imagined, that fable or tradition might ascribe to them a much later origin than the true one. This vulgar argument, therefore, against the eternity of the world, seems a little precarious.[4]

10 But here appears to be the foundation of a better argument. *Lucullus*[5] was the first that brought cherry trees from *Asia* to *Europe*; though that tree thrives so well in many *European* climates, that it grows in the woods without any culture. Is it possible, that throughout a whole eternity, no *European* had ever passed into *Asia*, and thought of transplanting so delicious a fruit into his own country? Or if the tree was once transplanted and propagated, how could it ever afterwards perish? Empires may rise and fall; liberty and slavery succeed alternately; ignorance and knowledge give place to each other; but the cherry tree will still remain in the woods of *Greece*, *Spain*, and *Italy*, and will never be affected by the revolutions of human society.

11 It is not two thousand years, since vines were transplanted into *France*; though there is no climate in the world more favourable to them. It is not three centuries since horses, cows, sheep, swine, dogs, corn were known in *America*. Is it possible, that, during the revolutions of a whole eternity, there never arose a *Columbus*, who might open the communication between *Europe* and that continent? We may as well imagine, that all men would wear stockings for ten thousand years, and never have the sense to think of garters to tie them. All these seem convincing proofs of the youth, or rather infancy of the world; as being founded on the operation of principles more constant and steady, than those by which human society [174] is governed and directed. Nothing less than a total convulsion of the elements will ever destroy all the *European* animals and vegetables, which are now to be found in the western world.

---

[3] *Constantinople* was the capital of the eastern Roman Empire and of Greek learning. After it was conquered by Turks in 1453, Greek learning spread across western Europe.

[4] Cf. Hume, "Of the Rise and Progress of the Arts and Sciences," in *Essays*, 56–77.

[5] According to Pliny the Elder (AD 24–70), the Roman general Lucullus (*c.* 110–57 BC) brought the cherry tree to Italy from Cerasus, Pontus (now Giresun, Turkey) to celebrate his victory over Mithridates VI, King of Pontus (73 BC).

12 And what argument have you against such convulsions? replied *Philo*. Strong and almost incontestable proofs may be traced over the whole earth that every part of this globe has continued for many ages entirely covered with water. And though order were supposed inseparable from matter, and inherent in it; yet may matter be susceptible of many and great revolutions, through the endless periods of eternal duration. The incessant changes, to which every part of it is subject, seem to intimate some such general transformations; though at the same time, it is observable, that all the changes and corruptions, of which we have ever had experience, are but passages from one state of order to another; nor can matter ever rest in total deformity and confusion. What we see in the parts, we may infer in the whole; at least, that is the method of reasoning, on which you rest your whole theory. And were I obliged to defend any particular system of this nature (which I never willingly should do), I esteem none more plausible, than that which ascribes an eternal, inherent principle of order to the world; though attended with great and continual revolutions and alterations. This at once solves all difficulties; and if the solution, by being so general, is not entirely complete and satisfactory, it is, at least, a theory, that we must, sooner or later, have recourse to, whatever system we embrace. How could things have been as they are, were there not an original, inherent principle of order somewhere, in thought or in matter? And it is very indifferent to which of these we give the preference. Chance has no place, on any hypothesis, sceptical or religious. Everything is surely governed by steady, inviolable laws. And were the inmost essence of things laid open to us, we should then discover a scene, of which, at [175] present, we can have no idea. Instead of admiring the order of natural beings, we should clearly see that it was absolutely impossible for them, in the smallest article, ever to admit of any other disposition.

13 Were anyone inclined to revive the ancient pagan theology, which maintained, as we learn from *Hesiod*,[6] that this globe was governed by 30,000 deities, who arose from the unknown powers of nature: You would naturally object, *Cleanthes*, that nothing is gained by this hypothesis, and that it is as easy to suppose all men and animals, being more numerous, but less perfect, to have sprung immediately from a like origin. Push the same inference a step farther; and you will find a numerous society of

---

[6] *Hesiod* (fl. 700 BC): Early Greek poet whose two surviving poems are the *Theogony* and *Works and Days*. His *Theogony* concerns the origins of the world and the gods.

deities as explicable as one universal deity, who possesses, within himself, the powers and perfections of the whole society. All these systems, then, of scepticism, polytheism, and theism you must allow, on your principles, to be on a like footing, and that no one of them has any advantage over the others. You may thence learn the fallacy of your principles.

Part 7

1 But here, continued *Philo*, in examining the ancient system of the soul of the world, there strikes me, all on a sudden, a new idea, which, if just, must go near to subvert all your reasoning, and destroy even your first inferences, on which you repose such confidence. If the universe bears a greater likeness to animal bodies and to vegetables, than to the works of human art, it is more probable, that its cause resembles the cause of the former than that of the latter, and its origin ought rather to be ascribed to generation or vegetation than to reason or design. Your conclusion, even according to your own principles, is therefore lame and defective.

2 Pray open up this argument a little farther, said *Demea*. For I do not rightly apprehend it, in that concise manner, in which you have expressed it.

3 Our friend *Cleanthes*, replied *Philo*, as you have heard, asserts, that since no question of fact can be proved otherwise than by experience, the existence of a deity admits not of proof from any other medium. The world, says he, resembles the works of human contrivance: Therefore its cause must also resemble that of the other. Here we may remark, that the operation of one very small part of nature, to wit man, upon another very small part, to wit that inanimate matter lying within his reach, is the rule, by which *Cleanthes* judges of the origin of the whole; and he measures objects, so widely disproportioned, by the same individual standard. But to waive all objections, drawn from this topic; I affirm, that there are other parts of the universe (besides the machines of human invention) which bear still a greater resemblance to the fabric of the world, and which therefore afford a better conjecture concerning the universal origin of this system. These parts are animals and vegetables. The world plainly

resembles more an animal or a vegetable than it does a watch or a knitting-loom. Its cause, therefore, it is more probable, resembles the cause of the former. The cause of the former is generation or vegetation. The cause, therefore, of the world, we may infer to be something similar or analogous [177] to generation or vegetation.

4 But how is it conceivable, said *Demea*, that the world can arise from anything similar to vegetation or generation?

5 Very easily, replied *Philo*. In like manner as a tree sheds its seed into the neighbouring fields, and produces other trees; so the great vegetable, the world, or this planetary system, produces within itself certain seeds, which, being scattered into the surrounding chaos, vegetate into new worlds. A comet, for instance, is the seed of a world; and after it has been fully ripened, by passing from sun to sun, and star to star, it is at last tossed into the unformed elements, which everywhere surround this universe, and immediately sprouts up into a new system.[1]

6 Or if, for the sake of variety (for I see no other advantage) we should suppose this world to be an animal; a comet is the egg of this animal; and in like manner as an ostrich lays its egg in the sand, which, without any farther care, hatches the egg, and produces a new animal; so . . .

7 I understand you, says *Demea*: But what wild, arbitrary suppositions are these? What *data* have you for such extraordinary conclusions? And is the slight, imaginary resemblance of the world to a vegetable or an animal sufficient to establish the same inference with regard to both? Objects, which are in general so widely different; ought they to be a standard for each other?

8 Right, cries *Philo*: This is the topic on which I have all along insisted. I have still asserted, that we have no *data* to establish any system of cosmogony. Our experience, so imperfect in itself, and so limited both in extent and duration, can afford us no probable conjecture concerning the whole of things. But if we must needs fix on some hypothesis; by what rule, pray, ought we to determine our choice? Is there any other rule than the greater similarity of the objects compared? And does not a plant or an animal, which springs from vegetation or generation, bear a stronger resemblance to the world, than does any artificial machine, which arises from reason and design?

---

[1] Cf. William Whiston, *A New Theory of the Earth* (London, 1696), 73–78, 95, 185.

9 But what is this vegetation and generation, of which you talk? said *Demea*. Can you explain their operations, and anatomize that fine internal structure, on which they depend?

[178]   10 As much, at least, replied *Philo*, as *Cleanthes* can explain the operations of reason, or anatomize that internal structure, on which *it* depends. But without any such elaborate disquisitions, when I see an animal, I infer, that it sprang from generation; and that with as great certainty as you conclude a house to have been reared by design. These words, *generation, reason,* mark only certain powers and energies in nature, whose effects are known, but whose essence is incomprehensible; and one of these principles, more than the other, has no privilege for being made a standard to the whole of nature.

11 In reality, *Demea*, it may reasonably be expected, that the larger the views are which we take of things, the better will they conduct us in our conclusions concerning such extraordinary and such magnificent subjects. In this little corner of the world alone, there are four principles, *reason, instinct, generation, vegetation,* which are similar to each other, and are the causes of similar effects. What a number of other principles may we naturally suppose in the immense extent and variety of the universe, could we travel from planet to planet and from system to system, in order to examine each part of this mighty fabric? Any one of these four principles above mentioned (and a hundred others, which lie open to our conjecture) may afford us a theory, by which to judge of the origin of the world; and it is a palpable and egregious partiality to confine our view entirely to that principle, by which our own minds operate. Were this principle more intelligible on that account, such a partiality might be somewhat excusable: But reason, in its internal fabric and structure, is really as little known to us as instinct or vegetation; and perhaps even that vague, undeterminate word, nature, to which the vulgar refer everything, is not at the bottom more inexplicable. The effects of these principles are all known to us from experience: But the principles themselves, and their manner of operation, are totally unknown: Nor is it less intelligible, or less conformable to experience to say, that the world arose by vegetation from a seed shed by another world, than to say that it arose from a divine reason or contrivance, according to the sense in which *Cleanthes* understands it.

[179]   12 But methinks, said *Demea*, if the world had a vegetative quality, and could sow the seeds of new worlds into the infinite chaos, this

54

power would be still an additional argument for design in its author. For whence could arise so wonderful a faculty but from design? Or how can order spring from anything which perceives not that order which it bestows?

13 You need only look around you, replied *Philo*, to satisfy yourself with regard to this question. A tree bestows order and organization on that tree, which springs from it, without knowing the order: An animal, in the same manner, on its offspring: A bird, on its nest: And instances of this kind are even more frequent in the world, than those of order, which arise from reason and contrivance. To say that all this order in animals and vegetables proceeds ultimately from design is begging the question; nor can that great point be ascertained otherwise than by proving *a priori*, both that order is, from its nature, inseparably attached to thought, and that it can never, of itself, or from original unknown principles, belong to matter.

14 But farther, *Demea*; this objection, which you urge, can never be made use of by *Cleanthes*, without renouncing a defence, which he has already made against one of my objections. When I enquired concerning the cause of that supreme reason and intelligence, into which he resolves everything; he told me, that the impossibility of satisfying such enquiries could never be admitted as an objection in any species of philosophy. *We must stop somewhere*, says he; *nor is it ever within the reach of human capacity to explain ultimate causes, or show the last connections of any objects. It is sufficient, if the steps, so far as we go, are supported by experience and observation.* Now that vegetation and generation, as well as reason, are [181] experienced to be principles of order in nature, is undeniable. If I rest my system of cosmogony on the former, preferably to the latter, it is at my choice. The matter seems entirely arbitrary. And when *Cleanthes* asks me what is the cause of my great vegetative or generative faculty, I am equally entitled to ask him the cause of his great reasoning principle. These questions we have agreed to forbear on both sides; and it is chiefly his interest on the present occasion to stick to this agreement. Judging by our limited and imperfect experience, generation has some privileges above reason: For we see every day the latter arise from the former, never [180] the former from the latter.

15 Compare, I beseech you, the consequences on both sides. The world, say I, resembles an animal, therefore it is an animal, therefore it arose from generation. The steps, I confess, are wide; yet there is some small

55

appearance of analogy in each step. The world, says *Cleanthes*, resembles a machine; therefore it is a machine, therefore it arose from design. The steps are here equally wide, and the analogy less striking. And if he pretends to carry on *my* hypothesis a step farther, and to infer design or reason from the great principle of generation, on which I insist; I may, with better authority, use the same freedom to push farther his hypothesis, and infer a divine generation or theogony from his principle of reason. I have at least some faint shadow of experience, which is the utmost, that can ever be attained in the present subject. Reason, in innumerable instances, is observed to arise from the principle of generation, and never to arise from any other principle.

16 *Hesiod*, and all the ancient mythologists, were so struck with this analogy, that they universally explained the origin of nature from an animal birth, and copulation. *Plato*, too, so far as he is intelligible, seems to have adopted some such notion in his *Timaeus*.[2]

17 The *Brahmins* assert, that the world arose from an infinite spider, who spun this whole complicated mass from his bowels, and annihilates afterwards the whole or any part of it, by absorbing it again, and resolving it into his own essence. Here is a species of cosmogony, which appears to us ridiculous; because a spider is a little contemptible animal, whose operations we are never likely to take for a model of the whole universe.[3] But still here is a new species of analogy, even in our globe. And were there a planet, wholly inhabited by spiders (which is very possible), this inference would there appear as natural and irrefragable as that which in our planet ascribes the origin of all things to design and intelligence, as explained by *Cleanthes*. Why an orderly system may not be spun from [181] the belly as well as from the brain, it will be difficult for him to give a satisfactory reason.

18 I must confess, *Philo*, replied *Cleanthes*, that, of all men living, the task which you have undertaken, of raising doubts and objections, suits you best, and seems, in a manner, natural and unavoidable to you.[4] So great is your fertility of invention, that I am not ashamed to acknowledge myself unable, on a sudden, to solve regularly such out-of-the-way difficulties as you incessantly start upon me: Though I clearly see, in general, their

[2] Plato, *Timaeus* 29d–31b, in *The Collected Dialogues of Plato*, ed. Edith Hamilton and Huttington Cairns (New York: Pantheon Books, 1961).
[3] Cf. Bayle, *Dictionary Historical and Critical*, s.v. "Spinoza," note A, IV:201.
[4] Cf. LE2, 120.

fallacy and error. And I question not, but you are yourself, at present, in the same case, and have not the solution so ready as the objection; while you must be sensible, that common sense and reason is entirely against you, and that such whimsies, as you have delivered, may puzzle, but never can convince us.[5]

5 Cf. MacLaurin, *An Account of Sir Isaac Newton's Philosophical Discoveries*, 381.

Part 8

1 What you ascribe to the fertility of my invention, replied *Philo*, is entirely owing to the nature of the subject. In subjects, adapted to the narrow compass of human reason, there is commonly but one determination, which carries probability or conviction with it; and to a man of sound judgement, all other suppositions, but that one, appear entirely absurd and chimerical.[1] But in such questions, as the present, a hundred contradictory views may preserve a kind of imperfect analogy; and invention has here full scope to exert itself. Without any great effort of thought, I believe that I could, in an instant, propose other systems of cosmogony, which would have some faint appearance of truth; though it is a thousand, a million to one, if either yours or any one of mine be the true system.

2 For instance; what if I should revive the old *Epicurean* hypothesis?[2] This is commonly, and I believe, justly, esteemed the most absurd system, that has yet been proposed;[3] yet, I know not, whether, with a few alterations, it might not be brought to bear a faint appearance of probability. Instead of supposing matter infinite, as *Epicurus* did; let us suppose it finite. A finite number of particles is only susceptible of finite transpositions: And it must happen, in an eternal duration, that every possible order or position must be tried an infinite number of times. This world, therefore, with all its events, even the most minute, has before been produced and destroyed, and will again be produced and destroyed, without any bounds

[1] Cf. Newton, *Principia*, Bk. 3, Rule 4, p. 796.
[2] *Epicurus* (341–270 BC): A major philosopher of the Hellenistic period. On the "Epicurean hypothesis," see Lucretius, *The Nature of Things*, 1.1021–37.
[3] Cf. Clarke, *A Demonstration*, 44.

and limitations. No one, who has a conception of the powers of infinite, in comparison of finite, will ever scruple this determination.

3 But this supposes, said *Demea*, that matter can acquire motion, without any voluntary agent or first mover.

4 And where is the difficulty, replied *Philo*, of that supposition? Every event, before experience, is equally difficult and incomprehensible; and every event, after experience, is equally easy and intelligible. Motion, in many instances, from gravity, from elasticity, from electricity, begins in matter, without any known voluntary agent; and to suppose always, in these cases, an unknown voluntary agent is mere hypothesis; and hypo- [183] thesis attended with no advantages. The beginning of motion in matter itself is as conceivable *a priori* as its communication from mind and intelligence.

5 Besides; why may not motion have been propagated by impulse through all eternity, and the same stock of it, or nearly the same, be still upheld in the universe? As much is lost by the composition of motion, as much is gained by its resolution. And whatever the causes are, the fact is certain, that matter is, and always has been in continual agitation, as far as human experience or tradition reaches. There is not probably, at present, in the whole universe, one particle of matter at absolute rest.

6 And this very consideration too, continued *Philo*, which we have stumbled on in the course of the argument, suggests a new hypothesis of cosmogony, that is not absolutely absurd and improbable. Is there a system, an order, an economy of things, by which matter can preserve that perpetual agitation, which seems essential to it, and yet maintain a constancy in the forms, which it produces? There certainly is such an economy: For this is actually the case with the present world. The continual motion of matter, therefore, in less than infinite transpositions, must produce this economy or order; and by its very nature, that order, when once established, supports itself, for many ages, if not to eternity. But wherever matter is so poised, arranged, and adjusted as to continue in perpetual motion, and yet preserve a constancy in the forms, its situation must of necessity have all the same appearance of art and contrivance, which we observe at present. All the parts of each form must have a relation to each other, and to the whole: And the whole itself must have a relation to the other parts of the universe; to the element, in which the form subsists; to the materials, with which it repairs its waste and decay; and to every other form, which is hostile or friendly. A defect in any of these

particulars destroys the form; and the matter, of which it is composed, is again set loose, and is thrown into irregular motions and fermentations, till it unite itself to some other regular form. If no such form be prepared to receive it, and if there be a great quantity of this corrupted matter in [184] the universe, the universe itself is entirely disordered; whether it be the feeble embryo of a world in its first beginnings, that is thus destroyed, or the rotten carcass of one, languishing in old age and infirmity. In either case, a chaos ensues; till finite, though innumerable revolutions produce at last some forms, whose parts and organs are so adjusted as to support the forms amidst a continued succession of matter.

7 Suppose (for we shall endeavour to vary the expression), that matter were thrown into any position, by a blind, unguided force; it is evident that this first position must in all probability be the most confused and most disorderly imaginable, without any resemblance to those works of human contrivance, which, along with a symmetry of parts, discover an adjustment of means to ends and a tendency to self-preservation. If the actuating force cease after this operation, matter must remain forever in disorder, and continue an immense chaos, without any proportion or activity. But suppose, that the actuating force, whatever it be, still continues in matter, this first position will immediately give place to a second, which will likewise in all probability be as disorderly as the first, and so on, through many successions of changes and revolutions. No particular order or position ever continues a moment unaltered. The original force, still remaining in activity, gives a perpetual restlessness to matter. Every possible situation is produced, and instantly destroyed. If a glimpse or dawn of order appears for a moment, it is instantly hurried away and confounded, by that never-ceasing force, which actuates every part of matter.

8 Thus the universe goes on for many ages in a continued succession of chaos and disorder. But is it not possible that it may settle at last, so as not to lose its motion and active force (for that we have supposed inherent in it), yet so as to preserve a uniformity of appearance, amidst the continual motion and fluctuation of its parts? This we find to be the case with the universe at present. Every individual is perpetually changing, and every part of every individual, and yet the whole remains, in appearance, the same. May we not hope for such a position, or rather be assured of it, from the eternal revolutions of unguided matter, and may not this account for all the appearing wisdom and contrivance, which is in the universe? Let

us contemplate the subject a little, and we shall find, that this adjustment, [185] if attained by matter, of a seeming stability in the forms, with a real and perpetual revolution or motion of parts, affords a plausible, if not a true solution of the difficulty.

9 It is in vain, therefore, to insist upon the uses of the parts in animals or vegetables and their curious adjustment to each other. I would fain know how an animal could subsist, unless its parts were so adjusted? Do we not find, that it immediately perishes whenever this adjustment ceases, and that its matter corrupting tries some new form? It happens, indeed, that the parts of the world are so well adjusted, that some regular form immediately lays claim to this corrupted matter: And if it were not so, could the world subsist? Must it not dissolve as well as the animal, and pass through new positions and situations; till in a great, but finite succession, it falls at last into the present or some such order?

10 It is well, replied *Cleanthes*, you told us, that this hypothesis was suggested on a sudden, in the course of the argument. Had you had leisure to examine it, you would soon have perceived the insuperable objections, to which it is exposed. No form, you say, can subsist, unless it possess those powers and organs, requisite for its subsistence: Some new order or economy must be tried, and so on, without intermission; till at last some order, which can support and maintain itself, is fallen upon. But according to this hypothesis, whence arise the many conveniences and advantages, which men and all animals possess? Two eyes, two ears, are not absolutely necessary for the subsistence of the species. Human race might have been propagated and preserved, without horses, dogs, cows, sheep,[4] and those innumerable fruits and products, which serve to our satisfaction and enjoyment. If no camels had been created for the use of man in the sandy deserts of *Africa* and *Arabia*, would the world have been dissolved? If no loadstone had been framed to give that wonderful and useful direction to the needle, would human society and the human kind have been immediately extinguished? Though the maxims of nature be in general very frugal, yet instances of this kind are far from being rare; and any one of them is a sufficient proof of design, and of a benevolent design, which gave rise to the order and arrangement of the universe.

11 At least, you may safely infer, said *Philo*, that the foregoing hypo- [186] thesis is so far incomplete and imperfect; which I shall not scruple to allow.

---

4 Similar wording appears in More, *Divine Dialogues*, 12–15.

But can we ever reasonably expect greater success in any attempts of this nature? Or can we ever hope to erect a system of cosmogony, that will be liable to no exceptions, and will contain no circumstance repugnant to our limited and imperfect experience of the analogy of nature? Your theory itself cannot surely pretend to any such advantage; even though you have run into *anthropomorphism*, the better to preserve a conformity to common experience. Let us once more put it to trial. In all instances which we have ever seen, ideas are copied from real objects, and are ectypal, not archetypal,[5] to express myself in learned terms: You reverse this order, and give thought the precedence. In all instances which we have ever seen, thought has no influence upon matter, except where that matter is so conjoined with it, as to have an equal reciprocal influence upon it. No animal can move immediately anything but the members of its own body; and indeed, the equality of action and reaction seems to be a universal law of nature: But your theory implies a contradiction to this experience. These instances, with many more, which it were easy to collect (particularly the supposition of a mind or system of thought that is eternal, or in other words, an animal ingenerable and immortal), these instances, I say, may teach, all of us, sobriety in condemning each other, and let us see, that as no system of this kind ought ever to be received from a slight analogy, so neither ought any to be rejected on account of a small incongruity. For that is an inconvenience, from which we can justly pronounce no one to be exempted.

12 All religious systems, it is confessed, are subject to great and insuperable difficulties. Each disputant triumphs in his turn; while he carries on an offensive war, and exposes the absurdities, barbarities, and pernicious tenets of his antagonist. But all of them, on the whole, prepare a complete triumph for the sceptic, who tells them, that no system ought ever to be embraced with regard to such subjects: For this plain reason, that no absurdity ought ever to be assented to with regard to any subject. A total [187] suspense of judgement is here our only reasonable resource.[6] And if every attack, as is commonly observed, and no defence, among theologians, is successful; how complete must be *his* victory, who remains always, with all mankind, on the offensive, and has himself no fixed station or abiding city, which he is ever, on any occasion, obliged to defend?

---

[5] *Ectypal, not archetypal*: Having the nature of a copy, not that of an original or archetype.
[6] Cf. Hume, *NHR*, Sec. xv, p. 136.

Part 9 [188]

1 But if so many difficulties attend the argument *a posteriori*, said *Demea*; had we not better adhere to that simple and sublime argument *a priori*, which, by offering to us infallible demonstration, cuts off at once all doubt and difficulty? By this argument too, we may prove the INFINITY of the divine attributes, which, I am afraid, can never be ascertained with certainty from any other topic. For how can an effect, which either is finite, or, for aught we know, may be so; how can such an effect, I say, prove an infinite cause? The unity too of the divine nature, it is very difficult, if not absolutely impossible, to deduce merely from contemplating the works of nature; nor will the uniformity alone of the plan, even were it allowed, give us any assurance of that attribute. Whereas the argument *a priori* . . .

2 You seem to reason, *Demea*, interposed *Cleanthes*, as if those advantages and conveniences in the abstract argument were full proofs of its solidity. But it is first proper, in my opinion, to determine what argument of this nature you choose to insist on; and we shall afterwards, from itself, better than from its *useful* consequences, endeavour to determine what value we ought to put upon it.

3 The argument, replied *Demea*, which I would insist on, is the common one.[1] Whatever exists must have a cause or reason of its existence; it being absolutely impossible for anything to produce itself, or be the cause of its own existence. In mounting up, therefore, from effects to causes, we must either go on in tracing an infinite succession, without any ultimate cause at all, or must at last have recourse to some ultimate cause, that is *necessarily* existent: Now that the first supposition is absurd may be thus

---

[1] Demea's argument is drawn from Clarke, *A Demonstration*, Secs. I–III.

proved. In the infinite chain or succession of causes and effects, each single effect is determined to exist by the power and efficacy of that cause, which immediately preceded; but the whole eternal chain or succession, taken together, is not determined or caused by anything: And yet it is evident that it requires a cause or reason, as much as any particular object, which begins to exist in time. The question is still reasonable, why this particular [189] succession of causes existed from eternity, and not any other succession, or no succession at all. If there be no necessarily existent being, any supposition, which can be formed, is equally possible; nor is there any more absurdity in nothing's having existed from eternity, than there is in that succession of causes, which constitutes the universe. What was it then, which determined something to exist rather than nothing, and bestowed being on a particular possibility, exclusive of the rest? *External causes*, there are supposed to be none. *Chance* is a word without a meaning. Was it *nothing*? But that can never produce anything. We must, therefore, have recourse to a necessarily existent being, who carries the REASON of his existence in himself; and who cannot be supposed not to exist without an express contradiction. There is consequently such a being, that is, there is a deity.

4 I shall not leave it to *Philo*, said *Cleanthes* (though I know that the starting objections is his chief delight), to point out the weakness of this metaphysical reasoning. It seems to me so obviously ill-grounded, and at the same time of so little consequence to the cause of true piety and religion, that I shall myself venture to show the fallacy of it.

5 I shall begin with observing, that there is an evident absurdity in pretending to demonstrate a matter of fact, or to prove it by any arguments *a priori*. Nothing is demonstrable, unless the contrary implies a contradiction. Nothing, that is distinctly conceivable, implies a contradiction. Whatever we conceive as existent, we can also conceive as non-existent. There is no being, therefore, whose non-existence implies a contradiction. Consequently there is no being, whose existence is demonstrable.[2] I propose this argument as entirely decisive, and am willing to rest the whole controversy upon it.

6 It is pretended, that the deity is a necessarily existent being, and this necessity of his existence is attempted to be explained by asserting, that, if we knew his whole essence or nature, we should perceive it to be as

___
[2] Cf. *T* 1.3.7.3; *EHU* 4.2.

impossible for him not to exist, as for twice two not to be four. But it is evident, that this can never happen, while our faculties remain the same as at present. It will still be possible for us, at any time, to conceive the non-existence of what we formerly conceived to exist; nor can the mind ever lie under a necessity of supposing any object to remain always in being; in the same manner as we lie under a necessity of always conceiving twice [190] two to be four. The words, therefore, *necessary existence*, have no meaning; or, which is the same thing, none that is consistent.

7 But farther; why may not the material universe be the necessarily existent being, according to this pretended explication of necessity? We dare not affirm that we know all the qualities of matter; and for aught we can determine, it may contain some qualities, which, were they known, would make its non-existence appear as great a contradiction as that twice two is five. I find only one argument employed to prove, that the material world is not the necessarily existent being; and this argument is derived from the contingency both of the matter and the form of the world. "Any particle of matter," it is said,[a] "may be *conceived* to be annihilated; and any form may be *conceived* to be altered. Such an annihilation or alteration, therefore, is not impossible." But it seems a great partiality not to perceive, that the same argument extends equally to the deity, so far as we have any conception of him; and that the mind can at least imagine him to be non-existent, or his attributes to be altered. It must be some unknown, inconceivable qualities, which can make his non-existence appear impossible, or his attributes unalterable: And no reason can be assigned, why these qualities may not belong to matter. As they are altogether unknown and inconceivable, they can never be proved incompatible with it.

8 Add to this, that in tracing an eternal succession of objects, it seems absurd to enquire for a general cause or first author. How can anything that exists from eternity, have a cause; since that relation implies a priority in time, and a beginning of existence?[3]

9 In such a chain too, or succession of objects, each part is caused by that which preceded it, and causes that which succeeds it. Where then is the difficulty? But the WHOLE, you say, wants a cause. I answer, that the uniting of these parts into a whole, like the uniting of several distinct countries into one kingdom, or several distinct members into one body,

---

[a] Dr. Clarke. [Clarke, *A Demonstration*, Sec. III, p. 18.]
[3] Cf. *T* 1.3.2.7; *EHU* 7.29.

is performed merely by an arbitrary act of the mind, and has no influence on the nature of things. Did I show you the particular causes of each individual in a collection of twenty particles of matter, I should think it [191] very unreasonable, should you afterwards ask me, what was the cause of the whole twenty. This is sufficiently explained in explaining the cause of the parts.[4]

10 Though the reasonings, which you have urged, *Cleanthes*, may well excuse me, said *Philo*, from starting any farther difficulties; yet I cannot forbear insisting still upon another topic. It is observed by arithmeticians, that the products of 9 compose always either 9 or some lesser product of 9; if you add together all the characters, of which any of the former products is composed. Thus, of 18, 27, 36, which are products of 9, you make 9 by adding 1 to 8, 2 to 7, 3 to 6. Thus, 369 is a product also of 9; and if you add 3, 6, and 9 you make 18, a lesser product of 9.[b] To a superficial observer, so wonderful a regularity may be admired as the effect either of chance or design; but a skillful algebraist immediately concludes it to be the work of necessity, and demonstrates, that it must forever result from the nature of these numbers. Is it not probable, I ask, that the whole economy of the universe is conducted by a like necessity, though no human algebra can furnish a key, which solves the difficulty? And instead of admiring the order of natural beings, may it not happen, that, could we penetrate into the intimate nature of bodies, we should clearly see why it was absolutely impossible, they could ever admit of any other disposition?[5] So dangerous is it to introduce this idea of necessity into the present question! And so naturally does it afford an inference directly opposite to the religious hypothesis!

11 But dropping all these abstractions, continued *Philo*, and confining ourselves to more familiar topics; I shall venture to add an observation, that the argument *a priori* has seldom been found very convincing, except to people of a metaphysical head, who have accustomed themselves to abstract reasoning, and who finding from mathematics, that the understanding frequently leads to truth, through obscurity and contrary to

---

[b] *République des Lettres*, Août, 1685. [Pierre Bayle, ed., *Nouvelles de la République des Lettres*, September 1685, art. 2, in *Œuvres diverses de Mr. Pierre Bayle*, 4 vols. (The Hague: Compagnie des libraires, 1737), 1:363. The article is by Fontenelle, published in September, 1685, not in August, as Hume's note indicates.]

[4] Cf. *T* 1.2.2.3.

[5] Cf. *NHR*, Sec. III, p. 127.

192] first appearances, have transferred the same habit of thinking to subjects, where it ought not to have place. Other people, even of good sense and the best inclined to religion, feel always some deficiency in such arguments, though they are not perhaps able to explain distinctly where it lies.[6] A certain proof, that men ever did, and ever will derive their religion from other sources than from this species of reasoning.

[6] Cf. *Letter from a Gentleman*, p. 23.

Part 10

1 It is my opinion, I own, replied *Demea*, that each man feels, in a manner, the truth of religion within his own breast; and from a consciousness of his imbecility and misery, rather than from any reasoning, is led to seek protection from that being, on whom he and all nature is dependent. So anxious or so tedious are even the best scenes of life, that futurity is still the object of all our hopes and fears. We incessantly look forward, and endeavour, by prayers, adoration, and sacrifice, to appease those unknown powers, whom we find, by experience, so able to afflict and oppress us. Wretched creatures that we are! What resource for us amidst the innumerable ills of life, did not religion suggest some methods of atonement, and appease those terrors, with which we are incessantly agitated and tormented?[1]

2 I am indeed persuaded, said *Philo*, that the best and indeed the only method of bringing everyone to a due sense of religion is by just representations of the misery and wickedness of men. And for that purpose a talent of eloquence and strong imagery is more requisite than that of reasoning and argument. For is it necessary to prove, what everyone feels within himself? It is only necessary to make us feel it, if possible, more intimately and sensibly.

3 The people, indeed, replied *Demea*, are sufficiently convinced of this great and melancholy truth. The miseries of life, the unhappiness of man, the general corruptions of our nature, the unsatisfactory enjoyment of pleasures, riches, honours; these phrases have become almost proverbial

---

[1] Cf. *NHR*, Sec. III, pp. 127–130. For Hume's account of the psychological origin of hope and fear, see *T* 2.3.9.

68

in all languages. And who can doubt of what all men declare from their own immediate feeling and experience?

4 In this point, said *Philo*, the learned are perfectly agreed with the vulgar; and in all letters,[2] *sacred* and *profane*, the topic of human misery has been insisted on with the most pathetic eloquence, that sorrow and melancholy could inspire. The poets, who speak from sentiment, without a system, and whose testimony has therefore the more authority, abound in images of this nature. From Homer down to Dr. Young,[3] the whole inspired tribe have ever been sensible, that no other representation of **[194]** things would suit the feeling and observation of each individual.

5 As to authorities, replied *Demea*, you need not seek them. Look round this library of *Cleanthes*. I shall venture to affirm, that, except authors of particular sciences, such as chemistry or botany, who have no occasion to treat of human life, there is scarce one of those innumerable writers, from whom the sense of human misery has not, in some passage or other, extorted a complaint and confession of it. At least, the chance is entirely on that side; and no one author has ever, so far as I can recollect, been so extravagant as to deny it.

6 There you must excuse me, said *Philo*: *Leibniz* has denied it; and is perhaps the first[a] who ventured upon so bold and paradoxical an opinion; at least, the first, who made it essential to his philosophical system.

7 And by being the first, replied *Demea*, might he not have been sensible of his error? For is this a subject, in which philosophers can propose to make discoveries, especially in so late an age? And can any man hope by a simple denial (for the subject scarcely admits of reasoning) to bear down the united testimony of mankind, founded on sense and consciousness?

8 And why should man, added he, pretend to an exemption from the lot of all other animals? The whole earth, believe me, *Philo*, is cursed and polluted. A perpetual war is kindled amongst all living creatures. Necessity,

---

[a] That sentiment had been maintained by *Dr. King* and some few others before *Leibniz*; though by none of so great a fame as that German philosopher who ventured upon so bold and paradoxical an opinion; at least, the first who made it essential to his philosophical system. [See William King (1650–1729), *The Origin of Evil* [*De Origine Mali* (Dublin, 1702)], trans. Edmund Law (London, 1731); Gottfried Wilhelm Leibniz (1641–1716), *Theodicy* [*Theodicée*] (Amsterdam, 1710). Many of Demea's remarks on evil are drawn from King.]

[2] *Letters*: Writings.

[3] Edward Young (1683–1765), a minor English poet who achieved international fame for his long poem, *The Complaint, or Night Thoughts on Life, Death, and Immortality* (1742–45), a Christian apologetic inspired by the deaths of his stepdaughter in 1736 and of his wife and his stepdaughter's husband in 1740.

hunger, want stimulate the strong and courageous: Fear, anxiety, terror agitate the weak and infirm. The first entrance into life gives anguish to the newborn infant and to its wretched parent: Weakness, impotence, distress attend each stage of that life: And it is at last finished in agony and horror.

9 Observe too, says *Philo*, the curious artifices of nature, in order to embitter the life of every living being. The stronger prey upon the weaker, and keep them in perpetual terror and anxiety. The weaker too, in their turn, often prey upon the stronger, and vex and molest them without relaxation. Consider that innumerable race of insects, which either are bred on the body of each animal, or flying about, infix their stings in [195] him. These insects have others still less than themselves, which torment them. And thus on each hand, before and behind, above and below, every animal is surrounded with enemies, which incessantly seek his misery and destruction.

10 Man alone, said *Demea*, seems to be, in part, an exception to this rule. For by combination in society, he can easily master lions, tigers, and bears, whose greater strength and agility naturally enable them to prey upon him.

11 On the contrary, it is here chiefly, cried *Philo*, that the uniform and equal maxims of nature are most apparent. Man, it is true, can, by combination, surmount all his *real* enemies, and become master of the whole animal creation: But does he not immediately raise up to himself *imaginary* enemies, the demons of his fancy, who haunt him with superstitious terrors, and blast every enjoyment of life? His pleasure, as he imagines, becomes, in their eyes, a crime: His food and repose give them umbrage and offence: His very sleep and dreams furnish new materials to anxious fear: And even death, his refuge from every other ill, presents only the dread of endless and innumerable woes. Nor does the wolf molest more the timid flock, than superstition does the anxious breast of wretched mortals.

12 Besides, consider, *Demea*; this very society, by which we surmount those wild beasts, our natural enemies; what new enemies does it not raise to us? What woe and misery does it not occasion? Man is the greatest enemy of man. Oppression, injustice, contempt, contumely, violence, sedition, war, calumny, treachery, fraud; by these they mutually torment each other: And they would soon dissolve that society which they had

formed, were it not for the dread of still greater ills, which must attend their separation.

13 But though these external insults, said *Demea*, from animals, from men, from all the elements which assault us, form a frightful catalogue of woes, they are nothing in comparison of those, which arise within ourselves, from the distempered condition of our mind and body. How many lie under the lingering torment of diseases. Hear the pathetic enumeration of the great poet.

> Intestine stone and ulcer, colic-pangs,
> Daemoniac frenzy, moping melancholy,
> And moon-struck madness, pining atrophy,
> Marasmus, and wide-wasting pestilence.
> Dire was the tossing, deep the groans: DESPAIR   [196]
> Tended the sick, busiest from couch to couch.
> And over them triumphant DEATH his dart
> Shook, but delayed to strike, though oft invoked
> With vows, as their chief good and final hope.⁴

14 The disorders of the mind, continued *Demea*, though more secret, are not perhaps less dismal and vexatious. Remorse, shame, anguish, rage, disappointment, anxiety, fear, dejection, despair; who has ever passed through life without cruel inroads from these tormentors? How many have scarcely ever felt any better sensations? Labour and poverty, so abhorred by everyone, are the certain lot of the far greater number: And those few privileged persons, who enjoy ease and opulence, never reach contentment or true felicity. All the goods of life united would not make a very happy man: But all the ills united would make a wretch indeed; and any one of them almost (and who can be free from everyone?) nay often the absence of one good (and who can possess all?) is sufficient to render life ineligible.

15 Were a stranger to drop, on a sudden, into this world, I would show him, as a specimen of its ills, a hospital full of diseases, a prison crowded with malefactors and debtors,⁵ a field of battle strewed with carcasses, a fleet foundering in the ocean, a nation languishing under tyranny, famine, or pestilence. To turn the gay side of life to him, and give him a notion

---

⁴ Milton, *Paradise Lost*, Bk. 11, 484–493. Hume's quote appears to omit line 488.
⁵ Cf. "Bayle on Manicheanism," 146; More, *Divine Dialogues*, 233–234.

of its pleasures; whither should I conduct him? To a ball, to an opera, to court? He might justly think, that I was only showing him a diversity of distress and sorrow.

16 There is no evading such striking instances, said *Philo*, but by apologies, which still farther aggravate the charge. Why have all men, I ask, in all ages, complained incessantly of the miseries of life? . . . They have no just reason, says one: These complaints proceed only from their discontented, repining, anxious disposition . . . And can there possibly, I reply, be a more certain foundation of misery, than such a wretched temper?

17 But if they were really as unhappy as they pretend, says my antagonist, why do they remain in life? –

Not satisfied with life, afraid of death.[6]

[197] This is the secret chain, say I, that holds us. We are terrified, not bribed to the continuance of our existence.

18 It is only a false delicacy, he may insist, which a few refined spirits indulge, and which has spread these complaints among the whole race of mankind . . . And what is this delicacy, I ask, which you blame? Is it anything but a greater sensibility to all the pleasures and pains of life? And if the man of a delicate, refined temper, by being so much more alive than the rest of the world, is only so much more unhappy; what judgement must we form in general of human life?

19 Let men remain at rest, says our adversary; and they will be easy. They are willing artificers of their own misery . . . No! reply I; an anxious languor follows their repose: Disappointment, vexation, trouble, their activity and ambition.

20 I can observe something like what you mention in some others, replied *Cleanthes*: But I confess, I feel little or nothing of it in myself; and hope that it is not so common as you represent it.[7]

21 If you feel not human misery yourself, cried *Demea*, I congratulate you on so happy a singularity. Others, seemingly the most prosperous, have not been ashamed to vent their complaints in the most melancholy strains. Let us attend to the great, the fortunate emperor, *Charles* the fifth,

---

[6] Matthew Prior (1664–1721), *Solomon on the Vanity of the World*, Bk. 3, line 683, in *The Literary Works of Matthew Prior*, ed. H. Bunker Wright and Monroe K. Spears, 2nd edn., 2 vols. (Oxford: Clarendon Press, 1971).

[7] Francis Hutcheson, *An Essay on the Nature and Conduct of the Passions and Affections, with Illustrations of the Moral Sense* (London, 1728), Sec. 6, art. 4.

when, tired with human grandeur, he resigned all his extensive dominions into the hands of his son. In the last harangue, which he made on that memorable occasion, he publicly avowed, *that the greatest prosperities which he had ever enjoyed, had been mixed with so many adversities, that he might truly say he had never enjoyed any satisfaction or contentment.*[8] But did the retired life, in which he sought for shelter, afford him any greater happiness? If we may credit his son's account, his repentance commenced the very day of his resignation.

22 *Cicero's* fortune, from small beginnings, rose to the greatest lustre and renown; yet what pathetic complaints of the ills of life do his familiar letters, as well as philosophical discourses, contain? And suitably to his own experience, he introduces *Cato*, the great, the fortunate *Cato*, protesting in his old age, that, had he a new life in his offer, he would reject the present.[9]

23 Ask yourself, ask any of your acquaintance, whether they would live over again the last ten or twenty years of their life. No! But the next twenty, they say, will be better:

> And from the dregs of life, hope to receive [198]
> What the first sprightly running could not give.[10]

Thus at last they find (such is the greatness of human misery; it reconciles even contradictions) that they complain, at once, of the shortness of life, and of its vanity and sorrow.

24 And is it possible, *Cleanthes*, said *Philo*, that after all these reflections, and infinitely more, which might be suggested, you can still persevere in your anthropomorphism, and assert the moral attributes of the deity, his justice, benevolence, mercy, and rectitude, to be of the same nature with these virtues in human creatures? His power we allow infinite: Whatever he wills is executed: But neither man nor any other animal is happy: Therefore he does not will their happiness. His wisdom is infinite: He is never mistaken in choosing the means to any end: But the course of nature tends not to human or animal felicity: Therefore it is not established for that purpose. Through the whole compass of human knowledge, there are no inferences more certain and infallible than these. In what respect,

---

[8] *Charles V* (1500–58): King of Spain and the Holy Roman Emperor. Cf. Bayle, *Dictionary*, s.v. "Charles V."

[9] Cicero, *On Old Age* (*De Senectute*), 23, 83–84.

[10] John Dryden, *Aureng-Zebe*, Act 4, Scene 1, 41–42.

then, do his benevolence and mercy resemble the benevolence and mercy of men?

25 *Epicurus'* old questions are yet unanswered. Is he willing to prevent evil, but not able? then is he impotent. Is he able, but not willing? then is he malevolent. Is he both able and willing? Whence then is evil?[11]

26 You ascribe, *Cleanthes*, (and I believe justly) a purpose and intention to nature. But what, I beseech you, is the object of that curious artifice and machinery, which she has displayed in all animals? The preservation alone of individuals and propagation of the species. It seems enough for her purpose, if such a rank be barely upheld in the universe, without any care or concern for the happiness of the members, that compose it. No resource for this purpose: No machinery, in order merely to give pleasure or ease: No fund of pure joy and contentment: No indulgence without some want or necessity, accompanying it. At least, the few phenomena of this nature are overbalanced by opposite phenomena of still greater importance.

27 Our sense of music, harmony, and indeed beauty of all kinds, gives satisfaction, without being absolutely necessary to the preservation and propagation of the species. But what racking pains, on the other hand, arise from gouts, gravels, megrims, toothaches, rheumatisms;[12] where the injury to the animal-machinery is either small or incurable? Mirth, laughter, play, frolic seem gratuitous satisfactions, which have no farther tendency: Spleen, melancholy, discontent, superstition are pains of the same nature. How then does the divine benevolence display itself, in the sense of you anthropomorphites? None but we mystics, as you were pleased to call us, can account for this strange mixture of phenomena, by deriving it from attributes, infinitely perfect, but incomprehensible.

[199]

28 And have you, at last, said *Cleanthes* smiling, betrayed your intentions, *Philo*? Your long agreement with *Demea* did indeed a little surprise me; but I find you were all the while erecting a concealed battery against me. And I must confess, that you have now fallen upon a subject, worthy of your noble spirit of opposition and controversy. If you can make out the present point, and prove mankind to be unhappy or corrupted, there is an end at once of all religion. For to what purpose establish the natural attributes of the deity, while the moral are still doubtful and uncertain?[13]

---

[11] See Bayle, *Dictionary*, s.v. "Paulicians," note E, IV:513.   [12] Fragment, III.
[13] Cf. Cicero, *The Nature of the Gods*, 2.25, 27; 3.38; Fragment, 109.

29 You take umbrage very easily, replied *Demea*, at opinions the most innocent, and the most generally received even amongst the religious and devout themselves: And nothing can be more surprising than to find a topic like this, concerning the wickedness and misery of man, charged with no less than atheism and profaneness. Have not all pious divines and preachers, who have indulged their rhetoric on so fertile a subject; have they not easily, I say, given a solution of any difficulties which may attend it? This world is but a point in comparison of the universe: This life but a moment in comparison of eternity. The present evil phenomena, therefore, are rectified in other regions, and in some future period of existence. And the eyes of men, being then opened to larger views of things, see the whole connection of general laws, and trace, with adoration, the benevolence and rectitude of the deity, through all the mazes and intricacies of his providence.

30 No! replied *Cleanthes*, No! These arbitrary suppositions can never be admitted, contrary to matter of fact, visible and uncontroverted. Whence can any cause be known but from its known effects? Whence can any hypothesis be proved but from the apparent phenomena? To establish one [200] hypothesis upon another is building entirely in the air; and the utmost we ever attain, by these conjectures and fictions, is to ascertain the bare possibility of our opinion; but never can we, upon such terms, establish its reality.[14]

31 The only method of supporting divine benevolence (and it is what I willingly embrace) is to deny absolutely the misery and wickedness of man. Your representations are exaggerated: Your melancholy views mostly fictitious: Your inferences contrary to fact and experience. Health is more common than sickness: Pleasure than pain: Happiness than misery. And for one vexation which we meet with, we attain, upon computation, a hundred enjoyments.

32 Admitting your position, replied *Philo*, which yet is extremely doubtful; you must, at the same time, allow, that, if pain be less frequent than pleasure, it is infinitely more violent and durable. One hour of it is often able to outweigh a day, a week, a month of our common insipid enjoyments:[15] And how many days, weeks, and months are passed by several in the most acute torments? Pleasure, scarcely in one instance, is ever

---

[14] Cf. *EHU* 11.21; Shaftesbury, "The Moralists," Part II, Sec. 3, in *Characteristics*, 270–271.
[15] Similar wording appears in Bayle, *Dictionary*, s.v. "Xenophanes," note F, V:579.

able to reach ecstasy and rapture: And in no one instance can it continue for any time at its highest pitch and altitude. The spirits evaporate; the nerves relax; the fabric is disordered; and the enjoyment quickly degenerates into fatigue and uneasiness. But pain often, good God, how often! rises to torture and agony; and the longer it continues, it becomes still more genuine agony and torture. Patience is exhausted; courage languishes; melancholy seizes us; and nothing terminates our misery but the removal of its cause, or another event, which is the sole cure of all evil, but which, from our natural folly, we regard with still greater horror and consternation.[16]

33 But not to insist upon these topics, continued *Philo*, though most obvious, certain, and important; I must use the freedom to admonish you, *Cleanthes*, that you have put the controversy upon a most dangerous issue, and are unawares introducing a total scepticism into the most essential articles of natural and revealed theology. What! no method of fixing a just foundation for religion, unless we allow the happiness of human life, and maintain a continued existence even in this world, with all our present [201] pains, infirmities, vexations, and follies, to be eligible and desirable! But this is contrary to everyone's feeling and experience: It is contrary to an authority so established as nothing can subvert: No decisive proofs can ever be produced against this authority; nor is it possible for you to compute, estimate, and compare all the pains and all the pleasures in the lives of all men and of all animals: And thus, by your resting the whole system of religion on a point, which, from its very nature, must forever be uncertain, you tacitly confess, that that system is equally uncertain.[17]

34 But allowing you, what never will be believed; at least, what you never possibly can prove, that animal, or at least, human happiness in this life, exceeds its misery; you have yet done nothing: For this is not, by any means, what we expect from infinite power, infinite wisdom, and infinite goodness. Why is there any misery at all in the world? Not by chance surely. From some cause then. Is it from the intention of the deity? But he is perfectly benevolent. Is it contrary to his intention? But he is almighty. Nothing can shake the solidity of this reasoning, so short, so clear, so decisive; except we assert, that these subjects exceed all human capacity, and that our common measures of truth and falsehood are not applicable to them; a topic which I have all along insisted on, but which you have, from the beginning, rejected with scorn and indignation.

[16] Fragment, 110–111.   [17] Fragment, 110.

35 But I will be contented to retire still from this entrenchment: For I deny that you can ever force me in it. I will allow, that, pain or misery in man is *compatible* with infinite power and goodness in the deity, even in your sense of these attributes: What are you advanced by all these concessions? A mere possible compatibility is not sufficient. You must *prove* these pure, unmixed, and uncontrollable attributes from the present mixed and confused phenomena, and from these alone. A hopeful undertaking! Were the phenomena ever so pure and unmixed, yet being finite, they would be insufficient for that purpose. How much more, where they are also so jarring and discordant!

36 Here, *Cleanthes*, I find myself at ease in my argument. Here I triumph. Formerly, when we argued concerning the natural attributes of [202] intelligence and design, I needed all my sceptical and metaphysical subtlety to elude your grasp. In many views of the universe, and of its parts, particularly the latter, the beauty and fitness of final causes strike us with such irresistible force, that all objections appear (what I believe they really are) mere cavils and sophisms; nor can we then imagine how it was ever possible for us to repose any weight on them. But there is no view of human life or of the condition of mankind, from which, without the greatest violence, we can infer the moral attributes, or learn that infinite benevolence, conjoined with infinite power and infinite wisdom, which we must discover by the eyes of faith alone. It is your turn now to tug the labouring oar, and to support your philosophical subtleties against the dictates of plain reason and experience.

Part 11

1 I scruple not to allow, said *Cleanthes*, that I have been apt to suspect the frequent repetition of the word, infinite, which we meet with in all theological writers, to savour more of panegyric than of philosophy, and that any purposes of reasoning, and even of religion, would be better served, were we to rest contented with more accurate and more moderate expressions. The terms, *admirable, excellent, superlatively great, wise*, and *holy*; these sufficiently fill the imaginations of men; and anything beyond, besides that it leads into absurdities, has no influence on the affections or sentiments. Thus, in the present subject, if we abandon all human analogy, as seems your intention, *Demea*, I am afraid we abandon all religion, and retain no conception of the great object of our adoration. If we preserve human analogy, we must forever find it impossible to reconcile any mixture of evil in the universe with infinite attributes; much less, can we ever prove the latter from the former. But supposing the author of nature to be finitely perfect, though far exceeding mankind; a satisfactory account may then be given of natural and moral evil, and every untoward phenomenon be explained and adjusted. A less evil may then be chosen, in order to avoid a greater: Inconveniences be submitted to, in order to reach a desirable end: And in a word, benevolence, regulated by wisdom, and limited by necessity, may produce just such a world as the present. You, *Philo*, who are so prompt at starting views, and reflections, and analogics,[1] I would gladly hear, at length, without interruption, your opinion of this

---

[1] Cf. *EHU* 9.6 n. 20: "When we reason from analogies, the man, who has the greater experience or the greater promptitude of suggesting analogies, will be the better reasoner."

new theory; and if it deserve our attention, we may afterwards, at more leisure, reduce it into form.

2 My sentiments, replied *Philo*, are not worth being made a mystery of; and therefore, without any ceremony, I shall deliver what occurs to me, with regard to the present subject. It must, I think, be allowed, that, if a very limited intelligence, whom we shall suppose utterly unacquainted with the universe, were assured, that it were the production of a very good, wise, and powerful being, however finite, he would, from his conjectures, form *beforehand* a different notion of it from what we find it to be by [204] experience; nor would he ever imagine, merely from these attributes of the cause of which he is informed, that the effect could be so full of vice and misery and disorder, as it appears in this life. Supposing now, that this person were brought into the world, still assured, that it was the workmanship of such a sublime and benevolent being; he might, perhaps, be surprised at the disappointment; but would never retract his former belief, if founded on any very solid argument; since such a limited intelligence must be sensible of his own blindness and ignorance, and must allow that there may be many solutions of those phenomena, which will forever escape his comprehension. But supposing, which is the real case with regard to man, that this creature is not antecedently convinced of a supreme intelligence, benevolent, and powerful, but is left to gather such a belief from the appearances of things; this entirely alters the case, nor will he ever find any reason for such a conclusion. He may be fully convinced of the narrow limits of his understanding, but this will not help him in forming an inference concerning the goodness of superior powers, since he must form that inference from what he knows, not from what he is ignorant of.[2] The more you exaggerate his weakness and ignorance, the more diffident you render him, and give him the greater suspicion, that such subjects are beyond the reach of his faculties. You are obliged, therefore, to reason with him merely from the known phenomena, and to drop every arbitrary supposition or conjecture.

3 Did I show you a house or palace, where there was not one apartment convenient or agreeable; where the windows, doors, fires, passages, stairs, and the whole economy of the building were the source of noise, confusion, fatigue, darkness, and the extremes of heat and cold; you would certainly

[2] Contrast with Joseph Butler, *The Analogy of Religion*, ed. Ernest C. Mossner (New York: F. Ungar Pub. Cp., 1961), Bk. I, Ch. VIII, p. 111: "It is easy to see distinctly how our ignorance . . . is really a satisfactory answer to all objections against the justice and goodness of Providence."

blame the contrivance, without any farther examination. The architect would in vain display his subtlety, and prove to you, that if this door or that window were altered, greater ills would ensue. What he says, may be strictly true: The alteration of one particular, while the other parts of the building remain, may only augment the inconveniences. But still you would assert in general, that, if the architect had had skill and good intentions, he might have formed such a plan of the whole, and might have adjusted the parts in such a manner, as would have remedied all or

[205] most of these inconveniences. His ignorance or even your own ignorance of such a plan, will never convince you of the impossibility of it. If you find any inconveniences and deformities in the building, you will always, without entering into any detail, condemn the architect.[3]

4 In short, I repeat the question: Is the world, considered in general, and as it appears to us in this life, different from what a man or such a limited being would, *beforehand*, expect from a very powerful, wise, and benevolent deity? It must be strange prejudice to assert the contrary. And from thence I conclude, that, however consistent the world may be, allowing certain suppositions and conjectures, with the idea of such a deity, it can never afford us an inference concerning his existence. The consistency is not absolutely denied, only the inference. Conjectures, especially where infinity is excluded from the divine attributes, may, perhaps, be sufficient to prove a consistence; but can never be foundations for any inference.

5 There seem to be *four* circumstances, on which depend all, or the greatest part of the ills, that molest sensible creatures; and it is not impossible but all these circumstances may be necessary and unavoidable. We know so little beyond common life, or even of common life, that, with regard to the economy of a universe, there is no conjecture, however wild, which may not be just; nor any one, however plausible, which may not be erroneous. All that belongs to human understanding, in this deep ignorance and obscurity, is to be sceptical, or at least cautious; and not to admit of any hypothesis, whatever; much less, of any which is supported by no appearance of probability. Now this I assert to be the case with regard to all the causes of evil, and the circumstances, on which it depends. None of them appear to human reason, in the least degree, necessary or unavoidable; nor can we suppose them such, without the utmost license of imagination.

---

[3] Cf. Memoranda, 26, p. 107.

6 The *first* circumstance, which introduces evil, is that contrivance or economy of the animal creation, by which pains, as well as pleasures, are employed to excite all creatures to action, and make them vigilant in the great work of self-preservation. Now pleasure alone, in its various degrees, seems to human understanding sufficient for this purpose. All animals might be constantly in a state of enjoyment; but when urged by any of the necessities of nature, such as thirst, hunger, weari ness; instead [206] of pain, they might feel a diminution of pleasure, by which they might be prompted to seek that object, which is necessary to their subsistence. Men pursue pleasure as eagerly as they avoid pain; at least, might have been so constituted. It seems, therefore, plainly possible to carry on the business of life without any pain.[4] Why then is any animal ever rendered susceptible of such a sensation? If animals can be free from it an hour, they might enjoy a perpetual exemption from it; and it required as particular a contrivance of their organs to produce that feeling, as to endow them with sight, hearing, or any of the senses. Shall we conjecture, that such a contrivance was necessary, without any appearance of reason? And shall we build on that conjecture as on the most certain truth?

7 But a capacity of pain would not alone produce pain, were it not for the *second* circumstance, *viz.*, the conducting of the world by general laws; and this seems no wise necessary to a very perfect being.[5] It is true; if everything were conducted by particular volitions, the course of nature would be perpetually broken, and no man could employ his reason in the conduct of life. But might not other particular volitions remedy this inconvenience? In short, might not the deity exterminate all ill, wherever it were to be found; and produce all good, without any preparation or long progress of causes and effects?

8 Besides, we must consider, that, according to the present economy of the world, the course of nature, though supposed exactly regular, yet to us appears not so, and many events are uncertain, and many disappoint our expectations. Health and sickness, calm and tempest, with an infinite number of other accidents, whose causes are unknown and variable, have a great influence both on the fortunes of particular persons and on the prosperity of public societies: And indeed all human life, in a manner, depends on such accidents. A being, therefore, who knows the secret springs of the universe, might easily, by particular volitions, turn

[4] Cf. ibid., 19, p. 107.   [5] Cf. ibid., 20, p. 107.

all these accidents to the good of mankind, and render the whole world happy, without discovering himself in any operation. A fleet, whose purposes were salutary to society, might always meet with a fair wind: Good princes enjoy sound health and long life: Persons, born to power and authority, be framed with good tempers and virtuous dispositions. A few [207] such events as these, regularly and wisely conducted, would change the face of the world; and yet would no more seem to disturb the course of nature or confound human conduct, than the present economy of things, where the causes are secret, and variable, and compounded. Some small touches, given to *Caligula's* brain in his infancy, might have converted him into a *Trajan*.[6] One wave, a little higher than the rest, by burying *Caesar* and his fortune in the bottom of the ocean, might have restored liberty to a considerable part of mankind. There may, for aught we know, be good reasons why providence interposes not in this manner; but they are unknown to us: And though the mere supposition, that such reasons exist, may be sufficient to *save* the conclusion concerning the divine attributes, yet surely it can never be sufficient to *establish* that conclusion.

9 If everything in the universe be conducted by general laws, and if animals be rendered susceptible of pain, it scarcely seems possible but some ill must arise in the various shocks of matter, and the various concurrence and opposition of general laws: But this ill would be very rare, were it not for the *third* circumstance which I proposed to mention, *viz.* the great frugality, with which all powers and faculties are distributed to every particular being. So well adjusted are the organs and capacities of all animals, and so well fitted to their preservation, that, as far as history or tradition reaches, there appears not to be any single species, which has yet been extinguished in the universe. Every animal has the requisite endowments; but these endowments are bestowed with so scrupulous an economy, that any considerable diminution must entirely destroy the creature. Wherever one power is increased, there is a proportional abatement in the others. Animals, which excel in swiftness, are commonly defective in force. Those, which possess both, are either imperfect in some of their senses, or are oppressed with the most craving wants. The human species,

---

[6] *Caligula*: Gaius Caesar (AD 12–41), Roman emperor (AD 37–41) whose scandalous actions and cruelty led many to conclude he was insane. *Trajan* (AD 53–117): Roman emperor (AD 98–117) whose reign was marked by extensive building projects of great benefit to the people and by his compassionate treatment of the poor.

whose chief excellency is reason and sagacity, is of all others the most necessitous; and the most deficient in bodily advantages; without clothes, [208] without arms, without food, without lodging, without any convenience of life, except what they owe to their own skill and industry. In short, nature seems to have formed an exact calculation of the necessities of her creatures; and like a *rigid master*, has afforded them little more powers or endowments, than what are strictly sufficient to supply those necessities. An *indulgent parent* would have bestowed a large stock, in order to guard against accidents, and secure the happiness and welfare of the creature, in the most unfortunate concurrence of circumstances. Every course of life would not have been so surrounded with precipices, that the least departure from the true path, by mistake or necessity, must involve us in misery and ruin. Some reserve, some fund would have been provided to ensure happiness; nor would the powers and the necessities have been adjusted with so rigid an economy. The author of nature is inconceivably powerful: His force is supposed great, if not altogether inexhaustible: Nor is there any reason, as far as we can judge, to make him observe this strict frugality in his dealings with his creatures. It would have been better, were his power extremely limited, to have created fewer animals, and to have endowed these with more faculties for their happiness and preservation. A builder is never esteemed prudent, who undertakes a plan, beyond what his stock will enable him to finish.

10 In order to cure most of the ills of human life, I require not that man should have the wings of the eagle, the swiftness of the stag, the force of the ox, the arms of the lion, the scales of the crocodile or rhinoceros; much less do I demand the sagacity of an angel or cherubim. I am contented to take an increase in one single power or faculty of his soul. Let him be endowed with a greater propensity to industry and labour; a more vigorous spring and activity of mind; a more constant bent to business and application. Let the whole species possess naturally an equal diligence with that which many individuals are able to attain by habit and reflection; and the most beneficial consequences, without any allay of ill, is the immediate and [209] necessary result of this endowment. Almost all the moral, as well as natural evils of human life arise from idleness; and were our species, by the original constitution of their frame, exempt from this vice or infirmity, the perfect cultivation of land, the improvement of arts and manufactures, the exact execution of every office and duty, immediately follow; and men at once may fully reach that state of society, which is so imperfectly attained by

the best regulated government. But as industry is a power, and the most valuable of any, nature seems determined, suitably to her usual maxims, to bestow it on men with a very sparing hand; and rather to punish him severely for his deficiency in it, than to reward him for his attainments. She has so contrived his frame, that nothing but the most violent necessity can oblige him to labour; and she employs all his other wants to overcome, at least in part, the want of diligence, and to endow him with some share of a faculty, of which she has thought fit naturally to bereave him. Here our demands may be allowed very humble, and therefore the more reasonable. If we required the endowments of superior penetration and judgement, of a more delicate taste of beauty, of a nicer sensibility to benevolence and friendship; we might be told, that we impiously pretend to break the order of nature, that we want to exalt ourselves into a higher rank of being, that the presents which we require, not being suitable to our state and condition, would only be pernicious to us. But it is hard; I dare to repeat it, it is hard, that being placed in a world so full of wants and necessities; where almost every being and element is either our foe or refuses its assistance; we should also have our own temper to struggle with, and should be deprived of that faculty, which can alone fence against these multiplied evils.

11 The *fourth* circumstance, whence arises the misery and ill of the universe, is the inaccurate workmanship of all the springs and principles of the great machine of nature.[7] It must be acknowledged, that there are few parts of the universe, which seem not to serve some purpose, and whose removal would not produce a visible defect and disorder in the whole. The parts hang all together; nor can one be touched without [210] affecting the rest, in a greater or less degree. But at the same time, it must be observed, that none of these parts or principles, however useful, are so accurately adjusted, as to keep precisely within those bounds, in which their utility consists; but they are, all of them, apt, on every occasion, to run into the one extreme or the other. One would imagine, that this grand production had not received the last hand of the maker; so little finished is every part, and so coarse are the strokes, with which it is executed. Thus, the winds are requisite to convey the vapours along the surface of the globe, and to assist men in navigation: But how oft, rising

---

[7] Cf. Leibniz's Fourth Letter to Clarke, art. 40, in *The Leibniz–Clarke Correspondence*, ed. H. G. Alexander (Barnes & Noble, NY: Manchester University Press, 1956), 42.

up to tempests and hurricanes, do they become pernicious? Rains are necessary to nourish all the plants and animals of the earth: But how often are they defective? how often excessive? Heat is requisite to all life and vegetation; but is not always found in the due proportion. On the mixture and secretion of the humours and juices of the body depend the health and prosperity of the animal: But the parts perform not regularly their proper function. What more useful than all the passions of the mind, ambition, vanity, love, anger? But how oft do they break their bounds, and cause the greatest convulsions in society? There is nothing so advantageous in the universe, but what frequently becomes pernicious, by its excess or defect; nor has nature guarded, with the requisite accuracy, against all disorder or confusion. The irregularity is never, perhaps, so great as to destroy any species; but is often sufficient to involve the individuals in ruin and misery.

12 On the concurrence, then, of these *four* circumstances does all, or the greatest part of natural evil depend. Were all living creatures incapable of pain, or were the world administered by particular volitions, evil never could have found access into the universe: And were animals endowed with a large stock of powers and faculties, beyond what strict necessity requires; or were the several springs and principles of the universe so accurately framed as to preserve always the just temperament and medium; there must have been very little ill in comparison of what we feel at present. What then shall we pronounce on this occasion? Shall we say, that these circumstances are not necessary, and that they might easily have been altered in the contrivance of the universe? This decision seems too presumptuous for creatures, so blind and ignorant. Let us be [211] more modest in our conclusions. Let us allow, that, if the goodness of the deity (I mean a goodness like the human) could be established on any tolerable reasons *a priori*, these phenomena, however untoward, would not be sufficient to subvert that principle; but might easily, in some unknown manner, be reconcilable to it. But let us still assert, that as this goodness is not antecedently established, but must be inferred from the phenomena, there can be no grounds for such an inference, while there are so many ills in the universe, and while these ills might so easily have been remedied, as far as human understanding can be allowed to judge on such a subject. I am sceptic enough to allow, that the bad appearances, notwithstanding all my reasonings, may be compatible with such attributes as you suppose: But surely they can never prove these attributes. Such a conclusion cannot

85

result from scepticism; but must arise from the phenomena, and from our confidence in the reasonings, which we deduce from these phenomena.

13 Look round this universe. What an immense profusion of beings, animated and organized, sensible and active! You admire this prodigious variety and fecundity. But inspect a little more narrowly these living existences, the only beings worth regarding. How hostile and destructive to each other! How insufficient all of them for their own happiness! How contemptible or odious to the spectator! The whole presents nothing but the idea of a blind nature, impregnated by a great vivifying principle, and pouring forth from her lap, without discernment or parental care, her maimed and abortive children.

14 Here the *Manichaean* system[8] occurs as a proper hypothesis to solve the difficulty: And no doubt, in some respects, it is very specious, and has more probability than the common hypothesis, by giving a plausible account of the strange mixture of good and ill, which appears in life. But if we consider, on the other hand, the perfect uniformity and agreement of the parts of the universe, we shall not discover in it any marks of the combat

[212] of a malevolent with a benevolent being. There is indeed an opposition of pains and pleasures in the feelings of sensible creatures: But are not all the operations of nature carried on by an opposition of principles, of hot and cold, moist and dry, light and heavy?[9] The true conclusion is, that the original source of all things is entirely indifferent to all these principles, and has no more regard to good above ill than to heat above cold, or to drought above moisture, or to light above heavy.

15 There may *four* hypotheses be framed concerning the first causes of the universe; *that* they are endowed with perfect goodness, *that* they have perfect malice, *that* they are opposite and have both goodness and malice, *that* they have neither goodness nor malice. Mixed phenomena can never prove the two former unmixed principles. And the uniformity and steadiness of general laws seem to oppose the third. The fourth, therefore, seems by far the most probable.

---

[8] *Manichaean* system: A dualistic religious movement founded in Persia in the third century AD by Mani, who taught that the universe is a battlefield for control between two independent deities, an evil material god and a good immaterial god. Cf. "Bayle on Manicheanism," 145–152.

[9] *Hot, cold, moist, dry, light and heavy*: According to Aristotelian science, all terrestrial matter is composed of some combination of four elements: earth, water, fire, air, which have a natural tendency to separate in space. Earth elements are heavy and, therefore, low; fire elements are light and located up high; air and water have intermediate positions.

16 What I have said concerning natural evil will apply to moral, with little or no variation; and we have no more reason to infer, that the rectitude of the supreme being resembles human rectitude than that his benevolence resembles the human.[10] Nay, it will be thought, that we have still greater cause to exclude from him moral sentiments, such as we feel them; since moral evil, in the opinion of many, is much more predominant above moral good than natural evil above natural good.

17 But even though this should not be allowed, and though the virtue, which is in mankind, should be acknowledged much superior to the vice; yet so long as there is any vice at all in the universe, it will very much puzzle you anthropomorphites, how to account for it. You must assign a cause for it, without having recourse to the first cause. But as every effect must have a cause, and that cause another; you must either carry on the progression *in infinitum*, or rest on that original principle, who is the ultimate cause of all things . . .

18 Hold! hold! cried *Demea*: Whither does your imagination hurry you? I joined in alliance with you, in order to prove the incomprehensible nature of the divine being, and refute the principles of *Cleanthes*, who would measure everything by human rule and standard. But I now find you running into all the topics of the greatest libertines and infidels; [213] and betraying that holy cause, which you seemingly espoused. Are you secretly, then, a more dangerous enemy than *Cleanthes* himself?

19 And are you so late in perceiving it? replied *Cleanthes*. Believe me, *Demea*; your friend *Philo*, from the beginning, has been amusing himself at both our expense; and it must be confessed, that the injudicious reasoning of our vulgar theology has given him but too just a handle of ridicule. The total infirmity of human reason, the absolute incomprehensibility of the divine nature, the great and universal misery, and still greater wickedness of man; these are strange topics surely to be so fondly cherished by orthodox divines and doctors. In ages of stupidity and ignorance, indeed, these principles may safely be espoused; and perhaps, no views of things are more proper to promote superstition, than such as encourage the blind amazement, the diffidence, and melancholy of mankind. But at present . . .

20 Blame not so much, interposed *Philo*, the ignorance of these reverend gentlemen. They know how to change their style with the times. Formerly it was a most popular theological topic to maintain, that human life was

---

[10] Cf. Memoranda, 23–25, p. 107.

vanity and misery, and to exaggerate all the ills and pains, which are incident to men. But of late years, divines, we find, begin to retract this position, and maintain, though still with some hesitation, that there are more goods than evils, more pleasures than pains, even in this life. When religion stood entirely upon temper and education, it was thought proper to encourage melancholy; as indeed, mankind never have recourse to superior powers so readily as in that disposition. But as men have now learned to form principles, and to draw consequences, it is necessary to change the batteries, and to make use of such arguments as will endure, at least, some scrutiny and examination. This variation is the same (and from the same causes) with that which I formerly remarked with regard to scepticism.[11]

21 Thus *Philo* continued to the last his spirit of opposition, and his censure of established opinions. But I could observe, that *Demea* did not at all relish the latter part of the discourse; and he took occasion soon after, on some pretence or other, to leave the company.

[11] See *D* 1.12.

Part 12

1 After *Demea*'s departure, *Cleanthes* and *Philo* continued the conversation, in the following manner. Our friend, I am afraid, said *Cleanthes*, will have little inclination to revive this topic of discourse, while you are in company; and to tell truth, *Philo*, I should rather wish to reason with either of you apart on a subject, so sublime and interesting. Your spirit of controversy, joined to your abhorrence of vulgar superstition, carries you strange lengths, when engaged in an argument; and there is nothing so sacred and venerable, even in your own eyes, which you spare on that occasion.

2 I must confess, replied *Philo*, that I am less cautious on the subject of natural religion than on any other; both because I know that I can never, on that head, corrupt the principles of any man of common sense, and because no one, I am confident, in whose eyes I appear a man of common sense, will ever mistake my intentions.[1] You, in particular, *Cleanthes*, with whom I live in unreserved intimacy; you are sensible, that, notwithstanding the freedom of my conversation, and my love of singular arguments, no one has a deeper sense of religion impressed on his mind, or pays more profound adoration to the divine being, as he discovers himself to reason, in the inexplicable contrivance and artifice of nature. A purpose, an intention, a design strikes everywhere the most careless, the most stupid thinker; and no man can be so hardened in absurd systems, as at all times to reject it.[2] *That nature does nothing in vain*, is a maxim established in all the schools, merely from the contemplation of the works of nature,

---

[1] Cf. Bayle, "A General and Preliminary Observation," from *Explanations*, in *Dictionary Historical and Critical*, V:811.

[2] Cf. *NHR*, pp. 124–125, 134. See also *Letter from a Gentleman*, 25–26; *T* 1.3.14 n.

without any religious purpose; and, from a firm conviction of its truth, an anatomist, who had observed a new organ or canal, would never be satisfied, till he had also discovered its use and intention. One great foundation of the Copernican system is the maxim, *that nature acts by the simplest methods, and chooses the most proper means to any end*; and astronomers often, without thinking of it, lay this strong foundation of piety and religion. The same thing is observable in other parts of philosophy: And thus all

[215] the sciences almost lead us insensibly to acknowledge a first intelligent author; and their authority is often so much the greater, as they do not directly profess that intention.

3 It is with pleasure I hear *Galen* reason concerning the structure of the human body. The anatomy of a man, says he,[a] discovers above 600 different muscles; and whoever duly considers these, will find, that in each of them nature must have adjusted at least ten different circumstances, in order to attain the end, which she proposed; proper figure, just magnitude, right disposition of the several ends, upper and lower position of the whole, the due insertion of the several nerves, veins, and arteries: So that in the muscles alone, above 6000 several views and intentions must have been formed and executed. The bones he calculates to be 284: The distinct purposes, aimed at in the structure of each, above forty. What a prodigious display of artifice, even in these simple and homogeneous parts? But if we consider the skin, ligaments, vessels, glandules, humours, the several limbs and members of the body; how must our astonishment rise upon us, in proportion to the number and intricacy of the parts so artificially adjusted? The farther we advance in these researches, we discover new scenes of art and wisdom: But descry still, at a distance, farther scenes beyond our reach; in the fine internal structure of the parts, in the economy of the brain, in the fabric of the seminal vessels. All these artifices are repeated in every different species of animal, with wonderful variety, and with exact propriety, suited to the different intentions of nature, in framing each species. And if the infidelity of *Galen*, even when these natural sciences were still imperfect, could not withstand such striking appearances; to what pitch of pertinacious obstinacy must

[a] *De formatione foetus* [*On the Formation of the Foetus*. Claudius Galen (AD 129–216) was the most famous physician of the Roman Empire and originator of the experimental method in medical investigation. His theories emphasized purposeful creation by a single creator, for which reason he was regarded as a proto-Christian.]

a philosopher in this age have attained, who can now doubt of a supreme intelligence?[3]

4 Could I meet with one of this species (who, I thank God, are very rare) I would ask him: Supposing there were a God, who did not discover himself immediately to our senses; were it possible for him to give stronger proofs of his existence, than what appear on the whole face of nature? What indeed could such a divine being do, but copy the present economy of things; render many of his artifices so plain, that no stupidity could mistake them; afford glimpses of still greater artifices, which [216] demonstrate his prodigious superiority above our narrow apprehensions; and conceal altogether a great many from such imperfect creatures? Now according to all rules of just reasoning, every fact must pass for undisputed, when it is supported by all the arguments, which its nature admits of; even though these arguments be not, in themselves, very numerous or forcible: How much more, in the present case, where no human imagination can compute their number, and no understanding estimate their cogency?

5 I shall farther add, said *Cleanthes*, to what you have so well urged, that one great advantage of the principle of theism, is, that it is the only system of cosmogony, which can be rendered intelligible and complete, and yet can throughout preserve a strong analogy to what we every day see and experience in the world. The comparison of the universe to a machine of human contrivance is so obvious and natural, and is justified by so many instances of order and design in nature, that it must immediately strike all unprejudiced apprehensions, and procure universal approbation. Whoever attempts to weaken this theory, cannot pretend to succeed by establishing in its place any other, that is precise and determinate: It is sufficient for him, if he start doubts and difficulties; and by remote and abstract views of things, reach that suspense of judgement, which is here the utmost boundary of his wishes. But besides, that this state of mind is in itself unsatisfactory, it can never be steadily maintained against such striking appearances, as continually engage us into the religious hypothesis. A false, absurd system, human nature, from the force of prejudice, is capable of adhering to, with obstinacy and perseverance: But no system at

---

3 This entire paragraph echoes comments by John Wilkins and Samuel Clarke on Galen. See Wilkins, *Of the Principles and Duties of Natural Religion*, 4th edn. (London, 1699), Ch. 6, p. 81; Clarke, *A Demonstration*, Sec. XI, p. 81.

all, in opposition to a theory, supported by strong and obvious reason, by natural propensity, and by early education, I think it absolutely impossible to maintain or defend.

6 So little, replied *Philo*, do I esteem this suspense of judgement in the present case to be possible, that I am apt to suspect there enters somewhat of a dispute of words into this controversy, more than is usually imagined. That the works of nature bear a great analogy to the productions of art is evident; and according to all the rules of good reasoning, we ought to infer, [217] if we argue at all concerning them, that their causes have a proportional analogy. But as there are also considerable differences, we have reason to suppose a proportional difference in the causes; and in particular ought to attribute a much higher degree of power and energy to the supreme cause than any we have ever observed in mankind. Here then the existence of a DEITY is plainly ascertained by reason; and if we make it a question, whether, on account of these analogies, we can properly call him a *mind* or *intelligence*, notwithstanding the vast difference, which may reasonably be supposed between him and human minds; what is this but a mere verbal controversy? No man can deny the analogies between the effects: To restrain ourselves from enquiring concerning the causes is scarcely possible: From this enquiry, the legitimate conclusion is, that the causes have also an analogy: And if we are not contented with calling the first and supreme cause a GOD or DEITY, but desire to vary the expression; what can we call him but MIND or THOUGHT, to which he is justly supposed to bear a considerable resemblance?

7 All men of sound reason are disgusted with verbal disputes, which abound so much in philosophical and theological enquiries; and it is found, that the only remedy for this abuse must arise from clear definitions, from the precision of those ideas which enter into any argument, and from the strict and uniform use of those terms which are employed. But there is a species of controversy, which, from the very nature of language and of human ideas, is involved in perpetual ambiguity, and can never, by any precaution or any definitions, be able to reach a reasonable certainty or precision. These are the controversies concerning the degrees of any quality or circumstance. Men may argue to all eternity, whether *Hannibal* be a great, or a very great, or a superlatively great man, what degree of beauty *Cleopatra* possessed, what epithet of praise *Livy* or *Thucydides* is entitled to, without bringing the controversy to any

determination.[4] The disputants may here agree in their sense and differ in the terms, or *vice versa*; yet never be able to define their terms, so as to enter into each other's meaning: Because the degrees of these qualities are [218] not, like quantity or number, susceptible of any exact mensuration, which may be the standard in the controversy. That the dispute concerning theism is of this nature, and consequently is merely verbal, or, perhaps, if possible, still more incurably ambiguous, will appear upon the slightest enquiry. I ask the theist, if he does not allow, that there is a great and immeasurable, because incomprehensible difference between the *human* and the *divine* mind: The more pious he is, the more readily will he assent to the affirmative, and the more will he be disposed to magnify the difference: He will even assert, that the difference is of a nature, which cannot be too much magnified. I next turn to the atheist, who, I assert, is only nominally so, and can never possibly be in earnest; and I ask him, whether from the coherence and apparent sympathy in all the parts of this world, there be not a certain degree of analogy among all the operations of nature, in every situation and in every age; whether the rotting of a turnip, the generation of an animal, and the structure of human thought, be not energies that probably bear some remote analogy to each other: It is impossible he can deny it: He will readily acknowledge it. Having obtained this concession, I push him still farther in his retreat; and I ask him, if it be not probable, that the principle which first arranged, and still maintains order in this universe, bears not also some remote inconceivable analogy to the other operations of nature, and among the rest, to the economy of human mind and thought. However reluctant, he must give his assent. Where then, cry I to both these antagonists, is the subject of your dispute? The theist allows, that the original intelligence is very different from human reason: The atheist allows, that the original principle of order bears some remote analogy to it. Will you quarrel, Gentlemen, about the degrees, and enter into a controversy, which admits not of any precise meaning, nor consequently of any determination? If you should be so obstinate, I should not be surprised to find you insensibly change sides; while the theist on the one hand exaggerates the

---

[4] *Hannibal* (247–183 BC): Carthaginian general who crossed the Alps in 218 BC with elephants and about 35,000 men to fight the Romans. *Cleopatra* (69–30 BC): Egyptian queen (51–49 BC and 48–30 BC). *Livy* (Titus Livius, 59 BC–AD 17): Roman historian; *Thucydides* (c. 460–400 BC): Greek historian.

dissimilarity between the supreme being and frail, imperfect, variable, fleeting, and mortal creatures; and the atheist on the other magnifies the analogy among all the operations of nature, in every period, every situation, and every position. Consider then, where the real point of con-

[219] troversy lies, and if you cannot lay aside your disputes, endeavour, at least, to cure yourselves of your animosity.[5]

8 And here I must also acknowledge, *Cleanthes*, that, as the works of nature have a much greater analogy to the effects of *our* art and contrivance, than to those of *our* benevolence and justice; we have reason to infer that the natural attributes of the deity have a greater resemblance to those of man, than his moral have to human virtues. But what is the consequence? Nothing but this, that the moral qualities of man are more defective in their kind than his natural abilities. For as the supreme being is allowed to be absolutely and entirely perfect, whatever differs most from him departs the farthest from the supreme standard of rectitude and perfection.[b]

9 These, *Cleanthes*, are my unfeigned sentiments on this subject; and these sentiments, you know, I have ever cherished and maintained. But in proportion to my veneration for true religion, is my abhorrence of vulgar superstitions; and I indulge a peculiar pleasure, I confess, in pushing such principles, sometimes into absurdity, sometimes into impiety. And you are sensible, that all bigots, notwithstanding their great aversion to the latter above the former, are commonly equally guilty of both.

10 My inclination, replied *Cleanthes*, lies, I own, a contrary way. Religion, however corrupted, is still better than no religion at all. The doctrine of a future state is so strong and necessary a security to morals, that we never ought to abandon or neglect it. For if finite and temporary rewards and punishments have so great an effect, as we daily

---

[b] It seems evident, that the dispute between the sceptics and dogmatists is entirely verbal, or at least regards only the degrees of doubt and assurance, which we ought to indulge with regard to all reasoning: And such disputes are commonly, at the bottom, verbal and admit not of any precise determination. No philosophical dogmatist denies, that there are difficulties both with regard to the senses and to all science, and that these difficulties are in a regular, logical method, absolutely insolvable. No sceptic denies, that we lie under an absolute necessity, notwithstanding these difficulties, of thinking, and believing, and reasoning with regard to all kinds of subjects, and even of frequently assenting with confidence and security. The only difference, then, between these sects, if they merit that name, is that the sceptic, from habit, caprice, or inclination, insists most on the difficulties; the dogmatist, for like reasons, on the necessity.

[5] Added in 1776, the year of Hume's death, this paragraph, the longest in the work, "takes on a special significance as his dying testament to posterity" (M. A. Stewart, "The Dating of Hume's Manuscripts," in M. A. Stewart and John P. Wright, eds., *Hume and Hume's Connexions* (University Park, PA: Pennsylvania State University Press, 1995), 303.

find: How much greater must be expected from such as are infinite and [220] eternal?

11 How happens it then, said *Philo*, if vulgar superstition be so salutary to society, that all history abounds so much with accounts of its pernicious consequences on public affairs? Factions, civil wars, persecutions, subversions of government, oppression, slavery; these are the dismal consequences which always attend its prevalency over the minds of men. If the religious spirit be ever mentioned in any historical narration, we are sure to meet afterwards with a detail of the miseries, which attend it. And no period of time can be happier or more prosperous, than those in which it is never regarded, or heard of.

12 The reason of this observation, replied *Cleanthes*, is obvious. The proper office of religion is to regulate the heart of men, humanize their conduct, infuse the spirit of temperance, order, and obedience; and as its operation is silent, and only enforces the motives of morality and justice, it is in danger of being overlooked, and confounded with these other motives.[6] When it distinguishes itself, and acts as a separate principle over men, it has departed from its proper sphere, and has become only a cover to faction and ambition.

13 And so will all religion, said *Philo*, except the philosophical and rational kind. Your reasonings are more easily eluded than my facts. The inference is not just, because finite and temporary rewards and punishments have so great influence, that therefore such as are infinite and eternal must have so much greater. Consider, I beseech you, the attachment, which we have to present things, and the little concern which we discover for objects, so remote and uncertain.[7] When divines are declaiming against the common behaviour and conduct of the world, they always represent this principle as the strongest imaginable (which indeed it is) and describe almost all humankind as lying under the influence of it, and sunk into the deepest lethargy and unconcern about their religious interests. [221] Yet these same divines, when they refute their speculative antagonists, suppose the motives of religion to be so powerful, that, without them, it were impossible for civil society to subsist; nor are they ashamed of so palpable a contradiction. It is certain, from experience, that the smallest grain of natural honesty and benevolence has more effect on men's

[6] Cf. Hume, *History of England* (London, 1756), II:449n.
[7] Cf. Hume's discussion of the effects of remoteness and uncertainty on human passions in *T* 2.3.7–9.

conduct than the most pompous views, suggested by theological theories and systems. A man's natural inclination works incessantly upon him; it is forever present to the mind; and mingles itself with every view and consideration: Whereas religious motives, where they act at all, operate only by starts and bounds; and it is scarcely possible for them to become altogether habitual to the mind.[8] The force of the greatest gravity, say the philosophers, is infinitely small, in comparison of that of the least impulse; yet it is certain, that the smallest gravity will, in the end, prevail above a great impulse; because no strokes or blows can be repeated with such constancy as attraction and gravitation.

14 Another advantage of inclination: It engages on its side all the wit and ingenuity of the mind; and when set in opposition to religious principles, seeks every method and art of eluding them: In which it is almost always successful. Who can explain the heart of man, or account for those strange salvos and excuses, with which people satisfy themselves, when they follow their inclinations, in opposition to their religious duty? This is well understood in the world; and none but fools ever repose less trust in a man, because they hear, that, from study and philosophy, he has entertained some speculative doubts with regard to theological subjects. And when we have to do with a man, who makes a great profession of religion and devotion; has this any other effect upon several, who pass for prudent, than to put them on their guard, lest they be cheated and deceived by him?

15 We must farther consider, that philosophers, who cultivate reason and reflection, stand less in need of such motives to keep them under the restraint of morals: And that the vulgar, who alone may need them, are utterly incapable of so pure a religion, as represents the deity to be pleased with nothing but virtue in human behaviour. The recommendations to [222] the divinity are generally supposed to be either frivolous observances, or rapturous ecstasies, or a bigoted credulity. We need not run back into antiquity, or wander into remote regions, to find instances of this degeneracy. Amongst ourselves, some have been guilty of that atrociousness, unknown to the *Egyptian* and *Grecian* superstitions, of declaiming in express terms, against morality, and representing it as a sure forfeiture of the divine favour, if the least trust or reliance be laid upon it.

---

[8] See Bayle, Explanation 1, in *Dictionary*, v:812.

16 But even though superstition or enthusiasm[9] should not put itself in direct opposition to morality; the very diverting of the attention, the raising up a new and frivolous species of merit, the preposterous distribution which it makes of praise and blame, must have the most pernicious consequences, and weaken extremely men's attachment to the natural motives of justice and humanity.

17 Such a principle of action likewise, not being any of the familiar motives of human conduct, acts only by intervals on the temper, and must be roused by continual efforts, in order to render the pious zealot satisfied with his own conduct, and make him fulfil his devotional task.[10] Many religious exercises are entered into with seeming fervour, where the heart, at the time, feels cold and languid: A habit of dissimulation is by degrees contracted: And fraud and falsehood become the predominant principle. Hence the reason of that vulgar observation, that the highest zeal in religion and the deepest hypocrisy, so far from being inconsistent, are often or commonly united in the same individual character.

18 The bad effects of such habits, even in common life, are easily imagined: But where the interests of religion are concerned, no morality can be forcible enough to bind the enthusiastic zealot: The sacredness of the cause sanctifies every measure, which can be made use of to promote it.

19 The steady attention alone to so important an interest as that of eternal salvation is apt to extinguish the benevolent affections, and beget a narrow, contracted selfishness. And when such a temper is encouraged, it easily eludes all the general precepts of charity and benevolence.

20 Thus the motives of vulgar superstition have no great influence on [223] general conduct; nor is their operation very favourable to morality, in the instances, where they predominate.

21 Is there any maxim in politics more certain and infallible, than that both the number and authority of priests should be confined within very narrow limits, and that the civil magistrate ought, forever, to keep his

---

[9] See Hume, "Of Superstition and Enthusiasm" [1741], in *Essays*, 73–79. Hume identifies superstition and enthusiasm as two ways true religion is corrupted. Superstition originates in "weakness, fear, melancholy, together with ignorance" and manifests itself in "rituals, mortifications, sacrifices, presents or any practice, however absurd and frivolous," conceived as methods to appease divine powers that are feared to bring harm or hoped to bring protection. Enthusiasm, which in the eighteenth century was considered synonymous with fanaticism, originates "in hope, pride, presumption, a warm imagination, together with ignorance" and expresses itself in "raptures, transports and surprising flights of fancy," that are falsely taken as signs of divine favor.
[10] Cf. Memoranda, 39, p. 108; LM, 116; "Of Superstition and Enthusiasm," in *Essays*, p. 77.

fasces and axes[11] from such dangerous hands?[12] But if the spirit of popular religion were so salutary to society, a contrary maxim ought to prevail. The greater number of priests, and their greater authority and riches, will always augment the religious spirit. And though the priests have the guidance of this spirit; why may we not expect a superior sanctity of life, and greater benevolence and moderation, from persons, who are set apart for religion, who are continually inculcating it upon others, and who must themselves imbibe a greater share of it? Whence comes it then, that in fact, the utmost a wise magistrate can propose with regard to popular religions, is, as far as possible, to make a saving game of it, and to prevent their pernicious consequences with regard to society? Every expedient which he tries for so humble a purpose is surrounded with inconveniences. If he admits only one religion among his subjects, he must sacrifice, to an uncertain prospect of tranquillity, every consideration of public liberty, science, reason, industry, and even his own independency. If he gives indulgence to several sects, which is the wiser maxim, he must preserve a very philosophical indifference to all of them, and carefully restrain the pretensions of the prevailing sect; otherwise he can expect nothing but endless disputes, quarrels, factions, persecutions, and civil commotions.

22 True religion, I allow, has no such pernicious consequences: But we must treat of religion, as it has commonly been found in the world; nor have I anything to do with that speculative tenet of theism, which, as it is a species of philosophy, must partake of the beneficial influence of that principle, and at the same time must lie under a like inconvenience, of being always confined to very few persons.

[224]   23 Oaths are requisite in all courts of judicature; but it is a question whether their authority arises from any popular religion. It is the solemnity and importance of the occasion, the regard to reputation, and the reflecting on the general interests of society, which are the chief restraints upon mankind. Custom-house oaths and political oaths are but little regarded even by some who pretend to principles of honesty and religion: And a Quaker's asseveration is with us justly put upon the same footing with

---

[11] *Fasces and axes*: A bundle of rods surrounding an axe, symbolizing political authority and power over life and death.

[12] For examples of Hume's contempt for the authority of priests or clergy, see "Of Parties in General," "Of Superstition and Enthusiasm," and "Of National Characters," in *Essays*, 61–63, 73–79, 198–201, respectively.

the oath of any other person. I know, that *Polybius*[c] ascribes the infamy of *Greek* faith to the prevalency of the *Epicurean* philosophy; but I know also, that *Punic* faith had as bad a reputation in ancient times as *Irish* evidence has in modern;[13] though we cannot account for these vulgar observations by the same reason. Not to mention, that *Greek* faith was infamous before the rise of the *Epicurean* philosophy; and *Euripides*,[d] in a passage which I shall point out to you, has glanced a remarkable stroke of satire against his nation, with regard to this circumstance.

24 Take care, *Philo*, replied *Cleanthes*, take care: Push not matters too far: Allow not your zeal against false religion to undermine your veneration for the true. Forfeit not this principle, the chief, the only great comfort in life; and our principal support amidst all the attacks of adverse fortune. The most agreeable reflection, which it is possible for human imagination to suggest, is that of genuine theism, which represents us as the workmanship of a being perfectly good, wise, and powerful; who created us for happiness, and who, having implanted in us immeasurable desires of good, will prolong our existence to all eternity, and will transfer us into an infinite variety of scenes, in order to satisfy those desires, and render our felicity complete and durable. Next to such a being himself (if the comparison be allowed) the happiest lot which we can imagine, is that of being under his guardianship and protection.

25 These appearances, said *Philo*, are most engaging and alluring; and with regard to the true philosopher, they are more than appearances. But it happens here, as in the former case, that, with regard to the greater part of mankind, the appearances are deceitful, and that the terrors of religion commonly prevail above its comforts.

26 It is allowed, that men never have recourse to devotion so readily as [225] when dejected with grief or depressed with sickness. Is not this a proof, that the religious spirit is not so nearly allied to joy as to sorrow?

27 But men, when afflicted, find consolation in religion, replied *Cleanthes*. Sometimes, said *Philo*: But it is natural to imagine, that they will form a notion of those unknown beings, suitably to the present gloom

[c] Lib. 6 Cap. 54. [Polybius (203–120 BC), *The Histories*, Bk. 6, Ch. 56, not, as Hume's citation indicates, Ch. 54.]

[d] *Iphigenia in Tauride*. [Euripides (*c*. 480–406 BC), together with Sophocles and Aeschylus, was one of the three greatest tragedians of ancient Greece. Philo never does point out the passage from *Iphigenia*, but he is probably referring to vv. 1200–1205.]

13 *Greek faith*: Associated with greed and dishonesty. *Punic faith*: Faith having the treacherous character attributed to the Carthaginians by the Romans. *Irish evidence*: False witness; perjury.

and melancholy of their temper, when they betake themselves to the contemplation of them. Accordingly, we find the tremendous images to predominate in all religions; and we ourselves, after having employed the most exalted expression in our descriptions of the deity, fall into the flattest contradiction, in affirming, that the damned are infinitely superior in number to the elect.

28 I shall venture to affirm, that there never was a popular religion, which represented the state of departed souls in such a light, as would render it eligible for humankind, that there should be such a state. These fine models of religion are the mere product of philosophy. For as death lies between the eye and the prospect of futurity, that event is so shocking to nature, that it must throw a gloom on all the regions which lie beyond it; and suggest to the generality of mankind the idea of *Cerberus* and Furies;[14] devils, and torrents of fire and brimstone.

29 It is true; both fear and hope enter into religion; because both these passions, at different times, agitate the human mind, and each of them forms a species of divinity, suitable to itself. But when a man is in a cheerful disposition, he is fit for business or company or entertainment of any kind; and he naturally applies himself to these, and thinks not of religion. When melancholy, and dejected, he has nothing to do but brood upon the terrors of the invisible world, and to plunge himself still deeper in affliction. It may, indeed, happen, that after he has, in this manner, engraved the religious opinions deep into his thought and imagination, there may arrive a change of health or circumstances, which may restore his good humour, and raising cheerful prospects of futurity, make him run into the other extreme of joy and triumph. But still it must be acknowledged, that, as [226] terror is the primary principle of religion, it is the passion which always predominates in it, and admits but of short intervals of pleasure.

30 Not to mention, that these fits of excessive, enthusiastic joy, by exhausting the spirits, always prepare the way for equal fits of superstitious terror and dejection; nor is there any state of mind so happy as the calm and equable. But this state it is impossible to support, where a man thinks, that he lies, in such profound darkness and uncertainty, between an eternity of happiness and an eternity of misery. No wonder that such an opinion disjoints the ordinary frame of the mind, and throws it into the utmost

---

[14] *Cerberus*: The three-headed dog guarding the entrance to Hades. *Furies*: The three goddesses with serpentine hair who punish those whose crimes have not yet been avenged by hounding them until they die in a "furor" of torment.

confusion. And though that opinion is seldom so steady in its operation as to influence all the actions; yet it is apt to make a considerable breach in the temper, and to produce that gloom and melancholy, so remarkable in all devout people.

31 It is contrary to common sense to entertain apprehensions or terrors, upon account of any opinion whatsoever, or to imagine that we run any risk hereafter, by the freest use of our reason. Such a sentiment implies both an *absurdity* and an *inconsistency*. It is an absurdity to believe the deity has human passions, and one of the lowest of human passions, a restless appetite for applause. It is an inconsistency to believe, that, since the deity has this human passion, he has not others also; and in particular, a disregard to the opinions of creatures so much inferior.

32 *To know God*, says *Seneca, is to worship him.*[15] All other worship is indeed absurd, superstitious, and even impious. It degrades him to the low condition of mankind, who are delighted with entreaty, solicitation, presents, and flattery. Yet is this impiety the smallest of which superstition is guilty. Commonly, it depresses the deity far below the condition of mankind, and represents him as a capricious demon, who exercises his power without reason and without humanity! And were that divine being disposed to be offended at the vices and follies of silly mortals, who are his own workmanship; ill would it surely fare with the votaries of most popular superstitions. Nor would any of human race merit his *favour*, but a very few, the philosophical theists, who entertain, or rather indeed endeavour to entertain, suitable notions of his divine [227] perfections: As the only persons, entitled to his *compassion* and *indulgence*, would be the philosophical sceptics, a sect almost equally rare, who, from a natural diffidence of their own capacity, suspend, or endeavour to suspend all judgement with regard to such sublime and such extraordinary subjects.

33 If the whole of natural theology, as some people seem to maintain, resolves itself into one simple, though somewhat ambiguous, at least undefined proposition, *that the cause or causes of order in the universe probably bear some remote analogy to human intelligence*: If this proposition be not capable of extension, variation, or more particular explication: If it affords

---

[15] *Seneca* (5 BC–AD 65): Roman Stoic philosopher, writer, and tutor of Nero. What Seneca actually said was *Primus est deorum cultus deos credere*, or "The first way to worship the gods is to believe in the gods." *The Epistles of Seneca*, trans. R. M. Gummere, 3 vols. (Cambridge, MA: Harvard University Press, 1996–2001), III:89.

no inference that affects human life, or can be the source of any action or forbearance: And if the analogy, imperfect as it is, can be carried no farther than to the human intelligence; and cannot be transferred, with any appearance of probability, to the other qualities of the mind: If this really be the case, what can the most inquisitive, contemplative, and religious man do more than give a plain, philosophical assent to the proposition, as often as it occurs; and believe, that the arguments, on which it is established, exceed the objections, which lie against it? Some astonishment, indeed, will naturally arise from the greatness of the object: Some melancholy from its obscurity: Some contempt of human reason, that it can give no solution more satisfactory with regard to so extraordinary and magnificent a question. But believe me, *Cleanthes*, the most natural sentiment, which a well-disposed mind will feel on this occasion, is a longing desire and expectation, that heaven would be pleased to dissipate, at least alleviate this profound ignorance, by affording some more particular revelation to mankind, and making discoveries of the nature, attributes, and operations of the divine object of our faith. A person, seasoned with a just sense of the imperfections of natural reason, will fly to revealed truth with the greatest avidity: While the haughty dogmatist, persuaded, that he can [228] erect a complete system of theology by the mere help of philosophy, disdains any farther aid, and rejects this adventitious instructor. To be a philosophical sceptic is, in a man of letters, the first and most essential step towards being a sound, believing Christian;[16] a proposition, which I would willingly recommend to the attention of *Pamphilus*: And I hope *Cleanthes* will forgive me for interposing so far in the education and instruction of his pupil.

34 *Cleanthes* and *Philo* pursued not this conversation much farther; and as nothing ever made greater impression on me, than all the reasonings of that day; so, I confess, that, upon a serious review of the whole, I cannot but think, that *Philo*'s principles are more probable than *Demea*'s; but that those of *Cleanthes* approach still nearer to the truth.[17]

Finis.

[16] Cf. Bayle, *Dictionary*, s.v. "Pyrrho," note c, IV:656. Contrast with Shaftesbury, "The Moralists," in *Characteristics*, 242–243: "For as averse as I am to the cause of theism or name of "deist" when taken in a sense exclusive of revelation, I consider still that, in strictness, the root of all is theism and that, to be a settled Christian, it is necessary to be first of all a good theist."
[17] Cf. Cicero, *The Nature of the Gods*, 3.95.

Other writings

From Hume's memoranda

Editor's note: Hume's memoranda are notes he made from his readings during the period after his return from France in 1737 when he was finishing his final editing of the *Treatise* and possibly continuing into the early 1740s. The following selection is transcribed from the group of notes appearing under the heading "Philosophy." The memoranda were first published by E. C. Mossner in "Hume's Early Memoranda: The Complete Text," *Journal of the History of Ideas* 9 (1948), 492–518. M. A. Stewart corrects Mossner's dating and organization of the notes in "The Dating of Hume's Manuscripts," in Paul Wood, ed., *The Scottish Enlightenment: Essays in Reinterpretation* (Rochester: University of Rochester Press, 2000), 276–288. To facilitate cross-referencing to Mossner's article, the same entry numbering used by Mossner is included.

Philosophy

1 Notwithstanding the cruelty of the gladiatorian spectacles, the Romans show many signs of humanity. It was regarded as a piece of cruelty to burn a slave with a hot iron for stealing table linen. *Juv[enal]. Sat[ire]*. 14.

2 Too careful and elaborate an education prejudicial; because it learns one to trust to others for one's judgement. *L'Abbé Dubos*.

3 For a young man, who applies himself to the arts and sciences, the slowness with which he forms himself for the world is a good sign. *Id*.

4 Though the ancients speak often of God in the singular number, that proves not they believed in his unity, since Christians speak in the same manner of the devil. *Bayle*.

5 The testimony of idolators cannot be united to that of Christians against the atheists; since they never formed one proposition that there is a God and afterwards that there is more than one. These two propositions are not the same. *Id.*

6 Men love pleasure more than they hate pain. *Id.*

7 Men are vicious; but hate a religion that authorizes vice. *Id.*

8 The center of unity of all men with relation to religion is, That there is a first cause. As you augment the propositions you find non-conformists. Atheists, Epicureans, idolators, those who maintain the extension, composition, necessity of the first cause, etc. *Id.*

9 Those who deny the *Peccatum philosophicum* of the Jesuits maintain that men may deserve eternal punishment for their errors, though they never had sufficient means of instructing themselves.

10 Atheists plainly make a distinction between good reasoning and bad. Why not between vice and virtue? *Bayle.*

11 The accounts we have of the sentiments of the ancient philosophers not very distinct nor consistent. Cicero contradicts himself in two sentences in saying that Thales allowed the ordering of the world by a mind, and in saying that Anaxagoras was the first.

12 Three kinds of atheist according to some. 1. Who deny the existence of a God. Such as Diagoras, Theodorus. 2. Who deny a providence, such as the Epicureans and the Ionic sect. 3. Who deny the free will of the deity, such as Aristotle, the Stoics, etc.

13 The most probable account we have of the sentiments of the Ionic sect is that Thales maintained the origin of everything from water. Anaximander from the infinity of things: Anaximenes from air; Anaxagoras from his homœomeries. Heraclitus of a different sect from fire.

14 Strato's atheism the most dangerous of the ancient, holding the origin of the world from nature, or a matter endued with activity. Bayle thinks there are none but the Cartesians can refute this atheism.

15 A Stratonician could retort the arguments of all the sects of philosophy. Of the Stoics, who maintained their God to be fiery and compound and of the Platonicians who asserted the Ideas to be distinct from the deity. The same question, Why the parts or Ideas of God had that particular arrangement? Is as difficult as why the world had.

16 The argument *a priori*. That no necessary existent being can be limited is only conclusive that there is an intelligent being who antecedently

forms the idea of infinite perfection and resolves to work up to his model: Which implies a contradiction. *Bayle*.

17 Plato and Cicero maintained the eternity of the soul *a parte ante* as well as *a parte post*; and ought also to have maintained that of beasts.

18 Three kinds of ill according to King. Ills of privation, pain, and vice. The first no blemish in the creation; since there must be different ranks of creatures.

19 Men might have been determined to avoid things harmful and seek the useful by the augmentation and diminution of pleasure as well as by pain. In heaven men are supposed to be liable to no pain. *Bayle*.

20 Those who solve the difficulties concerning the origin of ill by the apology of general laws suppose another motive beside goodness in the creation of the world.

21 Matter indifferent to all kinds of motion and direction. The soul a *carte blanche* indifferent to all perception. What necessity then for harmful motions or disagreeable perceptions? Many plans upon which the universe might be formed. Strange that none should be better than the present. *Bayle*.

22 King says that liberty consists in a power of rendering things agreeable or disagreeable as we please.

23 Liberty not a proper solution of moral ill: Because it might have been bound down, by motives like those of saints and angels. *Id*.

24 God could not be pleased by the actions of a creature without liberty. But can he be pleased with the abuses of that liberty? *Id*.

25 Did he give liberty to please men themselves? But men are as well pleased to be determined to good. *Id*.

26 The remedy of every inconvenience would become a new one. No solution. Comparison from a work planned with genius, where chance strikes out beauties.

27 It seems to be a kind of objection against the immortality of the soul to consider the trifling accidents of marriage, copulation, etc., that bring men into life.

28 It is a stronger objection to the argument against atheism drawn from the universal consent of mankind to find barbarous and ignorant nations atheists than learned and polite ones. *Bayle*.

29 The first supreme deity of the Romans was not Jupiter but Summanus, to whom they attributed the thunder by night. The beautiful temple of Jupiter turned the tables. *Id*.

30 Argument against liberty derived from this, that preservation is a continual creation, and consequently God must create the soul with every new modification. *Id.*

31 Whether a cause is necessary? Whether necessary to an eternal being? Whether necessary in every new moment of a successive being? Whether necessary in motion?

32 God could have prevented all abuses of liberty without taking away liberty. Therefore liberty no solution of difficulties. *Bayle.*

33 God does not will sin as sin, but in some other view according to Calvin. *Id.*

34 Contrary to reason; above reason. Human reason: Divine reason. *Id.*

35 Some pretend that there can be no necessity according to the system of atheism: Because even matter cannot be determined without something superior to determine it. *Fénelon.*

36 Being, and truth and goodness the same. *Id.*

37 Three proofs for the existence of a God. 1. Something necessarily existent, and what is so is infinitely perfect. 2. The idea of infinite must come from an infinite being. 3. The idea of infinite perfection implies that of actual existence. *Id.*

38 There is a remarkable story to confirm the Cartesian philosophy of the brain. A man hurt by the fall of a horse forgot about twenty years of his life, and remembered what went before in a much more lively manner than usual.

39 No religion can maintain itself in vigour without many observances to be practiced on all occasions. Hence the priests are stricter upon these than moral duties without knowing the reason. There is a secret instinct of this kind.

40 Four kinds of atheists according to Cudworth, The Democritic or atomical, the Anaximandrian or hylopathian, the Stratonic or hylozoic, the Stoic or cosmo-plastic. To which he might have added the Pyrrhonian or sceptic. And the Spinozist or metaphysical. One might perhaps add the Anaxagorian or chymical.

Fragment on evil

Editor's note: The fragment is a remnant from a manuscript Hume was composing around the time he was completing his *Treatise*. It may have been late writing for the *Treatise*, subsequently excised, or writing for a second edition of the *Treatise* or some other project that was later abandoned. The first publication of the fragment, along with evidence concerning the dating of its composition, appeared only as recently as five years before the start of the twenty-first century. See M. A. Stewart, "Hume's Early Fragment on Evil," in John Wright and M. A. Stewart, eds., *Hume and Hume's Connexions* (University Park, PA: Pennsylvania State University Press, 1995), Ch. 8.

Sect. 7

Fourth objection

The *fourth* objection is not leveled against the intelligence of the deity, but against his moral attributes, which are equally essential to the system of theism.

The attempt to prove the moral attributes from the natural, benevolence from intelligence, must appear vain, when we consider that these qualities are totally distinct and separate. *Reason* and *virtue* are not the same; nor do they appear to have any immediate connection, in the nature of things. Even in man, any degree of the one affords no presumption for an equal degree of the other. A sound understanding and a hard heart are very compatible. Allowing, therefore, the intelligence of the deity to be proved by phenomena, ever so clear and decisive; we can draw no inference concerning his benevolence, without a new set of phenomena, equally clear and decisive.

Whether the author of nature be benevolent or not can only be proved by the effects, and by the predominancy either of good or evil, of happiness or misery, in the universe. If good prevail much above evil, we may, perhaps, presume, that the author of the universe, if an intelligent, is also a benevolent principle. If evil prevail much above good, we may draw a contrary inference. This is a standard, by which we may decide such a question, with some appearance of certainty; but when the question is brought to that standard, and we would willingly determine the facts, upon which we must proceed in our reasoning; we find that it is very difficult, if not absolutely impossible, ever to ascertain them. For who is able to form an exact computation of all the happiness and misery, that are in the world, and to compare them exactly with each other? I know it is the common opinion, that evil prevails very much above good, even amongst mankind, who are the most favoured by nature of all sensible creatures: But still some think, they have reason to dispute this popular opinion. What one may safely pronounce on this head, is, that if we compare pains and pleasures in their *degrees*, the former are infinitely superior; there being many pains, and even durable ones, extremely acute; and no pleasure, that is at the same time very intense and very durable. Love betwixt the sexes is, I believe, the only one, that has any pretensions to the character of an exquisite and intense pleasure, whether we consider the bodily enjoyment which it affords, or the tenderness and elegance of that friendship, which it inspires. Perhaps men of strong genius may find as high pleasures in study and contemplation. But what is all this in comparison of those many cruel distempers and violent sorrows, to which human life is subject? In this view, therefore, pains and pleasures are not to be put into the balance with each other. On the other hand, if we compare the *frequency* of pains with that of pleasures, we shall find, that the latter have the advantage, and that small pleasures, to the greatest part of mankind, return oftener, than pain or uneasiness. When a man is in good health and in good humour, every common incident of life affords him satisfaction; to go to bed; to rise again; to eat; to drink; to converse; to enjoy the weather; to perform his business; to hear news; to retail them. These incidents compose the lives of most men; and these are not without enjoyment. But whether those pleasures, by their frequency, are able to compensate the acuteness of our pains, I must confess I am not able to determine with any certainty. When I consider the subject with the utmost impartiality, and take the most comprehensive view of it, I find myself more inclined to think, that evil predominates in the world, and am apt to regard human life as a scene of misery, according to the sentiments of the greatest sages as well as of the generality of mankind, from the beginning of the world to his day. I am sensible, however, that there are many circumstances, which are apt to pervert my judgement in this particular, and make me entertain melancholy views of things. What is evil alarms us more, and makes more lasting impression than what is agreeable; which we readily receive without enquiry, and which we think ourselves in some measure, entitled to. Besides, the greater intenseness of our pains has a much more powerful influence on the imagination than the frequency of our pleasures; and it is almost impossible for us to make a just compensation betwixt them. Should I enumerate all the evils, incident to human life, and display them, with eloquence, in their proper colours, I should certainly gain the cause with most readers, who would be apt to despise, as frivolous, all the pleasures, which could be placed in opposition to them. Victuals, wine, a fiddle, a warm bed, a coffee-house conversation make a pitiful figure, when compared with racks, gravels, infamy, solitude, and dungeons. But I take no advantage of this circumstance, and shall not employ any rhetoric in a philosophical argument, where reason alone ought to be hearkened to. I shall only infer, from the whole, that the facts are here so complicated and dispersed, that a certain conclusion can never be formed from them, and that no single convert will ever be made by any disputes upon this subject; but each disputant will still go off the field with a stronger confirmation of those opinions and prejudices, which he brought to it. Did a controversy arise whether more males or females are born; could this question ever be decided merely by our running over all the families of our acquaintance; without the assistance of any bills of mortality, which bring the matter to a certainty?

But though it be difficult to decide this question, whether there be more good or evil in the universe, we may, perhaps, find means, independent of it, to decide, in some tolerable manner, that other question concerning the benevolence of the deity. Were evil predominant in the world, there would evidently remain no proofs of benevolence in the supreme being. But even if good be predominate; since it prevails in so small a degree, and is counter balanced by so many ills; it can never afford any proof of that attribute. Pains and pleasures seem to be scattered indifferently through life, as heat and cold, moist and dry are dispersed through the universe; and if the one prevails a little above the other, this is what will naturally happen in any mixture of principles, where an exact equality is not expressly intended. On every occasion, nature seems to employ either.

Letter to Francis Hutcheson, March 16, 1740 (extract)

Editor's note: Francis Hutcheson (1694–1746), Professor of Moral Philosophy at the University of Glasgow and a popularizer of Shaftesbury's thought in Scotland, helped foster a more enlightened attitude among the Scottish clergy. Hume and Hutcheson shared the Shaftesburean conviction that moral judgments do not convey factual information but express disinterested emotions. Further, they both believed that moral sense is independent of religious belief. Hume sought Hutcheson's advice in preparing the third volume of his *Treatise of Human Nature* for publication. Hutcheson was very helpful to Hume in this regard, but four years later their disagreements about religion led Hutcheson to oppose Hume's candidacy for a faculty appointment at the University of Edinburgh.

Dear Sir:

... I must consult you in a point of prudence. I have concluded a reasoning with these two sentences. *When you pronounce any action or character to be vicious, you mean nothing but that from the particular constitution of your nature you have a feeling or sentiment of blame from the contemplation of it. Vice and virtue, therefore, may be compared to sounds, colours, heat and cold, which, according to modern philosophy, are not qualities in objects but perceptions in the mind: And this discovery in morals, like that other in physics, is to be regarded as a mighty advancement of the speculative sciences; though like that too, it has little or no influence on practice.* Is not this laid a little too strong? I desire your opinion of it, though I cannot entirely promise to conform myself to it. I wish from my heart, I could avoid concluding, that since morality, according to your opinion as well as mine, is determined merely by sentiment, it regards only human nature and human life. This has been often urged against you, and the consequences are very momentous. If you make any alterations on your performances, I can assure you, there are many who desire you would more fully consider this point; if you think that the truth lies on the popular side. Otherwise common prudence, your character, and situation forbid you touch upon it. If morality were determined by reason, that is the same to all rational beings: But nothing but experience can assure us, that the sentiments are the same. What experience have we with regard to superior beings? How can we ascribe to them any sentiments at all? They have implanted those sentiments in us for the conduct of life like our bodily sensations, which they possess not themselves. I expect no answer to these difficulties in the compass of a letter. It is enough if you have patience to read so long a letter as this. I am, Dear sir

Your most obedient humble servant, [etc.]

Letter to William Mure, June 30, 1743 (extract)

Editor's note: William Mure (1718–76) was one of Hume's lifelong friends. William Leechman (1706–85) became Mure's tutor about 1727. He was ordained as a minister in 1736 and was appointed Professor of Divinity at the University of Glasgow in 1743, shortly before Hume wrote this letter. He was a member of Francis Hutcheson's circle, contributing to the moderation of strict orthodoxy among the Scottish clergy. His sermon, about which Hume's letter comments, was published as *The Nature, Reasonableness, and Advantages of Prayer: A Sermon* (Glasgow, 1743).

I have read Mr. Leechman's sermon with a great deal of pleasure, and think it a very good one; though I am sorry to find the author to be a rank atheist. You know (or ought to know) that Plato says there are three kinds of atheists. The first who deny a deity, the second who deny his providence, the third who assert, that he is influenced by prayers or sacrifices. I find Mr. Leechman is an atheist of the last kind . . .

As to the argument I could wish Mr. Leechman would in the second edition answer this objection both to devotion and prayer, and indeed to everything we commonly call religion, except the practice of morality, and the assent of the understanding to the proposition *that God exists*.

It must be acknowledged that nature has given us a strong passion of admiration for whatever is excellent, and of love and gratitude for whatever is benevolent and beneficial, and that the deity possesses these attributes in the highest perfection and yet I assert he is not the natural object of any passion or affection. He is no object either of the senses or imagination, and very little of the understanding, without which it is impossible to excite any affection. A remote ancestor, who has left us estates and honours, acquired with virtue, is a great benefactor, and yet it is impossible to bear him any affection, because unknown to us; though in general we know him to be a man or a human creature, which brings him vastly nearer our comprehension than an invisible infinite spirit. A man, therefore, may have his heart perfectly well disposed towards every proper and natural object of affection, friends, benefactors, country, children, etc., and yet from this circumstance of the invisibility and incomprehensibility of the deity may feel no affection towards him. And indeed I am afraid, that all enthusiasts mightily deceive themselves. Hope and fear perhaps agitate their breast when they think of the deity: Or they degrade him into a resemblance with themselves, and by that means render him more comprehensible. Or they exult with vanity in esteeming themselves his peculiar favourites. Or at best they are actuated by a forced and strained affection, which moves by starts and bounds, and with a very irregular disorderly pace. Such an affection cannot be required of any man as his duty. Please to observe, that I not only exclude the turbulent passions, but the calm affections. Neither of them can operate without the assistance of the senses, and imagination, or at least a more complete knowledge of the object than we have of the deity. In most men this is the case; and a natural infirmity can never be a crime. But secondly were devotion never so much admitted, prayer must still be excluded. First the addressing of our virtuous wishes and desires to the deity, since the address has no influence on him, is only a kind of rhetorical figure, in order to render these wishes more ardent and passionate. This is Mr. Leechman's doctrine. Now the use of any figure of speech can never be a duty. Secondly this figure, like most figures of rhetoric, has an evident impropriety in it. For we can make use of no expression or even thought, in prayers and entreaties, which does not imply that these prayers have an influence. Thirdly. This figure is very dangerous and leads directly and even unavoidably to impiety and blasphemy. It is a natural infirmity of men to imagine, that their prayers have a direct influence, and this infirmity must be extremely fostered and encouraged by the constant use of prayer. Thus all wise men have excluded the use of images and pictures in prayer; though they certainly enliven devotion; because it is found by experience, that with the vulgar these visible representations draw too much towards them, and become the only objects of devotion. – Excuse this long letter, make my compliments to Mr. Leechman and all friends, and believe me to be Yours sincerely [etc.]

[P.S.] I have frequently in Edinburgh enquired for the *Dialogues on Devotion* published at Glasgow some time ago; but could not find them. If you have a copy send it me, and I shall restore it with the first occasion. It may be a means of my conversion.

Letters to Gilbert Elliot of Minto

Editor's note: Gilbert Elliot was one of Hume's close friends. Despite their religious differences, Elliot had supported Hume's candidacy for an academic appointment at the University of Glasgow in 1752, though Hume was again passed over because of his anti-religious views. Despite Elliot's support in this regard, he strongly advised Hume against publishing the *Dialogues*. His response to Hume's request for assistance in strengthening Cleanthes' argument did not go further than to echo views that Hume already had Cleanthes express in Part 3 of the *Dialogues*, such as that a survey of order and mutual adaptation among the parts of nature naturally leads to belief in an intelligent designer, a belief that strikes with a force like that of sensation, based more on feeling or sentiment than on subtle reasoning.

1. Letter of February 18, 1751 (extract)

Dear Sir,

Your notion of correcting subtlety by sentiment is certainly very just with regard to morals, which depend upon sentiment; and in politics and natural philosophy, whatever conclusion is contrary to certain matter of fact must certainly be wrong, and there must some error lie somewhere in the argument, whether we be able to show it or not. But in metaphysics or theology, I cannot see how either of these plain and obvious standards of truth can have place. Nothing there can correct bad reasoning but good reasoning: and sophistry must be opposed by syllogism. About seventy or eighty years ago, I observe, a principle like that which you advance prevailed very much in France amongst some philosophers and *beaux esprits*. The occasion of it was this. The famous Mons. Nicole of the Port Royal, in his *Perpétuité de la Foi*, pushed the Protestants very hard upon the impossibility of the people's reaching a conviction of their religion by the way of private judgement; which required so many disquisitions, reasonings, researches, erudition, impartiality, and penetration, as not one of a hundred, even amongst men of education, is capable of. Monsr. Claude and the Protestants answered him, not by solving his difficulties (which seems impossible) but by retorting them (which is very easy). They showed that to reach the way of authority, which the Catholics insist on, as long a train of acute reasoning and as great erudition was requisite as would be sufficient for a Protestant. We must first prove all the truths of natural religion, the foundation of morals, the divine authority of the scripture, the deference which it commands to the Church, the tradition of the Church, etc. The comparison of these controversial writings begot an idea in some, that it was neither by reasoning nor authority we learn our religion, but by sentiment. And certainly this were a very convenient way, and what a philosopher would be very well pleased to comply with, if he could distinguish sentiment from education. But to all appearance the sentiment of Stockholm, Geneva, Rome ancient and modern, Athens, and Memphis, have the same characters. And no thinking man can implicitly assent to any of them; but from the general principle, that as the truth in these subjects is beyond human capacity, and that as for one's own ease he must adopt some tenets, there is more satisfaction and convenience in holding to the catechism we have been first taught. Now this I have nothing to say against. I would only observe, that such a conduct is founded on the most universal and determined scepticism, joined to a little indolence. For more curiosity and research gives a direct opposite turn from the same principles . . .

I send you enclosed a little endeavour at drollery against some people who care not much to be joked upon.[1] I have frequently had it in my intentions to write a supplement to Gulliver, containing the ridicule of priests. It was certainly a pity that Swift was a parson. Had he been a lawyer or physician, we had nevertheless been entertained at the expense of these professions. But priests are so jealous, that they cannot bear to be touched on that head; and for a plain reason: Because they are conscious

---

[1] Hume's *The Bellman's Petition* (1752), a satire on the clergy.

they are really ridiculous. That part of the Doctor's subject is so fertile, that a much inferior genius, I am confident, might succeed in it . . .

I am Dear Sir yours sincerely, [etc.]

2. Letter of March 10, 1751 (extract)

Dear Sir,

You would perceive by the sample I have given you, that I make Cleanthes the hero of the dialogue. Whatever you can think of, to strengthen that side of the argument, will be most acceptable to me. Any propensity you imagine I have to the other side, crept in upon me against my will: And it is not long ago that I burned an old manuscript book, wrote before I was twenty; which contained, page after page, the gradual progress of my thoughts on that head. It began with an anxious search after arguments, to confirm the common opinion: Doubts stole in, dissipated, returned, were again dissipated, returned again; and it was a perpetual struggle of a restless imagination against inclination, perhaps against reason.

I have often thought, that the best way of composing a dialogue, would be for two persons that are of different opinions about any question of importance, to write alternately the different parts of the discourse, and reply to each other. By this means, that vulgar error would be avoided, of putting nothing but nonsense into the mouth of the adversary: And at the same time, a variety of character and genius being upheld, would make the whole look more natural and unaffected. Had it been my good fortune to live near you, I should have taken on me the character of Philo, in the dialogue, which you'll own I could have supported naturally enough: And you would not have been averse to that of Cleanthes. I believe, too, we could both of us have kept our temper very well; only, you have not reached an absolute philosophical indifference on these points. What danger can ever come from ingenious reasoning and enquiry? The worst speculative sceptic ever I knew, was a much better man than the best superstitious devotee and bigot. I must inform you, too, that this was the way of thinking of the ancients on this subject. If a man made profession of philosophy, whatever his sect was, they always expected to find more regularity in his life and manners, than in those of the ignorant and illiterate. There is a remarkable passage of Appian to this purpose. That historian observes, that notwithstanding the established prepossession in favour of learning, yet some philosophers, who have been trusted with absolute power, have very much abused it; and he instances in Critias, the most violent of the Thirty, and Ariston, who governed Athens in the time of Sylla. But I find, upon enquiry, that Critias was a professed atheist, and Ariston an Epicurean, which is little or nothing different: And yet Appian wonders at their corruption, as much as if they had been Stoics or Platonists. A modern zealot would have thought that corruption unavoidable.

I could wish that Cleanthes' argument could be so analyzed, as to be rendered quite formal and regular. The propensity of the mind towards it, unless that propensity were as strong and universal as that to believe in our senses and experience, will still, I am afraid, be esteemed a suspicious foundation. It is here I wish for your assistance. We must endeavour to prove that this propensity is somewhat different from our inclination to find our own figures in the clouds, our face in the moon, our passions and sentiments even in inanimate matter. Such an inclination may, and ought to be controlled, and can never be a legitimate ground of assent.

The instances I have chosen for Cleanthes are, I hope, tolerably happy, and the confusion in which I represent the sceptic seems natural. But *si quid novisti rectius*, etc.[2]

You ask me, if the idea of cause and effect is nothing but vicinity (you should have said constant vicinity, or regular conjunction), I would gladly know *whence is that farther idea of causation against which you argue?* This question is pertinent; but I hope I have answered it. We feel, after the constant conjunction, an easy transition from one idea to the other, or a connection in the imagination. And as it is usual for us to transfer our own feelings to the objects on which they are dependent, we attach the internal sentiment to the external objects. If no single instances of cause and effect appear to have any connection, but only repeated similar ones, you will find yourself obliged to have recourse to this theory.

I am sorry our correspondence should lead us into these abstract speculations. I have thought, and read, and composed very little on such questions of late. Morals, politics, and literature have employed all my time; but still the other topics I must think more curious, important, entertaining, and useful, than any geometry that is deeper than Euclid.

[2] A popular phrase from Horace, *Epistles*, Bk. 1, Epis. 6.67: "Si quid novisti rectius istis. Candidus imperti; si non, his utere mecum" ("If you can mend these precepts, do; if not, what serves for me may serve for you"). Translation by John Conington, in *The Satires, Epistles, and Art of Poetry of Horace* (London: G. Bell, 1892).

If in order to answer the doubts started, new principles of philosophy must be laid; are not these doubts themselves very useful? Are they not preferable to blind, and ignorant assent? I hope I can answer my own doubts: But if I could not, is it to be wondered at? To give myself airs, and speak magnificently, might I not observe, that Columbus did not conquer empires and plant colonies?

If I have not unraveled the knot so well, in these last papers I sent you, as perhaps I did in the former, it has not, I assure you, proceeded from want of good will; but some subjects are easier than others: At some times one is happier in his researches and enquiries than at others. Still I have recourse to the *si quid novisti rectius*. Not in order to pay you a compliment, but from a real philosophical doubt and curiosity.

I do not pay compliments, because I do not desire them. For this reason, I am very well pleased you speak so coldly of my *Petition*.[3] I had, however, given orders to have it printed, which perhaps may be executed: Though I believe I had better have left it alone. Not because it will give offence, but because it will not give entertainment: Not because it may be called profane; but because it may perhaps be deservedly called dull. To tell the truth, I was always so indifferent about fortune, and especially now, that I am more advanced in life, and am a little more at my ease, suited to my extreme frugality, that I neither fear nor hope any thing from any man, and am very indifferent either about offence or favour. Not only, I would not sacrifice truth and reason to political views, but scarce even a jest. You may tell me that I ought to have reversed the order of these points, and have put the jest first: As it is usual for people to be the fondest of their performances on subjects on which they are least made to excel. And that, consequently, I would give more to be thought a good droll, than to have the praises of erudition, and subtility, and invention. – This malicious insinuation, I will give no answer to, but proceed with my subject . . .

After you have done with these papers, please return them by the same carrier. But there is no hurry. On the contrary the longer you keep them, I shall still believe you are thinking the more seriously to execute what I desire of you. I am Dear Sir

Yours most sincerely, [etc.]

---

[3] See Hume's previous letter to Elliot, note 1 above.

P.S.

If you'll be persuaded to assist me in supporting Cleanthes, I fancy you need not take matters any higher than Part 3. He allows, indeed, in Part 2, that all our inference is founded on the similitude of the works of nature to the usual effects of mind. Otherwise they must appear a mere chaos. The only difficulty is, why the other dissimilitudes do not weaken the argument. And indeed it would seem from experience and feeling, that they do not weaken it so much as we might naturally expect. A theory to solve this would be very acceptable.

From *The Natural History of Religion*

Editor's note: Originally published in 1757, Hume's *Natural History of Religion* was controversial for its claims that there are societies that have no religious beliefs, that religion originates in psychological causes such as hope and fear rather than in philosophical contemplation of the order in nature, that polytheism historically preceded monotheism, and that both polytheism and monotheism have a bad influence on morality, although polytheism has the advantage of being more tolerant of other religious sects.

Introduction

As every enquiry, which regards religion, is of the utmost importance, there are two questions in particular, which challenge our attention, to wit, that concerning its foundation in reason, and that concerning its origin in human nature. Happily, the first question, which is the most important, admits of the most obvious, at least, the clearest, solution. The whole frame of nature bespeaks an intelligent author; and no rational enquirer can, after serious reflection, suspend his belief a moment with regard to the primary principles of genuine theism and religion. But the other question, concerning the origin of religion in human nature, is exposed to some more difficulty. The belief of invisible, intelligent power has been very generally diffused over the human race, in all places and in all ages; but it has neither perhaps been so universal as to admit of no exception, nor has it been, in any degree, uniform in the ideas, which it has suggested. Some nations have been discovered, who entertained no sentiments of religion, if travellers and historians may be credited; and no two nations, and scarce any two men, have ever agreed precisely in the same sentiments. It would appear, therefore, that this preconception springs not from an original instinct or primary impression of nature, such as gives rise to self-love, affection between the sexes, love of progeny, gratitude, resentment; since every instinct of this kind has been found absolutely universal in all nations and ages, and has always a precise determinate object, which it inflexibly pursues. The first religious principles must be secondary; such as may easily be perverted by various accidents and causes, and whose operation too, in some cases, may, by an extraordinary concurrence of circumstances, be altogether prevented. What those principles are, which give rise to the original belief, and what those accidents and causes are, which direct its operation, is the subject of our present enquiry . . .

II   Origin of polytheism

If we would, therefore, indulge our curiosity, in enquiring concerning the origin of religion, we must turn our thoughts towards polytheism, the primitive religion of uninstructed mankind.

Were men led into the apprehension of invisible, intelligent power by a contemplation of the works of nature, they could never possibly entertain any conception but of one single being, who bestowed existence and order on this vast machine, and adjusted all its parts, according to one regular plan or connected system. For though, to persons of a certain turn of mind, it may not appear altogether absurd, that several independent beings, endowed with superior wisdom, might conspire in the contrivance and execution of one regular plan; yet is this a merely arbitrary supposition, which, even if allowed possible, must be confessed neither to be supported by probability nor necessity. All things in the universe are evidently of a piece. Everything is adjusted to everything. One design prevails throughout the whole. And this uniformity leads the mind to acknowledge one author; because the conception of different authors, without any distinction of attributes or operations, serves only to give perplexity to the imagination, without bestowing any satisfaction on the understanding. The statue of LAOCOON, as we learn from PLINY, was the work of three artists: But it is certain, that, were we not told so, we should never have imagined, that a group of figures, cut from one stone, and united in one plan, was not the work and contrivance of one statuary. To ascribe any single effect to the combination of several causes, is not surely a natural and obvious supposition.

On the other hand, if, leaving the works of nature, we trace the footsteps of invisible power in the various and contrary events of human life, we are necessarily led into polytheism and to the acknowledgment of several limited and imperfect deities. Storms and tempests ruin what is nourished by the sun. The sun destroys what is fostered by the moisture of dews and rains. War may be favourable to a nation, whom the inclemency of the seasons afflicts with famine. Sickness and pestilence may depopulate a kingdom, amidst the most profuse plenty. The same nation is not, at the same time, equally successful by sea and by land. And a nation, which now triumphs over its enemies, may anon submit to their more prosperous arms. In short, the conduct of events, or what we call the plan of a particular providence, is so full of variety and uncertainty, that, if we suppose it immediately ordered by any intelligent beings, we must acknowledge a contrariety in their designs and intentions, a constant combat of opposite powers, and a repentance or change of intention in the same power, from impotence or levity. Each nation has its tutelar deity. Each element is subjected to its invisible power or agent. The province of each god is separate from that of another. Nor are the operations of the same god always certain and invariable. Today he protects: Tomorrow he abandons us. Prayers and sacrifices, rites and ceremonies, well or ill performed, are the sources of his favour or enmity, and produce all the good or ill fortune, which are to be found amongst mankind.

We may conclude, therefore, that, in all nations, which have embraced polytheism, the first ideas of religion arose not from a contemplation of the works of nature, but from a concern with regard to the events of life, and from the incessant hopes and fears, which actuate the human mind . . .

It must necessarily, indeed, be allowed, that, in order to carry men's intention beyond the present course of things, or lead them into any inference concerning invisible intelligent power, they must be actuated by some passion, which prompts their thought and reflection; some motive, which urges their first enquiry. But what passion shall we here have recourse to, for explaining an effect of such mighty consequences? Not speculative curiosity, surely, or the pure love of truth. That motive is too refined for such gross apprehensions; and would lead men into enquiries concerning the frame of nature, a subject too large and comprehensive for their narrow capacities. No passions, therefore, can be supposed to work upon such barbarians, but the ordinary affections of human life; the anxious concern for happiness, the dread of future misery, the terror of death, the thirst of revenge, the appetite for food and other necessaries. Agitated by hopes and fears of this nature, especially the latter, men scrutinize, with a trembling curiosity, the course of future causes, and examine the various and contrary events of human life. And in this disordered scene, with eyes still more disordered and astonished, they see the first obscure traces of divinity.

III   The same subject continued

We are placed in this world, as in a great theatre, where the true springs and causes of every event are entirely concealed from us; nor have we either sufficient wisdom to foresee, or power to prevent those ills, with which we are continually threatened. We hang in perpetual suspense between life and death, health and sickness, plenty and want; which are distributed amongst the human species by secret and unknown causes, whose operation is oft unexpected, and always unaccountable. These *unknown causes*, then, become the constant object of our hope and fear; and while the passions are kept in perpetual alarm by an anxious expectation of the events, the imagination is equally employed in forming ideas of those powers, on which we have so entire a dependence. Could men anatomize nature, according to the most probable, at least the most intelligible philosophy, they would find, that these causes are nothing but the particular fabric and structure of the minute parts of their own bodies and of external objects; and that, by a regular and constant machinery, all the events are produced, about which they are so much concerned. But this philosophy exceeds the comprehension of the ignorant multitude, who can only conceive the *unknown causes* in a general and confused manner; though their imagination, perpetually employed on the same subject, must labour to form some particular and distinct idea of them. The more they consider these causes themselves, and the uncertainty of their operation, the less satisfaction do they meet with in their researches; and, however unwilling, they must at last have abandoned so arduous an attempt, were it not for a propensity in human nature, which leads into a system, that gives them some satisfaction.

There is an universal tendency among mankind to conceive all beings like themselves, and to transfer to every object, those qualities, with which they are familiarly acquainted, and of which they are intimately conscious. We find human faces in the moon, armies in the clouds; and by a natural propensity, if not corrected by experience and reflection, ascribe malice or good-will to everything, that hurts or pleases us. Hence the frequency and beauty of the *prosopopoeia* in poetry; where trees, mountains and streams are personified, and the inanimate parts of nature acquire sentiment and passion. And though these poetical figures and expressions gain not on the belief, they may serve, at least, to prove a certain tendency in the imagination, without which they could neither be beautiful nor natural. Nor is a river-god or hamadryad always taken for a mere poetical or imaginary personage; but may sometimes enter into the real creed of the ignorant vulgar; while each grove or field is represented as possessed of a particular *genius* or invisible power, which inhabits and protects it. Nay, philosophers cannot entirely exempt themselves from this natural frailty; but have oft ascribed to inanimate matter the horror of a *vacuum*, sympathies, antipathies, and other affections of human nature. The absurdity is not less, while we cast our eyes upwards; and transferring, as is too usual, human passions and infirmities to the deity, represent him as jealous and revengeful, capricious and partial, and, in short, a wicked and foolish man, in every respect but his superior power and authority. No wonder, then, that mankind, being placed in such an absolute ignorance of causes, and being at the same time so anxious concerning their future fortune, should immediately acknowledge a dependence on invisible powers, possessed of sentiment and intelligence. The *unknown causes*, which continually employ their thought, appearing always in the same aspect, are all apprehended to be of the same kind or species. Nor is it long before we ascribe to them thought and reason and passion, and sometimes even the limbs and figures of men, in order to bring them nearer to a resemblance with ourselves.

In proportion as any man's course of life is governed by accident, we always find, that he increases in superstition; as may particularly be observed of gamesters and sailors, who, though, of all mankind, the least capable of serious reflection, abound most in frivolous and superstitious apprehensions. The gods, says CORIOLANUS in DIONYSIUS,[a] have an influence in every affair; but above all, in war; where the event is so uncertain. All human life, especially before the institution of order and

---

[a] Lib. viii. 33 [Dionysius of Halicarnassus, *Roman Antiquities*, Bk. VIII, Ch. 2, Sec. 2].

good government, being subject to fortuitous accidents; it is natural, that superstition should prevail everywhere in barbarous ages, and put men on the most earnest enquiry concerning those invisible powers, who dispose of their happiness or misery. Ignorant of astronomy and the anatomy of plants and animals, and too little curious to observe the admirable adjustment of final causes; they remain still unacquainted with a first and supreme creator, and with that infinitely perfect spirit, who alone, by his almighty will, bestowed order on the whole frame of nature. Such a magnificent idea is too big for their narrow conceptions, which can neither observe the beauty of the work, nor comprehend the grandeur of its author. They suppose their deities, however potent and invisible, to be nothing but a species of human creatures, perhaps raised from among mankind, and retaining all human passions and appetites, together with corporeal limbs and organs. Such limited beings, though masters of human fate, being, each of them, incapable of extending his influence everywhere, must be vastly multiplied, in order to answer that variety of events, which happen over the whole face of nature. Thus every place is stored with a crowd of local deities; and thus polytheism has prevailed, and still prevails, among the greatest part of uninstructed mankind.[b]

Any of the human affections may lead us into the notion of invisible, intelligent power; hope as well as fear, gratitude as well as affliction: But if we examine our own hearts, or observe what passes around us, we shall find, that men are much oftener thrown on their knees by the melancholy than by the agreeable passions. Prosperity is easily received as our due, and few questions are asked concerning its cause or author. It begets cheerfulness and activity and alacrity and a lively enjoyment of every social and sensual pleasure: And during this state of mind, men have little leisure or inclination to think of the unknown invisible regions. On the other hand, every disastrous accident alarms us, and sets us on enquiries concerning the principles whence it arose: Apprehensions spring up with regard to futurity: And the mind, sunk into diffidence, terror, and melancholy, has recourse to every method of appeasing those secret intelligent powers, on whom our fortune is supposed entirely to depend.

[b] The following lines of EURIPIDES are so much to the present purpose, that I cannot forbear quoting them: . . . Hecuba, 956: "There is nothing secure in the world; no glory, no prosperity. The gods toss all life into confusion; mix everything with its reverse; that all of us, from our ignorance and uncertainty, may pay them the more worship and reverence."

No topic is more usual with all popular divines than to display the advantages of affliction, in bringing men to a due sense of religion; by subduing their confidence and sensuality, which, in times of prosperity, make them forgetful of a divine providence. Nor is this topic confined merely to modern religions. The ancients have also employed it. *Fortune has never liberally, without envy,* says a GREEK historian,[c] *bestowed an unmixed happiness on mankind; but with all her gifts has ever conjoined some disastrous circumstance, in order to chastize men into a reverence for the gods, whom, in a continued course of prosperity, they are apt to neglect and forget* . . .

XIV   Bad influence of popular religions on morality

Here I cannot forbear observing a fact, which may be worth the attention of such as make human nature the object of their enquiry. It is certain, that, in every religion, however sublime the verbal definition which it gives of its divinity, many of the votaries, perhaps the greatest number, will still seek the divine favour, not by virtue and good morals, which alone can be acceptable to a perfect being, but either by frivolous observances, by intemperate zeal, by rapturous ecstasies, or by the belief of mysterious and absurd opinions. The least part of the *Sadder,* as well as of the *Pentateuch,* consists in precepts of morality; and we may also be assured, that that part was always the least observed and regarded. When the old ROMANS were attacked with a pestilence, they never ascribed their sufferings to their vices, or dreamed of repentance and amendment. They never thought, that they were the general robbers of the world, whose ambition and avarice made desolate the earth, and reduced opulent nations to want and beggary. They only created a dictator,[d] in order to drive a nail into a door; and by that means, they thought that they had sufficiently appeased their incensed deity.

In ÆGINA, one faction forming a conspiracy, barbarously and treach-erously assassinated seven hundred of their fellow-citizens; and carried their fury so far, that, one miserable fugitive having fled to the temple, they cut off his hands, by which he clung to the gates, and carrying him out of holy ground, immediately murdered him. *By this impiety,* says

---

[c] Diod. Sic. lib. iii. 47 [Diodorus Siculus, *Library of History*, Bk. III, Ch. 47].
[d] Called Dictator clavis figendae causa. T. Livii.l.vii.c.3. [Livy, *From the Founding of the City*, Bk. VII, Ch. 3, Sec. 3.]

HERODOTUS[e] (not by the other many cruel assassinations), *they offended the gods, and contracted an inexpiable guilt.*

Nay, if we should suppose, what never happens, that a popular religion were found, in which it was expressly declared, that nothing but morality could gain the divine favour; if an order of priests were instituted to inculcate this opinion, in daily sermons, and with all the arts of persuasion; yet so inveterate are the people's prejudices, that, for want of some other superstition, they would make the very attendance on these sermons the essentials of religion, rather than place them in virtue and good morals. The sublime prologue of ZALEUCUS' laws[f] inspired not the LOCRIANS, so far as we can learn, with any sounder notions of the measures of acceptance with the deity, than were familiar to the other GREEKS.

This observation, then, holds universally: But still one may be at some loss to account for it. It is not sufficient to observe, that the people, everywhere, degrade their deities into a similitude with themselves, and consider them merely as a species of human creatures, somewhat more potent and intelligent. This will not remove the difficulty. For there is no man so stupid, as that, judging by his natural reason, he would not esteem virtue and honesty the most valuable qualities, which any person could possess. Why not ascribe the same sentiment to his deity? Why not make all religion, or the chief part of it, to consist in these attainments?

Nor is it satisfactory to say, that the practice of morality is more difficult than that of superstition; and is therefore rejected. For, not to mention the excessive penances of the *Brachmans* and *Talapoins*; it is certain, that the *Rhamadan* of the TURKS, during which the poor wretches, for many days, often in the hottest months of the year, and in some of the hottest climates of the world, remain without eating or drinking from the rising to the setting sun; this *Rhamadan*, I say, must be more severe than the practice of any moral duty, even to the most vicious and depraved of mankind. The four Lents of the MUSCOVITES, and the austerities of some *Roman Catholics*, appear more disagreeable than meekness and benevolence. In short, all virtue, when men are reconciled to it by ever so little practice, is agreeable: All superstition is forever odious and burdensome.

---

[e] Lib. vi. 91 [Herodotus, *History*, Bk. VI, Ch. 91].
[f] To be found in Diod. Sic. lib. xii. 120 [Diodorus Siculus, *Library of History*, Bk. XII, Ch. 20–21].

Perhaps, the following account may be received as a true solution of the difficulty. The duties, which a man performs as a friend or parent, seem merely owing to his benefactor or children; nor can he be wanting to these duties, without breaking through all the ties of nature and morality. A strong inclination may prompt him to the performance: A sentiment of order and moral obligation joins its force to these natural ties: And the whole man, if truly virtuous, is drawn to his duty, without any effort or endeavour. Even with regard to the virtues, which are more austere, and more founded on reflection, such as public spirit, filial duty, temperance, or integrity; the moral obligation, in our apprehension, removes all pretension to religious merit; and the virtuous conduct is deemed no more than what we owe to society and to ourselves. In all this, a superstitious man finds nothing, which he has properly performed for the sake of his deity, or which can peculiarly recommend him to the divine favour and protection. He considers not, that the most genuine method of serving the divinity is by promoting the happiness of his creatures. He still looks out for some more immediate service of the supreme being, in order to allay those terrors, with which he is haunted. And any practice, recommended to him, which either serves to no purpose in life, or offers the strongest violence to his natural inclinations; that practice he will the more readily embrace, on account of those very circumstances, which should make him absolutely reject it. It seems the more purely religious, because it proceeds from no mixture of any other motive or consideration. And if, for its sake, he sacrifices much of his ease and quiet, his claim of merit appears still to rise upon him, in proportion to the zeal and devotion which he discovers. In restoring a loan, or paying a debt, his divinity is nowise beholden to him; because these acts of justice are what he was bound to perform, and what many would have performed, were there no god in the universe. But if he fast a day, or give himself a sound whipping; this has a direct reference, in his opinion, to the service of God. No other motive could engage him to such austerities. By these distinguished marks of devotion, he has now acquired the divine favour; and may expect, in recompense, protection and safety in this world, and eternal happiness in the next.

Hence the greatest crimes have been found, in many instances, compatible with a superstitious piety and devotion: Hence, it is justly regarded as unsafe to draw any certain inference in favour of a man's morals, from the fervour or strictness of his religious exercises, even though he himself believe them sincere. Nay, it has been observed, that enormities of the blackest dye have been rather apt to produce superstitious terrors, and increase the religious passion. BOMILCAR, having formed a conspiracy for assassinating at once the whole senate of CARTHAGE, and invading the liberties of his country, lost the opportunity, from a continual regard to omens and prophecies. *Those who undertake the most criminal and most dangerous enterprises are commonly the most superstitious*; as an ancient historian[g] remarks on this occasion. Their devotion and spiritual faith rise with their fears. CATILINE was not contented with the established deities and received rites of the national religion: His anxious terrors made him seek new inventions of this kind;[h] which he never probably had dreamed of, had he remained a good citizen, and obedient to the laws of his country.

To which we may add, that, after the commission of crimes, there arise remorses and secret horrors, which give no rest to the mind, but make it have recourse to religious rites and ceremonies, as expiations of its offences. Whatever weakens or disorders the internal frame promotes the interests of superstition: And nothing is more destructive to them than a manly, steady virtue, which either preserves us from disastrous, melancholy accidents, or teaches us to bear them. During such calm sunshine of the mind, these spectres of false divinity never make their appearance. On the other hand, while we abandon ourselves to the natural undisciplined suggestions of our timid and anxious hearts, every kind of barbarity is ascribed to the supreme being, from the terrors with which we are agitated; and every kind of caprice, from the methods which we embrace in order to appease him. *Barbarity, caprice*; these qualities, however nominally disguised, we may universally observe, form the ruling character of the deity in popular religions. Even priests, instead of correcting these depraved ideas of mankind, have often been found ready to foster and encourage them. The more tremendous the divinity is represented, the more tame and submissive do men become his ministers: And the more unaccountable the measures of acceptance required by him, the more necessary does it become to abandon our natural reason, and yield to their ghostly guidance and direction. Thus it may be allowed, that the artifices of men aggravate our natural infirmities and follies of this kind, but never originally beget them. Their root strikes deeper into the mind, and springs from the essential and universal properties of human nature.

[g] Diod. Sic. lib. xx. 43 [Diodorus Siculus, *Library of History*, Bk. xx, Ch. 43].

[h] Cic. Catil. i. 6, Sallust. de bello Catil. 22 [Cicero, First Speech, *Catiline Orations*; Sallust, *The War with Catiline*, Ch. 22].

XV General corollary

Though the stupidity of men, barbarous and uninstructed, be so great, that they may not see a sovereign author in the more obvious works of nature, to which they are so much familiarized; yet it scarcely seems possible, that any one of good understanding should reject that idea, when once it is suggested to him. A purpose, an intention, a design is evident in everything; and when our comprehension is so far enlarged as to contemplate the first rise of this visible system, we must adopt, with the strongest conviction, the idea of some intelligent cause or author. The uniform maxims too, which prevail throughout the whole frame of the universe, naturally, if not necessarily, lead us to conceive this intelligence as single and undivided, where the prejudices of education oppose not so reasonable a theory. Even the contrarieties of nature, by discovering themselves everywhere, become proofs of some consistent plan, and establish one single purpose or intention, however inexplicable and incomprehensible.

Good and ill are universally intermingled and confounded; happiness and misery, wisdom and folly, virtue and vice. Nothing is pure and entirely of a piece. All advantages are attended with disadvantages. An universal compensation prevails in all conditions of being and existence. And it is not possible for us, by our most chimerical wishes, to form the idea of a station or situation altogether desirable. The draughts of life, according to the poet's fiction, are always mixed from the vessels on each hand of JUPITER: Or if any cup be presented altogether pure, it is drawn only, as the same poet tells us, from the left-handed vessel.

The more exquisite any good is, of which a small specimen is afforded us, the sharper is the evil, allied to it; and few exceptions are found to this uniform law of nature. The most sprightly wit borders on madness; the highest effusions of joy produce the deepest melancholy; the most ravishing pleasures are attended with the most cruel lassitude and disgust; the most flattering hopes make way for the severest disappointments. And, in general, no course of life has such safety (for happiness is not to be dreamed of) as the temperate and moderate, which maintains, as far as possible, a mediocrity, and a kind of insensibility, in everything.

As the good, the great, the sublime, the ravishing are found eminently in the genuine principles of theism; it may be expected, from the analogy of nature, that the base, the absurd, the mean, the terrifying will be equally discovered in religious fictions and chimeras.

The universal propensity to believe in invisible, intelligent power, if not an original instinct, being at least a general attendant of human nature, may be considered as a kind of mark or stamp, which the divine workman has set upon his work; and nothing surely can more dignify mankind, than to be thus selected from all other parts of the creation, and to bear the image or impression of the universal creator. But consult this image, as it appears in the popular religions of the world. How is the deity disfigured in our representations of him! How much is he degraded even below the character, which we should naturally, in common life, ascribe to a man of sense and virtue!

What a noble privilege is it of human reason to attain the knowledge of the supreme being; and, from the visible works of nature, be enabled to infer so sublime a principle as its supreme creator? But turn the reverse of the medal. Survey most nations and most ages. Examine the religious principles, which have, in fact, prevailed in the world. You will scarcely be persuaded, that they are anything but sick men's dreams: Or perhaps will regard them more as the playsome whimsies of monkeys in human shape, than the serious, positive, dogmatical asseverations of a being, who dignifies himself with the name of rational.

Hear the verbal protestations of all men: Nothing so certain as their religious tenets. Examine their lives: You will scarcely think that they repose the smallest confidence in them.

The greatest and truest zeal gives us no security against hypocrisy: The most open impiety is attended with a secret dread and compunction.

No theological absurdities so glaring that they have not, sometimes, been embraced by men of the greatest and most cultivated understanding. No religious precepts so rigorous that they have not been adopted by the most voluptuous and most abandoned of men.

Ignorance is the mother of devotion: A maxim that is proverbial, and confirmed by general experience. Look out for a people, entirely destitute of religion: If you find them at all, be assured, that they are but a few degrees removed from brutes.

What so pure as some of the morals, included in some theological systems? What so corrupt as some of the practices, to which these systems give rise?

The comfortable views, exhibited by the belief of futurity, are ravishing and delightful. But how quickly vanish on the appearance of its terrors, which keep a more firm and durable possession of the human mind?

The whole is a riddle, an enigma, an inexplicable mystery. Doubt, uncertainty, suspense of judgement appear the only result of our most accurate scrutiny, concerning this subject. But such is the frailty of human reason, and such the irresistible contagion of opinion, that even this deliberate doubt could scarcely be upheld; did we not enlarge our view, and opposing one species of superstition to another, set them a quarreling; while we ourselves, during their fury and contention, happily make our escape, into the calm, though obscure, regions of philosophy.

Selections from Bayle

TRANSLATED BY JAMES DYE

1 Bayle on materialism *vs* intelligent design[1]

§CVI

Whether the opposing argument which the Stratonician athe-
ists could fashion from the argument drawn from the order and
symmetry of the world could not have embarrassed the pagan
philosophers.

To spare you useless toil, I am warning you of one thing which is
absolutely necessary if you want to use the proof which first comes to
mind and which is basically most excellent, namely that founded on the
beauty and regularity of the heavens and on the remarkable ingenuity of
animal machines, in which one can clearly see that their parts are directed
toward particular ends and are made to work together. Those Athenians
whom we suppose to adhere to the system of Strato were obliged to
say that a lifeless and unconscious nature produced all these beautiful
works and that, without knowing what it was doing, arranged them with
a symmetry and interdependence which clearly seem to be caused by a
very enlightened intelligence, deliberately choosing both its ends and its
means. Exactly here, you say, lies an objection or difficulty which would
have cured the atheism of those folks to the extent that the depravity

---

[1] *Continuation des pensées diverses*, Ch. CVI, in *Œuvres diverses de Mr. Pierre Bayle*, 4 vols. (The Hague,
1737), III:333–336.

of their will allowed them to seek their understanding's cure. With this proposal you are inaugurating a very lovely race course[2] for yourself, where you may run as many races or perform as many promenades as you please; but if you wish to profit from these exercises you must insert the condition I am about to point out into your plan. I do this just in case it would never occur to you on your own.

This is the proposition you must prove: *the order in nature was so completely capable of converting the Stratonicians, had they not a malicious predilection to flee from the light, that the objection against them based on that order would have infallibly converted them, EVEN IF THEY COULD HAVE TURNED THAT SAME EVIDENCE STILL MORE FORCEFULLY AGAINST THEIR OPPONENTS.* Pay special attention to these final capitalized words, for your project's entire success depends on them.

You must be aware that the human mind is so disposed that once persons embrace an hypothesis, the difficulties which follow from it do not make them abandon it, if they see that their opponents have the same difficulties or if these difficulties are no worse than those they would encounter elsewhere. One cannot reasonably blame those who do not surrender to an argument which they turn back on their opponents, since any argument which strikes equally against the doctrines of opponent and proponent proves too much and, because of that, proves nothing. Only an unreasonable rhetorician would characterize a man unwilling to change his opinion while his opponents remain subject to the same, or equally serious, difficulties as "a dogmatist maliciously blinding himself." The man's refusal is completely rational. Let us see then, Sir – and here is where your task starts –, if our young Athenians could turn the difficulty at issue to the disadvantage of their opponents. If they can do so, I do not see how you could possibly prove the thesis that I set before you. Perhaps you will then agree that it would be better to attribute their unwillingness to surrender to conceptual confusion rather than, as you suppose, to willful malice.

It seems to me that nothing could be more overwhelming for a Stratonician philosopher than showing him that a cause deprived of consciousness could not have made this world, containing an order so beautiful, a mechanism so exact, and laws of motion so precise and constant. For, since the most shoddy house has never been built without a cause which conceived

---

[2] race course: *carrière* can also mean "career"; the double sense is probably intentional.

it, and which directed its construction according to that conception, how would it be possible that the human body should have been organized by an unconscious cause or that the world, which is a product incomparably more complicated than animal bodies, should have been produced by an inanimate nature which is so far from being capable of directing forces that it is not even aware whether it has any? This question by itself would suffice to make Stratonicians aware that their hypothesis was incomprehensible and to reduce them to absurdity. They could retain only this consolation, namely, that they could reduce their adversaries to the same condition.

They would not have done this by maintaining that no intelligent cause produces the human body; for, even if one granted them that neither the father's soul, nor the mother's soul, nor the child's soul organizes the foetus, one could have responded to them that God organized it himself, or that he assigned the task to some generative spirit. Any other response would have been to the advantage of the Stratonicians – only this one would stop them. They could not have asked for anything better than recourse to seminal virtues, shaping faculties, and such other causes which know nothing of that which they carry out. But if the supposition of a spirit put in charge of animal formation ably repulses the initial attack, it could only serve to hasten the major battle, since the Stratonicians would not have failed to point out that their opponents had to appeal straightway to the first being, that is, to those other sects' primary explanatory principle. As an example, let us pit them against the Stoics for a while and suppose that they speak to them in the following manner.

"You allow two principles of everything, God and matter: God as active principle and matter as passive principle. According to you, God is an eternal everliving fire and is, therefore, an arrangement of highly agitated particles, since that is fire's essential nature. A whole composed of several actively moving physical particles cannot exist without those particles having some particular arrangement and some particular quantity of motion. A thing considered in general, devoid of any individual properties, can doubtless exist as a mental object but it cannot *really* exist outside our minds. Whatever really exists extramentally must be precisely this or that; and if it is an agitated body, each of its parts must have a particular shape and location and a definite quantity of motion, such or such rather than any other. Consequently, you should say that, from all eternity, the fiery particles which compose God's nature have had a certain arrangement and a certain quantity of motion, different from every other possible arrangement and quantity of motion. Please tell us from whence precisely this arrangement and this particular quantity of motion derive. Have they been chosen by an intelligent cause, preferred to every other possible combination of arrangement and quantity of motion by a nature which knew what it was doing and why it was doing it? You cannot say that; since that would be to say that God was produced by an antecedent cause, that he is not an uncreated being, that he is not the first efficient cause of all things, and that we must go on up to this antecedent cause, explaining to ourselves its essence, whether it is a fire, etc. Then the same question would come back, recursively, *ad infinitum*. Consequently, you have to stop at this fiery nature you call 'God' and agree that the arrangement and quantity of motion of its parts have not been arranged by a cause which knew what it arranged or moved about. So, given that this arrangement and this quantity of motion which are not derived from any intelligent and directing cause have nevertheless, according to you, managed to form the most perfect of all beings, a nature infinitely more completely realized than the world, why do you want the world not to be the work of a cause which acts without self-awareness? What right do you have to reject our principle of all things under the pretext that it is an inanimate principle? If it is not possible that the world be the work of such a principle, it will be even less possible that your Jupiter – a God who knows everything, who provides for everything, who disposes everything with sovereign goodness and infinite wisdom – should have acquired so many perfections without any intelligent cause being in charge of the arrangement and movement of the particles composing him. It is impossible that he himself should have been in charge, since his intelligence and will do not exist before he completely exists. He was a fire as soon as he was a God. The arrangement and determinate motion of the parts of this fire neither preceded nor followed Jupiter's intellectual perfections. Therefore they have no other cause than just that necessity of his nature which is the *raison d'être* of your active principle, which you Stoics distinguish from matter, although we do not. In short, if you wish to compel us to explain to you how there is order in nature without any intelligent being's guidance, we will compel you to explain to us how there is order in God's fiery particles without any intelligent cause's oversight. Your task will be more vexatious than ours, since you have to provide an explanation for an effect infinitely more perfected than nature or the world."

That is what Strato's disciples could say to the Stoics. It will please me a great deal if you will send me a really good rejoinder.

The other philosophical sects were scarcely less open than the Stoics to a similar reversal of their reasoning. Only Christian philosophers, especially the Cartesians, are prepared to reduce Strato's sect to ruins without fearing that their arguments could be turned back against them. It is easy to understand that all those who assigned a corporeal nature to God exposed themselves to the *ad hominem* argument against the Stoics I have just proposed. Nor could any of those who believed God to be the soul or intellect of matter avoid this reversal of their argument, since in the final analysis that soul was composed of parts each of which had its own particular powers and capabilities which God had not bestowed on it by a free act of his will. The necessary and eternal being does not have volition antecedent to his other attributes; he has power, understanding, and wisdom completely simultaneously with his volitional acts. So, if the soul of the world were God, it would have from all eternity all the powers of which it is capable, and it would have them without some other antecedent cause having ordered and distributed them deliberately and purposefully and without their being thus arranged by itself as an intelligent being.

Perhaps you believe that a Platonist who attributed an incorporeal nature to God would have easily rendered Strato's disciples speechless. But do not be too sure of that, for the following reasons:

1 There is no uniform Platonic doctrine of divinity in Plato's works; they contain so many incompatible pronouncements that one cannot tell which of them to accept as satisfactory.
2 Plato's doctrine is just a fabric woven of arbitrary suppositions which he pompously reels off without proving them.
3 He is so obscure that he discourages all those who only seek clear understanding. Cicero, who admires so many other parts of his works, was not even willing to pay him the honor of examining his hypothesis concerning divine nature.
4 Strato would have been able to pose this question to the Platonists: is it true that you recognize eternal ideas separate from God's substance? If so, you must say either that they exist on their own or that God has produced them as copies of original ideas which are not separate from his substance. If they exit on their own, then clearly there are some

things each of which, without depending on any cause endowed with oversight and life, have their own qualities, one being representative of man, another of horse, etc. From whence could they acquire this determinate quality to be this rather than that? From whence could come their differences, their relations and their subordinate positions, if it be true, as you claim, that no unconscious cause is capable of producing anything in which there is proportion and tendency toward a particular end? If they are only copies of original ideas intimately united with God's substance, the difficulty will fall back on the original ideas. All of these will have their own properties and there will be relations between them and some will be subordinate to others. Where is the principle for all that order? It is neither in the will of God (since he does not know things by virtue of free choice, but because knowing is a necessary aspect of his nature) nor in his understanding, which likewise has no freedom of indifference to know this or that or to know it in one way rather than in another.

The doctrine of Aristotle on the nature of God is so tangled with variations and obscurities that it is still disputed whether it is impious or not. Some experts believe it prepared the way for Strato's atheism. Therefore, it was hardly suitable for converting Stratonicians; and you would please me greatly if you show me that it has nothing to fear from their turning its own arguments against it.

The Stratonicians had the fatal advantage of being able to counter all their opponents with the commonly accepted assumption that nothing comes to be from nothing (*ex nihilo nihil fit*), from which it follows that matter must be uncaused. To suppose that completely unqualified matter exists by itself is no less plausible than supposing it to exist conjoined with an active principle. That is why Cicero's Cotta concluded that if matter was not the product of divine providence, neither were earth, water, air, and fire – instead, they must be nature's own doing (this passage from Cicero is from the lost portion of Book III of *On the Nature of the Gods*). Lactantius made some very good points against this remark of Cotta's, but most of them would have been weak coming from the mouth of a Stoic. I shall take time to consider only this one: Lactantius asked "what force could nature have, nothing having given it any?" If it has some force, it has received it from someone who can only be God. If it is completely unaware of what it does, it cannot produce anything. If it can produce something, it has some awareness of what it is doing, and therefore it is God. One cannot call the force which conceives and executes a plan anything else, since the power to make something can exist only in a thinking and skilled being. Nothing can be started or finished unless an intelligent cause directs its execution and has the ability and the will to work at it. Anything unconscious will stay forever inactive; nothing can arise from a source lacking voluntary motion.

> What force could it (matter) have, no one imparting it? What nature, no one begetting it? If it had force, it received it from someone. From whom could it obtain it, if not from God? But if it had a nature, which is, of course, said of that which is begotten or formed, it came into existence. Who, then, except God, could have brought it into existence? Indeed, nature, from which all things are said to arise, can accomplish nothing if it has no deliberative ability. However, if it is able to generate and make, it follows that it has deliberative ability; and therefore, necessarily, it becomes God. The force in which both providential planning and the skill and ability to make are found cannot be called by any other name.[3] . . . The power to make something can exist only in that which understands, which thinks, and which is affected. Nothing can be started, or made, or ended, unless it was first envisioned in a plan, either how it will take place before it exists or how it will be understood once it has been accomplished. In short, anyone who makes has a desire to create and craftsmanship to complete what he wanted to make. On the other hand, anything insensible always stays inert and torpid, and nothing can arise from that in which there is no voluntary motion.[4]

A Stoic reasoning on these principles would have been obliged to deny that matter existed independently from God, since he would have been asked the same question concerning its existence which he had proposed concerning its activity. If nothing exists without having been produced by an intelligent cause, a Stratonician would have asked, from whence then come the active powers of the fire which composes your Jupiter? Have they been conferred following an ideal pattern which preceded Jupiter? That would lead to an infinite regress; and one would never discover a first cause. If you wish to avoid this great abyss, you must

[3] Lactantius, Bk. 2, Ch. 8, 111–112.   [4] Ibid., 113.

agree that no idea or voluntary movement contributed to the existence of the eternal fire you call "God." Consequently, your objections prove too much. You recognize ordered forces in Nature which neither follow nor result from any conscious act, even if they be accompanied with consciousness. Then why do you think it wicked that we recognize an order or orderly force in a nature which is aware of nothing? Once this order exists without consciousness, it will continue like that forever – the hardest part is finished.

Take the trouble of reflecting on some words from Euripides which I quoted elsewhere;[5] in this passage you will find three quite remarkable claims: (1) Jupiter is there acknowledged as being incomprehensible to human minds. (2) He is invoked such as he may be, whether a necessity of nature or a human-like intelligence. (3) It is avowed that he justly leads everything by a path which is concealed from us. It is Hecuba who speaks, even though what she says is too philosophical for a woman. Nevertheless, we do not doubt that Euripides there gives us the character of certain people who, in order to play it safe, recommended themselves to God, despite their being uncertain whether he was an intelligent being or only the blind and necessary force of nature. Such people would still have invoked him, with greater zeal and more pleasure, had they been certain of his intelligent nature. So, it was the difficulty of the matter, rather than willful malice,[6] which kept them in a state of uncertainty.

I should add that when I supposed that the Stoics recognized matter as a passive principle distinct from God I was not unaware of these words Plutarch addresses to them:

> And your Jupiter, such as you depict and imagine him, is he not, when he makes use of his natural form, a big unceasing fire? But now he submits, he gives up, he metamorphoses into all things by a variety of mutations.

This is to say quite clearly that he was himself the matter of every material body, which one can also infer from another passage containing

---

[5] *Dictionaire historique et critique*, 5th edn., 4 vols. (Amsterdam, Leiden, The Hague, Utrecht, 1740), at the end of the remarks on the article, "Jupiter," II:906. Here is the passage from *The Trojan Women*, lines 884–8:
   Hecuba. O, support of Earth, having your throne upon her, it is difficult to guess what you may be! Zeus, whether a natural necessity or a human thought, I pray to you; for, walking on a soundless way, you guide all human affairs toward justice.
[6] willful malice: *une malice afectée de leur cœur.*

the definition of 'God' according to the Stoics. But, since it appears from other authorities that they allowed a distinction between God and matter, I believed myself obliged to consider their doctrine according to the less disadvantageous account.

2 Bayle on Manicheanism[7]

Translator's note: Zarathustra (called Zoroaster by the ancient Greeks and Bayle) was an ancient Persian prophet (dates uncertain, perhaps 7th century BC) whose teaching envisaged earthly life as a struggle between a good god of light, Ahura Mazda, and an evil principle of darkness, Ahriman. Zoroastrianism became the state religion of Persia, influenced many subsequent religious movements, and a version of it survives today among the Parsees in India. Mani (AD *c.* 210–276), also a Persian, founded Manicheanism, a syncretistic religion combining Zoroastrian and Christian elements. Manicheans identified the good principle with the Judeo-Christian God and the evil principle with Satan.

Note D

Logic teaches us[8] that a being which exists by itself, is necessary, and is eternal, must be unique, infinite, omnipotent, and endowed with every kind of perfection. Thus, considering these ideas, nothing is more absurd than the hypothesis of two eternal principles, each self-contained, of which one has no goodness and can obstruct the other's plans. This is an instance of what I term "*a priori* reasoning." It leads us necessarily to reject this hypothesis and to allow only one principle of everything. If the goodness of a system required nothing more than that, the trial would be declared over, to the embarrassment of Zoroaster and all his followers. However, to be good every system requires two things: that its concepts be distinct and that it be able to make sense of our experience. Therefore, we must see whether the phenomena of nature can be conveniently explained by the hypothesis of a single principle. The Manicheans are pitiable when they contend that there are necessarily two first principles because in the world we see several things which are contraries, such as cold and heat, white and black, light and darkness. The opposition found between these forms of

---

7 "Manichéens," Note D, *Dictionnaire historique et critique*, III:305–306.
8 Logic teaches us: *Les idées les plus sûres & les plus claires de l'ordre nous apprennent* . . .

existence, backed up as much as one might wish by so-called variations, disorders, and irregularities of nature, would not add up to half of an objection against the unity, simplicity, and immutability of God. All these things can be explained, either by the diverse capabilities God has given to bodies, or by the laws of motion which he has established, or by the joint action of the intelligent occasional causes by which it has pleased him to conduct his activity. This does not require the ethereal beings the rabbis have imagined and which have furnished an Italian bishop an *ad hominem* argument for the incarnation . . . They say God united himself with ten very pure intelligences called *Sefira* and that he works with them in such a way that all the variations and imperfections of the effects must be attributed to them . . . One can save the simplicity and immutability of divine providence[9] without the excessive expense of this hypothesis. Merely setting up occasional causes will suffice, provided that one only has to explain physical phenomena, exclusive of human behavior. The heavens and the rest of the universe proclaim the glory, power, and unity of God; humanity alone – that masterpiece of the visible works of the Creator –, only humanity, say I, furnishes serious objections against the unity of God. Here's how:

The human race is wicked and unhappy. Everyone is aware of this, both through acquaintance with one's own private thoughts and through the interactions one is required to have with one's neighbor. Living five or six years is enough to persuade one completely of the truth of these two claims; those who live long and who are heavily involved in business know it still more clearly. Travels provide perpetual lessons on this topic; they display everywhere monuments to the unhappiness and perversity of humanity – everywhere there are prisons, hospitals, gibbets, and beggars. Here you see the debris from a once flourishing city, at the location of another you cannot even find the ruins.

> Now a grain field is where Troy was; and a luxuriant harvest reaped
> From the fertile soil where Phrygian blood seeped.
> (Ovid, *Epistle of Penelope to Ulysses*, 53)

Read these fine words drawn from a letter written to Cicero:

> Returning from Asia, and sailing from Aegina towards Megara, I began to survey the regions surrounding me. Aegina was behind

---

[9] of divine providence: *des voies de Dieu*

me, Megara before me, on my right Piraeus, on my left Corinth, all towns which once upon a time were very prosperous, but now lie before our eyes overthrown and demolished. (Sulpicius, ad Ciceron, Ep. 5)

Scholars, without leaving their studies, are those who acquire the greatest understanding of these two claims because, in reading history, they consider all historical periods and all the world's countries. Properly speaking, history is only a digest of the crimes and misfortunes of humankind; but we note that these two evils, the one moral and the other physical, fill up neither the whole of history nor the totality of individual human experiences. Both moral and physical good are ubiquitous, and it is these instances of virtue and of happiness which create the difficulty. If there were only evil and unhappy people, there would be no need to resort to the hypothesis of two principles. It is the mixture of happiness and virtue with misery and vice which requires this hypothesis; and therein is the strong point of Zoroastrianism . . .

In order to see how difficult it would be to refute this false system and to conclude, therefore, that one must have recourse to revelation to destroy it, let us here imagine a dispute between Melissus and Zoroaster, both of whom were pagans and great philosophers. Melissus, who recognized only one principle, would begin by saying that his system is admirably logically consistent[10] – the necessary being is not limited, therefore it is infinite and omnipotent, and therefore it is unique. Thus, it would be monstrous and contradictory were it to possess no goodness and instead had the greatest of all vices, namely, essential maliciousness. I grant you, Zoroaster would respond, that your ideas are quite coherent; and I am completely willing to acknowledge that, in this respect, your hypotheses are superior to mine. I shall also abandon an objection which I could employ to my advantage, namely to say that since the infinite must include everything that really exists, and maliciousness being no less real than goodness, the universe requires that there be both evil and good beings; and since sovereign good and sovereign malice cannot subsist in one and the same subject, it was absolutely necessary that nature contain both an entity essentially good and another entity essentially evil. I repeat, I give up this objection; and I grant you the advantage of being more rigorously logical than I.[11] But give

[10] admirably logically consistent: *s'accorde admirablement avec les idées de l'ordre*
[11] more rigorously logical than I: *plus conforme que moi aux notions de l'ordre*

me a brief explanation, according to your hypothesis, of how humanity comes to be wicked, or so susceptible to pain and sorrow. I defy you to find the reason for this phenomenon in your principles, as I can in mine. Hereby I regain the advantage. You excel in the beauty of your ideas and in *a priori* reasoning, but I surpass you in explaining the phenomena and in *a posteriori* reasoning. Since the major characteristic of a good system is to be able to explain our experience, and by itself the inability to explain it is proof that an hypothesis is no good, however beautiful it may otherwise seem, you must agree that I, by admitting two principles, provide an explanation of these phenomena[12] and that you, by admitting just one, do not.

Now we are doubtless at the crucial juncture of the whole dispute and here lies a great opportunity for Melissus . . . But let us keep on making Zoroaster speak.

If humanity be the product of a single principle, supremely good, supremely holy, and supremely powerful, how can it be exposed to diseases, cold and heat, hunger and thirst, pain and sorrow? How can it have so many evil tendencies? How can it commit so many crimes? How can supreme holiness produce a criminal creature? How can supreme goodness produce an unhappy creature? Would not supreme power, added to infinite goodness, completely fill its production with goods and keep everything which could be offensive or distressful well away from it? If Melissus reasons logically,[13] he will respond that humanity was not at all wicked when created by God. He will say that humanity received a happy estate from God; but, not having followed the guiding light of conscience, which should have led it along the path of virtue as its author intended, mankind became wicked. Humanity then deserved that God, being as supremely just as he is supremely good, make it feel the effects of his righteous anger. Therefore God is not the cause of moral evil; but he is the cause of physical evil, i.e. of the punishment of moral evil. This punishment, far from being incompatible with the supremely good principle, emanates necessarily from one of his attributes, I mean from his justice, which is no less essential to him than his goodness. This reply, the most

[12] provide an explanation of these phenomena: *frapper au but* means to get to the heart of the matter, to divine the solution of a problem. Alternatively, or additionally, Zoroaster might mean he is "about to win the debate," since the goal in various games is *le but*. For example, in soccer *frapper au but* means kicking the ball in an attempt to score a goal.
[13] reasons logically: *consulte les notions de l'ordre*

reasonable that Melissus could make, is fundamentally elegant and sound. But it can be attacked by arguments of a somewhat more specious and dazzling character. Zoroaster would not fail to point out that, if humanity were the product of an infinitely good and holy principle, it would have been created, not only without any actual evil, but also without any inclination toward evil, since that inclination is a defect which cannot have such a principle as its cause. We must then say that humanity, coming from the hands of its creator, had only the power, by itself, to make up its mind to be wicked and, having determined to be wicked, it is alone the cause of the crime it committed and of the moral evil which thereby entered into the universe.

But (1) we have no clear idea which can enable us to understand how a being which does not exist by itself can nevertheless act by itself. Therefore Zoroaster will say that the free will given to humans is not capable of actual self-determination, since its existence depends, continually and completely, on the action of God. (2) He will pose this question: did God foresee that human beings would badly use their free will? If one answers "yes," he will reply that it does not seem at all possible that anything can foresee that which depends entirely on an indeterminate cause. But I am willing to agree with you, he will say, that God foresaw his creatures' sin, and from that I conclude that he would have prevented their sinning, since it is not logical[14] that an infinitely good and holy cause, capable of preventing the introduction of moral evil, would not prevent it, especially since in permitting it, it would be obliged to overwhelm its own creation with punishments. If God did not foresee humanity's fall, he at least deemed it possible. Then, were it to happen, he would have seen himself obliged to renounce his paternal goodness in order to make his children very miserable by acting as a severe judge of them. [To avoid this consequence,] he would have determined humanity toward the morally good, as he had determined it toward the physically good. He would not have left in the human soul any power to pursue sin, no more than he has left there any power to pursue unhappiness just to be unhappy. That is what we must conclude if we reason logically[15] when we follow, step by step, that which an infinitely good principle ought to do. For if a goodness as limited as that of human fathers necessarily requires that they

---

[14] it is not logical: *les idées de l'ordre ne souffrent pas*
[15] That is what we must conclude if we reason logically: *Voilà à quoi nous conduisent les idées claires & distinctes de l'ordre*

prevent, to the best of their ability, the misuse their children could make of the goods they have given them, *a fortiori* an infinite and omnipotent goodness will forestall the harmful consequences of its gifts. Rather than giving them free will, it will determine its creatures toward the good; or, if it gives them free will, it will always watch over them efficaciously in order to prevent their sinning. I certainly believe that Melissus would not forget what he would like to say, but any reply he might give would be immediately counterattacked with reasons as plausible as his own. So, their dispute would never be concluded.

Were he to resort to the tactic of turning this sort of argument back against its proponent, he could greatly bewilder Zoroaster. By once granting him his two principles, he would leave the way wide open for Zoroaster to unravel the problem of the origin of evil. Zoroaster would go back to the epoch of chaos, which was a state, with respect to his two principles, strongly resembling what Hobbes calls the state of nature, which he supposes to have preceded the establishment of societies. In this state of nature, man was a wolf to man, everything went to the first occupant, and no one was master of anything unless he happened to be the strongest. To exit this abyss, each agreed to give up his rights to everything in order that the others would grant him ownership of some particular thing; deals were made; warfare ceased. Similarly, the two principles, tired of chaos, in which each would confound and overturn what the other would like to do, made a mutually satisfactory agreement – each gave up something and each shared in the production of humanity and of the laws of the union of soul and body. The good principle obtained those properties which procure for humans a thousand pleasures and consented to those which expose them to a thousand pains. If it consented that moral goodness should be infinitely smaller than moral evil in humankind, it made up its loss with some other species of creatures in which vice would be correspondingly less than virtue. If many men have more misery than happiness in this life, this is repaid in another state; that which they lack while in human form, they recover in another form. By means of this agreement chaos was disentangled. Chaos, I note, was, as a passive principle, the battlefield of the two active principles. The poets depicted this disentangling through the metaphor of a settled quarrel. Here is what Zoroaster could claim, priding himself on not having attributed to the good principle the production, of its own accord, of a product which had to be so wicked and miserable. It created only after having experimentally ascertained that it could not do better, nor better oppose the horrible designs of the bad principle. To render his hypothesis less offensive, he could deny that there had been a long war between these two principles and shoo away all those battles and prisoners of which the Manicheans spoke. Everything might be reduced to the certain knowledge that the two principles would have had that each could ever obtain only such and such conditions from the other. The agreement could have been made, from all eternity, on that basis.

A thousand serious difficulties might be raised against this philosopher; but since he would find replies and would ultimately ask that he be provided with a better hypothesis and would maintain that he had soundly refuted the one proposed by Melissus, one could never win him over to the true conception of things. Human reason is too weak to do that; it is a destructive principle, not an instructive one. It is only able to raise doubts and to take alternate tacks in order to drag on a dispute. I do not think I would be mistaken were I to say of natural revelation or the light of reason, what the theologians say of the Mosaic dispensation. They say that it was only able to make human beings aware of their powerlessness and of the necessity for a redeemer and a merciful law. It was a pedagogue (these are their terms) to lead us to Jesus Christ. Let us say pretty much the same of reason – it is only able to make humans aware of their ignorance and impotence and the necessity of a different revelation, namely that in the Scripture. There we find the means of invincibly refuting the hypothesis of two principles and all of Zoroaster's objections. There we find the unity of God and his infinite perfections, the fall of the first humans and the consequences thereof. Should anyone mount an impressive assemblage of arguments to tell us that it is not possible that moral evil should arise in the world through the product of an infinitely good and holy principle, we shall reply that nevertheless it happened and consequently it is quite possible. Nothing is crazier than arguing against the facts; the axiom "whatever is actual must be possible"[16] is as evident as the proposition that $2 + 2 = 4$. The Manicheans were aware of the point I just made, and that is why they rejected the Old Testament. However, they retained enough of the Scripture to provide their orthodox

[16] *ab actu ad potentiam valet consequentia*

opponents with ample arms. Thus it did not take much effort to confound these heretics, who moreover were as hesitant and confused as children when they went into the details of their system. Now, since it is Scripture which provides us with the best solutions, I was not mistaken in saying that it would be difficult to defeat a pagan philosopher on this issue . . .

Index

Cambridge Texts in the History Of Philosophy

Titles published in the series thus far

Kant *The Metaphysics of Morals* (edited by Mary Gregor with an introduction by Roger Sullivan)

Kant *Prolegomena to any Future Metaphysics* (edited by Gary Hatfield)

Kant *Religion within the Boundaries of Mere Reason and Other Writings* (edited by Allen Wood and George di Giovanni with an introduction by Robert Merrihew Adams)

Kierkegaard *Fear and Trembling* (edited by C. Stephen Evans and Sylvia Walsh)

La Mettrie *Machine Man and Other Writings* (edited by Ann Thomson)

Leibniz *New Essays on Human Understanding* (edited by Peter Remnant and Jonathan Bennett)

Lessing *Philosophical and Theological Writings* (edited by H. B. Nisbet)

Malebranche *Dialogues on Metaphysics and on Religion* (edited by Nicholas Jolley and David Scott)

Malebranche *The Search after Truth* (edited by Thomas M. Lennon and Paul J. Olscamp)

Medieval Islamic Philosophical Writings (edited by Muhammad Ali Khalidi)

Melanchthon *Orations on Philosophy and Education* (edited by Sachiko Kusukawa, translated by Christine Salazar)

Mendelssohn *Philosophical Writings* (edited by Daniel O. Dahlstrom)

Newton *Philosophical Writings* (edited by Andrew Janiak)

Nietzsche *The Antichrist, Ecce Homo, Twilight of the Idols and Other Writings* (edited by Aaron Ridley and Judith Norman)

Nietzsche *Beyond Good and Evil* (edited by Rolf-Peter Horstmann and Judith Norman)

Nietzsche *The Birth of Tragedy and Other Writings* (edited by Raymond Geuss and Ronald Speirs)

Nietzsche *Daybreak* (edited by Maudemarie Clark and Brian Leiter, translated by R. J. Hollingdale)

Nietzsche *The Gay Science* (edited by Bernard Williams, translated by Josefine Nauckhoff)

Nietzsche *Human, All Too Human* (translated by R. J. Hollingdale with an introduction by Richard Schacht)

Nietzsche *Thus Spoke Zarathustra* (edited by Adrian Del Caro and Robert B. Pippin)

Nietzsche *Untimely Meditations* (edited by Daniel Breazeale, translated by R. J. Hollingdale)

Nietzsche *Writings from the Late Notebooks* (edited by Rüdiger Bittner, translated by Kate Sturge)

Novalis *Fichte Studies* (edited by Jane Kneller)

Reinhold *Letters on the Kantian Philosophy* (edited by Karl Ameriks, translated by James Hebbeler)

Schleiermacher *Hermeneutics and Criticism* (edited by Andrew Bowie)

Schleiermacher *Lectures on Philosophical Ethics* (edited by Robert Louden, translated by Louise Adey Huish)

Schleiermacher *On Religion: Speeches to its Cultured Despisers* (edited by Richard Crouter)

Schopenhauer *Prize Essay on the Freedom of the Will* (edited by Günter Zöller)